International Management Ethics

What can we learn about management ethics from other cultures and societies? In this textbook, cross-cultural management theory is applied and made relevant to management ethics. To help you understand different approaches that global businesses can take to operate successfully and ethically, there are chapters focusing on specific countries and regions. As well as giving you the wider geographical, political and cultural contexts, the book includes numerous examples in every chapter to help you critique universal assumptions of what is ethical. By taking a closer look at the way we view other cultures and their values, the author challenges us to rethink commonly held assumptions and approaches in cross-cultural management, and to apply a more critical approach.

Terence Jackson is Professor of Cross-cultural Management at Middlesex University Business School. He has spent many years researching and teaching on issues relating to cross-cultural management, particularly in sub-Saharan Africa. He is the author of *International HRM: A Cross-cultural Approach* (2002) and *Management and Change in Africa: A Cross-cultural Perspective* (2004).

International
Management Ethics

A Critical, Cross-cultural Perspective

Terence Jackson

CAMBRIDGE UNIVERSITY PRESS
Cambridge, New York, Melbourne, Madrid, Cape Town, Singapore,
São Paulo, Delhi, Dubai, Tokyo, Mexico City

Cambridge University Press
The Edinburgh Building, Cambridge CB2 8RU, UK

Published in the United States of America by Cambridge University Press, New York

www.cambridge.org
Information on this title: www.cambridge.org/9780521618656

First published 2011

Printed in the United Kingdom at the University Press, Cambridge

A catalogue record for this publication is available from the British Library

Library of Congress Cataloguing in Publication data
Jackson, Terence, 1952–
    International Management Ethics : A Critical, Cross-cultural Perspective / Terence Jackson.
      p.   cm
    Includes bibliographical references and index.
    ISBN 978-0-521-85344-6 – ISBN 978-0-521-61865-6 (pbk.)
    1. Business ethics–Cross-cultural studies.   2. Management–Moral and ethical
    aspects–Cross-cultural studies.   3. International business enterprises–Management–
    Social aspects.   4. Corporate culture–Cross-cultural studies.   I. Title.
    HF5387.J2974 2011
    174′.4–dc22
    2010045745

ISBN 978-0-521-85344-6 Hardback
ISBN 978-0-521-61865-6 Paperback

Contents

Part III   Managing ethically across cultures

      References   277
      Index   292

Figures

Tables

1 Introduction: ethics and cross-cultural management

Management studies, like education studies, has tended to follow the social and behavioural sciences rather than to lead them. It is true that various streams of critical management and organization studies have developed, but these have largely drawn on developments in sociology or politics or even literary studies. Perhaps compounding the lack of innovation in applied areas such as management, has been the lack of cross-over, and cross-fertilization with other applied areas. For example, in a globalized world, where much of the work of international managers will be in the so-called 'developing' countries (which, by the way, take up some 80 per cent of the world's land-mass), and within the world as a whole we can talk about living in a largely post-colonial world where North–South geopolitical dynamics have tended to dominate, management studies has very little connection with develop-ment studies. If this cross-over does take place, it is within the domain of a rather uncritical modernization theory.

The acceptance of a developing–developed world paradigm is strongly evident within both international management studies, and, regrettably, cross-cultural management. Centre stage to the critical debate should be what promised to be a rising star, auguring major contributions to critical knowledge in the area of international management studies: cross-cultural management.

It all started out well, albeit within a positivist paradigm. Hofstede (1980b) warned against the unquestioning transfer of management knowledge from Western (i.e. American) culture to other cultures, begging the question of its ethicality but not taking this up. Boyacigiller and Adler (1991) did a fairly good job at the time of explaining why American international managers might assume a universality for management policies and practice. This work hinted at a global power dynamic at work, but again did not take this up.

Since this fledging subdiscipline saw the light of day in the 1980s and 1990s, much of the work – perhaps influenced by the more positivistic tendencies in the parallel subdiscipline of cross-cultural psychology – built on numerous comparative cross-national studies that provided some basic descriptions, but explained practically nothing. Particularly since the turn of the new millennium some journal editors have taken a more critical line on these comparative studies, and asked for some kind of explanation: Why compare country X with country Y? How can you explain differences between country X and country Y? Certainly much of the justification for differences came with a reference to Hofstede's (1980a/2003) work. Within cross-cultural management itself, Hofstede's work began to come under criticism. But this did not by and large break out of the (positivist) paradigm. It was premised on details of method, samples, constructs and level of analysis. Hence bigger and better (and more modern) Hofstedian-type studies were developed and delivered. Now researchers could refer for example to the GLOBE studies (e.g. House *et al.*, 2004). These studies, still including Hofstede's, were also being used to explain why there might be differences in ethicality among different countries. The growing number of comparative studies focusing on ethics, the present author's work included, would provide cultural antecedent (independent variable) explanation of differences in ethicality, between, say, American and German managers in terms of Hofstede's *Power Distance, Uncertainty Avoidance, individualism–collectivism* and/or *masculinity–femininity*. This turned out to all be slightly banal and rather tautological, particularly as ethics is part of the value structure of a society, rather than a result of it. *Power Distance*, for example, can only act as a descriptor for a societal/cultural context; it cannot provide an explanation for why large inequalities are regarded as ethical in one society and not in another.

To a large extent cross-cultural management, in its positivistic interpretation, appears to have run its course. Although the focus on societal values, or work values, provides a direct link to ethics, this connection has not really been made by the main advocates of these types of large-scale studies (Hofstede, 1980a/2003; Schwartz, 1994, 1999; Trompenaars, particularly Smith, Dugan and Trompenaars, 1996; GLOBE, e.g. House *et al.*, 2004). It is likely that this connection has not been made as ethics takes social and behavioural scientists into the realm of 'what ought to be', rather than 'what is'. This is not a place where positivism wants to be. Hofstede's (1980a/2003) work, and subsequent similar studies, tells us that if we go to work in another country, its *Power Distance* may be higher than that in our home country. Therefore it is likely to have steeper organizational hierarchies, workers are likely to be told what to do, and there will be little democracy in the workplace. This may be a useful description, and may help a manager understand what to expect. Yet it does not tell us what to do. It does not enter into any debate about the desirability of accepting inequality and autocracy, or whether to try to change it. This is the realm of ethics. Some would also argue that it is the realm of politics. Others would argue that this is what social sciences is particularly good at, rather than trying to construct universal predictive science in an attempt to emulate the natural sciences.

Yet for many social and behavioural scholars, and for cross-cultural management scholars in particular, this would represent a huge leap in the dark. It would involve understanding phenomena, and academic subject areas, far beyond their normal remit. It would involve understanding inter-socio/cultural interaction at numerous levels, and particularly at the geopolitical level. It would involve having at least a limited grasp of history, politics, sociology and economics, and to approach these and their immediate subject matter in a critical and challenging manner. It would involve a radical reinterpretation of what they are doing and what they are trying to achieve in their work: what the contribution is and why this is important.

It is perhaps best at this point to start at the beginning: to explain where this has come from, and where it might lead.

Ethics is normally considered a subdivision of philosophy, yet I am not a philosopher. My undergraduate training was in social anthropology, with a little bit of political science thrown in. With a Masters in education in between, my PhD was then in organizational psychology. This whole process took me some twenty years, with ten years in between each degree. Apart from jobs in the UK civil service, in teaching and in a large international bank, and finally into higher education, these years were formative in developing me into a teacher and researcher in organizational behaviour, developing a specialism in cross-cultural management (as I could not see any other way of doing organizational behaviour in a globalized world), and then focusing specifically on the so-called 'developing' regions, in particular sub-Saharan Africa (because no one else seemed to be doing it, and it seemed important to me).

I started to focus on Africa about thirteen years ago when the Paris Chamber of Commerce and the French Foreign Ministry funded me to teach on a multicultural management development programme in Johannesburg, and then an administrative cooperative programme with universities in Cape Town in 1996. The following years took me also to Zimbabwe, Botswana, Kenya, Cameroon and more recently Ghana. These years had a profound effect on my scholarly work. I no longer believed it was possible to isolate theories and empirical work in the behavioural sciences from wider geopolitical influences. In Africa you notice power imbalances. You notice the impact of history. You feel the lasting effects of France in Cameroon, of the British in Kenya. Returning home to the UK and travelling on the London Underground and looking around at the diverse people, you know that Britain has had an empire, and that what Niall Ferguson has said in his book *Empire* that 'the world we know today is in large measure the product of Britain's age of Empire' (2003: xxvii), has a large element of truth.

I remember sitting in a house in Valencia where my family was staying for a couple of weeks in the early 1990s. I was reading Brady's excellent book *Ethical Management: Rules and Results*. Bullfighting came onto the television. My host asked if I would be interested in going to a bullfight. Valencia boasts a magnificent bullring. He explained that it was not something he would normally go to, but he would take me if I were interested. I declined. I am not sure if I would have been so quick to decline if he had been, like many Spaniards, an avid supporter of bullfighting. Perhaps I would have gone out of curiosity. After all, I was in Spain doing what Spanish people do (when in Rome do as the Romans do). Or, perhaps I would have taken the position that many English people would take, and judge bullfighting as being distasteful and perhaps cruel (and maybe not too dissimilar to foxhunting in the UK). Yet does this mean that Spanish people are bad?

When this argument is transposed to female circumcision, or the veiling of women, or within a work situation, child labour, does this mean that these societies are reprehensible or inherently bad? Does it mean that they are in some ways more primitive than Western societies? Then how do we judge alleged torture of terrorist suspects by the American military in Guantanamo Bay? Are the Americans justified in breaching articles of the Declaration of Human Rights that they were instrumental in introducing after World War II? Although some of these issues may be somewhat removed from the immediate concerns of international management, similar issues arise.

Two main issues arise: what do we make of ethical standards that are different to our own, and how do we understand them? And, armed with this knowledge, how do we understand how to manage cross-culturally across different value and ethical systems? Can we judge people as unethical because they take clients to bullfights, or segregate women from men in the workplace, employ children in factory work? What do we do about it? Is this a moralistic judgement or a cultural one? Perhaps the two are intertwined.

Brady's book provides an interesting framework contrasting a *rules* and *results* approach to judging the ethicality of decisions. There may be predefined rules that guide our view of whether a decision is ethical. There may be perceived outcomes: what are the costs or the benefits to us and others if we make a certain decision?

International management ethics is not simply about comparing the ethical values of one society with another. I cannot think of a less meaningful activity. It is about understanding the choices managers have when making decisions that affect people's lives. The fact that managers now need to do this internationally may be considered an added complication and a source of inconvenience. One of the main issues in cross-cultural management is that of ethnocentricity. If we have a choice in determining whose values are best, we will opt for our own. Many cross-national studies on ethics have been about who is ethical and who is not. Yet universal standards of ethical behaviour are always difficult to establish from some supposed position of neutrality.

I agree with Bent Flyvbjerg (2001) in his book *Making Social Science Matter* in assuming that in social sciences there cannot be a view from nowhere. It always has to be from somewhere. When looking internationally, particularly towards non-Western 'cultures', postcolonial theory tells us how distorting that view from 'nowhere' can be. African societies have for many centuries been overtly patronized. Yet the same is true today, even if we are only looking a short distance from Western to Eastern Europe. Systems of international aid perpetuate this negative regard for others, which is also reflected back on the diaspora in the so-called 'developed' countries, in both perceptions of the other, and self-perceptions. This has grown more ominous in the first decade of the twenty-first century, in America and Britain's 'war on terror' with an increased overt suspicion towards Muslims.

This book asks how we can understand management ethics internationally from a cross-cultural perspective that assumes that we can learn from others with different cultural spaces. What we mean by 'ethics' is best summed up by Singer (1993: v) in his Introduction to his edited book *A Companion to Ethics*.

Ethics deals with values, with good and bad, with right and wrong. We cannot avoid involvement with ethics, for what we do – and what we don't do – is always a possible subject of ethical evaluation. Anyone who thinks about *what he or she ought to do* is, consciously or unconsciously, involved in ethics.

In this quotation I, not the author, have emphasized 'what he or she ought to do'. So little social science is concerned with 'what ought to be'. It tends to be concerned with 'what is' (i.e. description) or perhaps 'what is going to be' (i.e. prediction), although it often does the latter badly. Here I return to

Flyvbjerg (2001). Much of the emphasis in his work on reforming the social sciences is concerned with the strength they have over the physical sciences in working with values and 'what ought to be'.

In the subdisciplinary area of cross-cultural management, much of the work is concerned with value, but it does so at the level of description, i.e. 'what is'. Hence Hofstede's (1980a/2003) seminal work on value dimensions across nations, which did so much to encourage us to think critically about the transferability of management theory and practice from one nation to another, is after all about description. It does help us make predictions about what might happen if we transfer management practices from, say, the UK to France, or to Malaysia, but it does not tell us what we ought to do. It also does not tell us much about the dynamics of cross-cultural interaction, through such processes as globalization and the exercise of power. Here 'what is' (say, institutions imposed by a colonial power) may come into conflict with what ought to be (say, the social values of local communities).

As discussed above, where cross-cultural ethical studies are undertaken a comparison of ethical values across nations (i.e. description) is frequently drawn, but at worse it is undertaken from a stance of one 'culture' being less ethical than another 'culture'. Even if positivistic social science of this sort professes to be neutral, it often ends up making implicit judgements that are not articulated and not explained. There is a compounding of the descriptive with the normative that actually hampers understanding. For example, there may be a judgement that managers from one nation who are seen to be more likely to pay bribes than managers from another, are perceived as less ethical. Even more controversial is an issue such as the veiling of women in the workplace in some Arab countries, or the segregation of the sexes, or even the lack of women in the workforce in Islamic countries. That this might be seen from the West as women being oppressed, may be part of a judgement that sees these practices as less ethical than those pertaining in the West.

How can these issues be researched by the Western researcher? How can they be managed by Western managers in Middle Eastern countries? Taking a view from somewhere, as advised by Flyvbjerg, does not mean degrading the cultural/religious values of others. I believe it means understanding the contribution of other value systems, cultures and civilizations.

This text is arranged thematically, rather than being a compendium/ geography of ethics by country or region. Part I focuses on the state of the art of cross-cultural and international comparative management ethics (Chapters 3 and 4), but from a critical stance (Chapter 2). Part II develops certain themes, within a structure that looks at the contributions made from particular countries and regions, including geopolitical power dynamics and influences on our perception of culture; social and institutional influences on our regard for ethics; religion as an influence on management ethics; the problems of giving voice to indigenous views; and the ambivalence towards 'the exotic' and implications for international management ethics.

Although not attempting to be comprehensive, it is hoped that many of the issues discussed will shed light on some of the critical issues of theory and methodology discussed in Chapter 2 and developed a little more in Chapter 5 from the perspective of the role and contributions of the United States. This chapter in particular questions why culture appears to have been rendered invisible, and why even this may be a misperception in the context of American society. In this regard, American 'culture' is rarely scrutinized, even though so many cross-country comparisons include the United States where the culture is almost assumed. Chapter 6 views Europe as being more conscious of its cultural differences, yet sometimes ethics is rendered almost invisible. It looks at the dynamics and explanations of this, why this might be changing, and explores how ethical differences might be discussed through a concept of discourse ethics. Chapter 7 puts religion centre stage in the context of Islam and the Middle East, exploring Arab cultures in particular. It also looks at the contributions made by Islam to gender relations, and discusses the controversial nature of this in the West.

The global dynamics of a post-colonial world are a recurrent theme of this book. In fact, in many respects the assumption of an inheritance of a colonial world is taken as a starting point, from which the dynamics of 'neo-colonialism' are developed, particularly in Chapter 5. A premise is that the type of relationships and consciousness of one's identity that these dynamics have created make it particularly difficult to do cross-cultural research, and for managers to manage across cultures. It is also premised on the scientific understanding that our studies should focus not on a so-called 'culture' as a fixed and concrete entity, but on the interfaces between different cultural spaces, and outcomes in terms of a hybrid Third Space in a constant power dynamic.

Chapter 8 focuses on Africa as a 'developing' region, and looks also at the dynamics of the South finding its voice, and speaking back. The difficulty of doing cross-cultural management research is again highlighted through postcolonial theory and the contradictions of the West's perception of 'the other' in terms of both its negativity and view of 'the exotic'. In Chapter 9 the recent concern with *guanxi*, or the use of social networks and connections in business relations in China, is an example of this, where some commentators are virtually heralding this as the latest management tool in the hands of management consultants, while some see this as ethically unacceptable and damaging to the social and economic fabric of China.

In doing cross-cultural research, or managing a business in China or in India, and trying to understand different concepts of management and business ethics, it is not irrelevant that both these countries boast civilizations going back many, many millennia. This is examined in order to throw light on the issue of *guanxi*, as well as what the inheritance of ancient civilizations might mean for modern corporations. Again, in this regard, an understanding of geopolitical dynamics, how these are changing, the new roles of China and India in the world, and South–South relations are all important for both international managers and indeed for cross-cultural management scholars.

In the concluding Chapter 10, the main issue is bringing this all together. Attempts have been made to provide models or formulae for managing ethically across cultures. These often try to provide a careful balance between approaches such as teleological and deontological ones (Hosmer, 1987) or some kind of decision algorithm (Donaldson, 1989). Particularly to be grappled with is the balance between universalism and relativism. Throughout this book, the implicit question that is constantly asked is: what can we learn, as international managers, or international scholars, from others' cultural spaces? This may be different to assuming a universal ethics, but it is not a relativist stance. At a general level much can be gained from the discourse ethics discussed in Chapter 6: that by engaging in a conversation about how 'the other' sees the world, trying not only to understand this, but to learn from this, and then arriving at a working compromise may be the way forward. Whether or not this is possible, particularly in light of the discussion in the ensuing chapters on the representation of others' cultural spaces, may still be open to question. Yet the first stage is understanding the geopolitical dynamics that have led to assumptions about universality, as well as the different manifestations of cultural and ethical systems that have arisen through these international dynamics.

Part I

Understanding values and management ethics across cultural space

2 Understanding culture and cultural interfaces

This book is based on a premise that the concept of ethics, or what constitutes 'ethicality' differs across the globe. What is regarded as ethical in one society may not be so regarded in another. This is not a straightforward assumption as it is also possible to assume that there is a universal ethic. For example, it is reasonable to suppose that all societies and cultures have a value which condemns murder and causing unnecessary suffering to other people. It may also be reasonable to suppose that a belief in universal human rights is indeed universal (from the UN's Universal Declaration of Human Rights, 1948, and subsequent United Nations declarations), and that this is a useful guide in differentiating what is acceptable and what is not acceptable in a society other than our own. Why this may not be a reasonable assumption is discussed later in Chapter 5.

An assumption of a universality of ethics, as well as an assumption of cultural variation in what constitutes ethicality, does not necessarily provide a contradiction. But it does cause problems for managers operating across different countries.

The current chapter is concerned with *why* concepts of ethicality differ across the globe: from country to country. A simple cross-cultural approach that explains variation in terms of 'culture' is not sufficient. Explaining variation by reference to Hofstede's (1980a/2003) value dimensions, for example, although useful, does not fully answer the question of why there is variation. The current chapter addresses this crucial question: *why does ethicality, or the meaning of what is ethical or not, differ among countries and regions?* Chapter 3 looks at *how* ethicality differs among nations, particularly exploring the link between culture, values and ethics. Chapter 4 focuses on the issue of cultural difference and the universality of ethics, albeit within a more traditional, positivistic cross-cultural management framework. To illustrate some of the issues and concerns of this chapter, we first turn to the case of the American legislation on paying bribes overseas.

Opening case: the US Foreign Corrupt Practices Act

The Foreign Corrupt Practices Act came about after the scandals in the United States in the 1970s including illegal payments to Richard Nixon's presidential campaign and the Watergate revelations. In the wake of this the Securities and Exchange Commission publicized the fact that leading US multinationals had been making questionable payments to senior foreign officials and concealing them in their company accounts. After coming into force in 1977, a subsequent voluntary disclosure programme revealed more than 400 companies, of which 117 were in the Fortune 500 list, admitting paying over US$300 million in bribes. The most telling revelation was that US$25 million had been paid by Lockheed to a Japanese official and to Prince Bernhard of the Netherlands to secure the sale of their Tristar L-1011 aircraft. This led to criminal conviction and the resignation of the Japanese Prime Minister (Theobold, 2002).

The Act makes it illegal for US companies to offer payments to foreign government officials to secure business: that is, payments made voluntarily to secure unlawful advantage. But the Act excludes payments made under duress or extortion; and 'grease' or 'speed' payments. Companies may pay small payments to low-level agents or officials to expedite actions more quickly. In this sense grease payments are deemed to be small and do not secure an unlawful competitive advantage. After 1988, companies also had to keep accurate records of such transactions. If convicted of 'grand corruption' companies can incur fines up to US$2 million, and managers can be jailed for up to five years and/or fined up to US$100,000 (Theobold, 2002).

The Act has come under criticism by US business people as providing unfair advantage to foreign competitors whose governments tolerate extra-territorial bribery, with some (including European governments) allowing firms to offset such payments against their tax liability. For example, in 1995 a CIA report claimed that US firms had lost out around US$36 billion to foreign competitors. Gradually, from the 1980s, European countries through an OECD initiative were persuaded of the principle to criminalize bribery of foreign officials, despite opposition from Germany, the UK and France. This gave rise to the Convention on Combating Bribery of Foreign Public Officials in International Business Transactions in 1997.

Despite the tardiness of some countries to implement the OECD's Convention recommendations, and although the incidence of bribery by American companies appears to have dropped since 1977, these firms are still paying bribes in highly competitive situations. Again, Lockheed was found guilty of paying a US$1 million bribe to an Egyptian official to secure the sale of three of its Hercules C130 aircraft, and fined US$21.8 million. In 1996 IBM was indicted for allegedly paying US$27 million to officials of Banco Nacion in Argentina, concealed in a subcontract between IBM Argentina and a local consultancy company. The case dragged on until the year 2000 with IBM agreeing to pay US$300,000 to settle the charges. In fact, Transparency International's Bribe Payers Index for 1999 suggests that US companies were perceived as more likely to pay bribes than those from Sweden, Australia, Canada, Austria, Switzerland, the Netherlands or the UK (Theobold, 2002).

What a number of comparative studies have highlighted (e.g. Becker and Fritzsche, 1987; Jackson and Calafell Artola, 1997) when comparing America, French and German managers in terms of their perceptions of gift giving in exchange for preferential treatments, is that American managers come out more favourably than French and German ones, and German managers come out the worst. In other words, Americans appear to frown on gift giving as unethical, whereas Germans appear to see this more favourably, or at least pragmatically. Does this mean that German managers are less ethical than Americans? We discuss some of the issues that should be addressed before attempting to answer this question.

Why does the concept of ethicality differ across the globe?

In addressing this question, this chapter focuses on the components of ethics and the process of ethical formulation. If one were simply to make a comparison of ethical attitudes in different countries, a conclusion could be drawn that managers from one country are less ethical than in another. Hence American managers could be seen to be more ethical than German managers where the former rate business gift giving and receiving as less acceptable than the latter (Jackson and Calafell Artola, 1997). Yet, such a conclusion could only be drawn if an assumption were made of a universal ethical principle that could be applied anywhere in the world. It is certainly the case that multinational corporations are publishing codes of ethics that, among other issues, ban business gift giving and receiving. It has also been demonstrated that managers' attitudes in different countries are not significantly influenced by such enactments by their corporations (Jackson, 2000), and they are more influenced by what they see their peers doing.

A far more useful approach in cross-national comparisons is looking at what is regarded as ethical by managers and staff in different countries. Hence gift giving and receiving might be more acceptable in some countries than in others. This acceptance may not be taken as a judgement that such people are less ethical. There may be reasons why ethicality is conceived differently in different countries and societies.

To consider this it is first necessary to focus on the elements of ethics. These could include: choice; values; rules; power; control; culture; institutions; objectives; and stakeholders. These aspects may well differ as we move from country to country and society to society. When we look across different nations and societies to how ethicality differs, the following questions might be asked:

1. What *choices* are available to individuals and organizations in the decisions they make?
2. What *values* influence or govern these choices?
3. What *rules* are followed (or not followed) in order to make such choices?
4. How do these rules *control* the levels and nature of choice in a society or an organization?
5. What are the *power* relations among the different stakeholders within the organization or society that control the rules and the values that influence choice?
6. What different *objectives* do the different *stakeholders* have that influence choice in decision making?

Why the answers to these questions might be different is first taken up in this chapter. To consider this, a descriptive model of the different variables we need to consider is developed. In Chapter 3, what the answers to these questions might be are investigated.

Developing a descriptive model of cross-cultural analysis

Descriptively it is possible to identify variables that may be important in cross-cultural analysis by a simple framework that considers both the nature of the analysis and the scale or magnitude of the analysis (Table 2.1).

Jackson (1993a) has suggested that it is possible to capture the essence of organizational phenomena by reference to three broad areas, namely the *context* of the phenomena involving structures and networks of rules, the *content* of the phenomena involving people's perceptions and interpretations of social action, their values, their expectations and belief patterns, and the *conduct* of such organizational and social phenomena, or people's observable

Table 2.1 Descriptive conceptualization of variables involved in cross-cultural analysis

	Macro	Meso	Micro
Context	• GDP/capita • Level of infrastructure • Political rights • Level of social inequality • Level of corruption at national/local government and business level • Human development • National health and life expectancy • Level of education and literacy rates • Ethnolinguistic fractionalization (see Jackson, 2004 – Africa)	• Industrial sector of organization • Organizational governance and decision making • Organizational structure, systems and rules • Leadership and management styles • Motivation and rewards structures • Intercultural management structures and systems	• Ethnicity • Religion/religiosity • Gender • Profession • Personality • Social/economic/educational background • Family background
Content	• National cultural values, beliefs, attitudes and knowledge • Level of diversity of cultural values, beliefs, attitudes and knowledge • Level and nature of hybridization (cultural convergence, divergence and crossvergence)	• Organizational values, attitudes, beliefs and knowledge • Homogeneity/heterogeneity of values, attitudes, beliefs and knowledge • Staff commitment and loyalty • Level of sharing of values, attitudes, beliefs and knowledge	• Individual's values, attitudes, beliefs and knowledge • Work-home/community value conflicts • Individual-group value conflicts
Conduct	• Intercontinental and international interactions	• Interorganizational interactions • Organizational stakeholders interactions • Organization-group-individual interactions	• Interpersonal interactions • Interaction and relation of individual to group and organization

behaviours and social interactions. In addition it is possible to use such a consideration in an eclectic approach that brings together at least two schools of thought in the social sciences, namely *structural–functionalism* or systems theory or institutional theory, and *phenomenological* theory or cultural theory. A third broad area was previously seen within the province of *behaviourism* (Jackson, 1993a). Yet this might be rather a narrow interpretation. This aspect is discussed in more detail below.

Context in cross-cultural analysis

Structuralism can be used here very broadly to represent the mainly socio-logical theories that emphasize the pre-eminence of social structure on human action. This makes an assumption that human beings are not free agents but act according to structures, norms and rules laid down within the society (at the macro level) (Parsons, 1949; Radcliffe-Brown, 1952) and within the social and work organizations in which people live and work (e.g. Katz and Kahn, 1978). Hence, in the framework presented in Table 2.1 societal level factors (at the macro level) such as infrastructural, political arrangements and governmental practices are pre-eminent factors in influencing the type of ethicality within a society and organization within that society. Similarly at the meso level of single organizations the characteristics of the sector of industrial activity, the governance and organizational structure, for example, are instrumental in determining the ethicality of individuals within the organization. However, there is also an interaction effect in structural–functionalism such that the component parts of the structure may in effect 'speak back'.

Structural–functionalism provides a theory of equilibrium. The component parts of the organization or society contribute to the maintenance of the social system as a self-perpetuating entity. When they do not they are deemed to be dysfunctional and ultimately destructive of the social organism. If they are not removed, corrected, or if the social entity does not change to accommodate the dysfunctional behaviour, this may lead to its destruction (Merton, 1949; Parsons, 1949, 1951). An example could be that of corruption. This could be damaging to a social entity such as a national state or a business organization, and may be stamped out, or accommodated by the gradual institutionalization of corruption where it is difficult to do business and compete without involvement in forms of corrupt practice (Utomi, 1998, for example, discusses this connection in Nigeria).

Structural–functionalism, which provides the analogy of a human organism, where the different organs and cells contribute to the maintenance and good health of the organism as a self-fulfilling entity, and cutting out dysfunctional cells or organs, has largely been incorporated within open systems theory in organizational science (Katz and Kahn, 1978). This allows for external inputs from the wider environment. From actions within and upon the environment, the organization learns from information provided within feedback loops, and is thus changed by its interactions with the wider environment (Katz and Kahn, 1978; and for example Argyris, 1992 in concepts of the 'learning organization'). This provides an opportunity for organizations to react to environmental feedback, and (in the case of the double-loop learning of Argyris, 1992) to change their fundamental values in the face of adverse stakeholder reaction to particular business practices.

Within current approaches and debate within cross-national organizational studies structural–functionalism has more latterly manifested itself as *institutional theory*. This approach has been contrasted to a *culturalist* approach (Sorge, 2004), which is explored in more detail below. Institutional approaches again view systems characteristics as primary in any explanation of cross-national differences in, for example, management attributes, how people are managed and presumably management ethics (despite a dearth of literature). For example, the Foreign Corrupt Practices Act of the United States may influence the ethical behaviour of American managers abroad. Similarly, the fact that German corporations could until recently offset against their tax liability bribes paid abroad for business purposes may have affected the ethical behaviour of German managers abroad. Yet the regard for ethicality in these two countries may also be influenced by America's free-market economy and by Germany's social market economy. Hence Jackson (2000) has argued that countries differ in the way market forces are regulated, where the USA has had a low regulation of market forces, yet strong ethical legislation, and Germany and France have governmental policies that curtail the extremes of an unabated free-market economy, yet little emphasis on legislating for ethical conduct of organizations. Hence American companies may have a more visible policy aimed at guiding managerial decision making which may otherwise try to 'bend the rules'. Companies operating in more regulated economies may not have a need to enact such corporate policies (Jackson, 2000).

The argument here would be that the level of regulation of a free-market economy (an institutional factor) would influence the regard for and nature of management ethicality. Institutional factors could be said to influence the choices available to individuals and organizations (question 1 above), and the rules available within the choice situation (questions 3 and 4 above).

Content in cross-cultural analysis

Phenomenological theories take a different approach, and a different starting point (Cicourel, 1964; Berger and Luckmann, 1966; Schutz, 1972).

Structural-functionalist and systems theories are criticized for reifying social institutions and work organizations (Silverman, 1970) or making a social entity concrete, whereas social institutions in fact comprise people, or are constituted through people, who make sense of social actions within social groups. Social perceptions are important. The way that interactions, communication and social life are interpreted and acted upon is fundamental. Individuals and groups have goals and objectives. Organizations or institutions as entities do not have goals, or values, attitudes and beliefs. They have executive members and groups that have such conceptions. These executive goals and values may be accepted and internalized by other individuals and groups within the organization (stakeholders). Equally there may be competing goals or values in an organization emanating from individuals or groups with informal power based for example on an ethnic group, a professional group or based on family background or socio-economic status.

Jackson (2004) found in sub-Saharan Africa that there is an articulation of organizational staff stepping outside their community/home culture and entering a 'foreign' culture when they go to work in the morning in formal work organizations. This has implications for organizational control. African staff could either be alienated from the work organization, or be compliant to the organization in terms of its values and objectives, or internalize those values and objectives, or indeed reject them. By approaching this from a phenomenological perspective it is possible to conceptualize this as conflicting perceptions and interpretations of the same social phenomenon. In Jackson's (2004) conceptualization, conflicting or competing world views or value systems lead to different hybrid approaches to managing the organization as a result of cultural crossvergence. Hence different perceptions and interpretations are accommodated within the organization by adaptation.

This is captured in Table 2.1 at the macro level in terms of the nature and diversity of values and beliefs at national level, and the degree of hybridization of such values and beliefs. At the meso level, the nature of values and beliefs within the organization is also bound up with the level of diversity and sharing of such values, and the level of staff commitment and loyalty. Work-home/community life conflicts are at the individual level. Individuals' perceptions and interpretations are bound up with their group membership in the workplace, as well as their community membership outside the workplace.

It was noted above that this phenomenological approach is often contrasted with a structural-functionalist/systems/institutionalist approach: differences across nations are either attributed to institutional arrangement, which are seen as fundamental (e.g. Hickson and McMillan, 1981); or, differences are attributed to cultural factors or, in Hofstedian parlance, to differences in the 'software of the mind' (Hofstede, 1991). Sorge (2004) believes that the two approaches should be complementary. He cites Giddens (1986) in saying that individual behaviour and social structure are reciprocally constituted, that is normative customs that are instituted to be binding are kept in place by acting individuals. Yet on the other hand, individuals do not make behavioural choices without regard to such norms. If individuals make a habit of breaking norms, this is for a specific reason, for example a reaction of an individual in a specific situation. Thence, the challenging of existing norms may become itself institutionalized. Laws enacted in the United States regarding payment of bribes abroad may be circumvented by paying a local consultant to handle all the details of a business deal. It may be necessary to do this to compete effectively, and may become an institutional way of dealing with such situations.

Sorge (2004) believes that such an integrative approach will consider both the construction of actors, that is people with values, preferences and knowledge, and the construction of social and societal systems as reciprocally related to an extent that they cannot be separated from each other. He terms such an approach 'societal analysis'. However, to see culturalist approaches as focusing 'on the mind of the individual as the place where differences reside', and institutionalist approaches focusing 'on wider norms and standards supported or enforced by institutional machineries' (2004: 119) may in itself be seeing the issue from an institutionalist approach.

Harré *et al.* (1985), for example, see an intimate connection between what they term the 'social order' (at the macro level) and 'deep structure of the mind' (at the micro level). They present this as a hierarchical structure of control of human action (Figure 2.1).

They suggest that structure of mind and the social order have developed hand in hand, mostly through the facility of language. The implied rules by which level 3 controls the two lower levels are discoverable. This has implications for the way we might view institutions and culture as being parts of the same phenomenon. This view can be traced back to the work of the sociologist Durkheim (1915/1971) on totemism among the indigenous societies of Australia and North America. The members of each clan worshipped a particular animal (e.g. crow), which was also the name of the clan. He argued that the origins of the religious beliefs by which the lives of the people in each clan were governed were derived from the identification with the society (clan). The clan was seen to be greater and more powerful than the individual people within the clan. Ritual (associated, for example, with dancing round

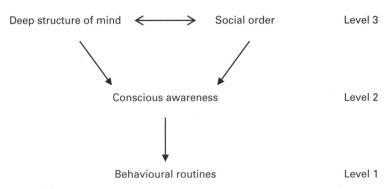

Figure 2.1   Hierarchical structure of control (from Harré *et al.*, 1985)

the totem pole) reinforced and drove these beliefs home. Thus the deep-seated beliefs that were acted upon unconsciously were no more than a set of implicit rules derived from the society in which the individual lived.

To a certain extent this 'deep structure' can be discerned through institutional manifestations. The structure of laws regulating the conduct of business may provide clues about the implicit rules that govern people's lives. For example Hofstede (1991), discussing the context of his cultural dimension of *Uncertainty Avoidance*, notes that Germany has laws for the event that all other laws might become unenforceable (*Notstandsgesetze*), whereas the UK does not even have a written constitution. He also points to the fact that German employment relations legislation is codified in details, while the UK has had difficulties in attempting to enact an Industrial Relations Act. The UK is lower in Hofstede's (1980a/2003) cultural values measure of *Uncertainty Avoidance* ('the extent to which the members of a culture feel threatened by uncertain or unknown situations') than Germany.

From this point of view the concept of culture should take in 'that complex whole which involves knowledge, beliefs, art, morals, law, customs and other capabilities and habits acquired by man as a member of society' (Tylor, 1871), or indeed the 'human-made part of the environment' (Herskovits, 1948). In other words, institutions as part of 'culture' are created by sentient human beings in interaction interpersonally, interorganizationally and internationally. Their rules reflect societal values, and the societal values reflect institutional rules.

However, again referring to sub-Saharan Africa, Dia (1996) takes the view that institutions were imposed on African societies during the colonial period. They have largely remained and evolved through the post-colonial period, and mostly are seen as still inappropriate to African societies and their context. Here, rules seem to be at odds with values.

There is no doubt that the introduction of institutions into Africa involved a number of elements: firstly the (cultural) background of the colonizing countries; secondly the interaction of colonizers with colonized societies and institutions (for example African institutions such as chiefdoms were integrated into colonial administrations, to enlist the help of local chiefs to keep law and order and to collect taxes: Gluckman, 1956/1970); and thirdly the wielding of power by the colonizers within the interactions with the local communities. There is no doubt also that these institutions have an influence on African communities today, and that they have helped to shape modern and urban African cultures. Through interactions these institutions have also been shaped by African cultural influences. The way these interactions might work at the interface of different cultural influences, at the macro, meso and micro levels, given that this takes place within a set of power relations, is discussed below under the heading of *conduct*.

But first to sum up, from a phenomenological view, the values that people have influence the choices they make (question 2 above). Yet what institutional rules they choose to follow may involve the extent to which their values come into conflict with such rules (questions 3 and 4 above) as in the case of post-colonial Africa discussed above. Within the organization, or society, the different stakeholders might have different objectives (question 6), and different values (question 2), and the distribution of power within different relations may influence choices made in decision making (question 6).

By focusing first on these two aspects, context (or an 'institutionalist' perspective) and content (a 'culturalist' perspective), and before moving on to consider a third aspect of conduct, it is possible to describe more fully the constituent parts of 'culture' (Figure 2.2).

Jack Goody (1994), a prominent British social anthropologist, points to the dichotomy in the American tradition of cultural anthropology between 'cultural studies' concerned with symbols and meaning, and the social (social structures, organizations, etc). He maintains that in the European tradition this dichotomy is not readily accepted, and has tended to treat these two categories as virtually synonymous. Certainly this is reflected in Tylor's classic definition (above), and for example Firth's (1951) view where culture is seen as the content of social relations, not as some distinct entity. This is the view taken here. Context both shapes meaning and is shaped by it. Both are what can be described as culture. Institutions are cultural constructs with rules that are applied in society, and they also shape and are shaped by

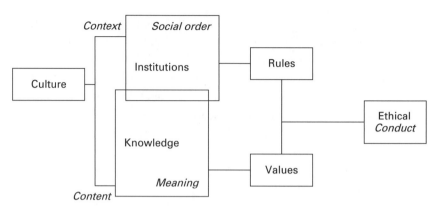

Figure 2.2   Culture and ethical conduct

values, which are part of the meaning systems of society. This is different, for example, from the conceptualization of the American cultural anthropologist Geertz (1973: 89) who sees culture as 'an historically transmitted pattern of meaning embodied in symbols of inherited conceptions expressed in symbolic forms by means which men communicate', and distinguishes between cultural symbols as 'vehicles of thought' and social structure as 'forms of human association' with a 'reciprocal interplay' occurring between them. Goody (1994: 252) therefore maintains that 'attempts to differentiate the cultural from the social, or the symbolic from other forms of human interaction, seem open to question. The terms may serve as general signposts to areas of interest within a wider field of social action.' This discussion highlights the role and importance of interaction, or in Silverman's (1970) terms 'meaningful action', as a component of culture. In a globalized world, with opportunity (or rather necessity) to interact across cultures, this becomes a core component of cross-cultural activity that can only be understood at the interface between knowledge and institutions.

Conduct in cross-cultural analysis

If institutional and culturalist theories have tended to separate context from content, behavioural theories have had the same effect in separating out *conduct* by seeing observable behaviour as the main subject of social interaction. Behavioural theories lie mainly in the province of psychology and social psychology, and mainly at the level of the individual. Overt behaviour is seen as the only means of explaining the psychology of the person: behaviour as a response to stimuli in the environment (Skinner, 1953). In social psychology, this has led to skills theory. For example, Argyle's (1967) social skills model is echoed later by systems theorists and theories of the learning organization (Argyris, 1992), which are aimed at the organizational or meso level. At the individual or micro level skilled performance is seen as a conscious process directed towards making changes in the environment. It requires motivation to drive the process, and attitudes directed towards specific goals may influence the process and its outcomes. It requires an ability to perceive the changes to be made and to understand how they might be achieved through rational thought processes, and then to formulate and carry out any actions that may be required to achieve the necessary goals (Argyle, 1967). As in Argyris's (1992) organizational learning model, the effects of actions on the outside world are fed back to the actors. From this feedback loop the individual learns: that is, reacts to the success in making changes to the outside world. Skills theory has been developed and adapted in the context of human resource management in organizations in many Western societies. The competences model (Boyatzis, 1982) is used extensively in defining how executive goals may be achieved by recruiting staff with necessary skills, attitudes and abilities, how they might be trained, and how they might be rewarded for acquiring and using a defined competences set.

By focusing on the behavioural level, ethical *conduct* for example may be seen as a trainable set of competences. This is reflected in training and educational courses that seek to develop ethical awareness and competences. Within the descriptive framework (Table 2.1) it provides a more fundamental and dynamic element. Rather than the three aspects, *context*, *content* and *conduct*, being separate facets of organizational and social phenomena, they are dynamically connected. In a globalized world, organizations and nations are also connected by numerous interactions. It is difficult to think of separate 'cultures' existing in isolation. Intellectually, it is more viable to think of cultural 'interfaces' at the macro, meso and micro levels of *conduct* (Table 2.1).

At the macro level international power dynamics play a major part in the way cultural interfaces are defined and developed. As was noted above, this is particularly apparent in emerging countries. Colonialism and imperialism have shaped the modern world in which global and local organizations operate. Empires continue to rise (for example, the global pre-eminence of the United States: commentators such as Ali, 2002, have pointed to neo-imperialism in this connection) and continue to fall (for example the Russian Soviet Empire; see Glenny, 1993). Recent global movements of this kind over the last decade and a half include the opening up of China first to international joint ventures, and an exponential growth in foreign investment from the early 1980s (Jackson and Bak, 1998). The collapse of the Soviet system at the end of the 1980s had global implications both directly and indirectly, for example the willingness to negotiate the end of apartheid in South Africa at the beginning of the 1990s together with a move away from a protected economy and an opening up of international trade (Jackson, 1999).

The liberalization of the Indian economy also took on a momentum at the beginning of the 1990s (Rohmetra, 1998), and this general trend towards market economics in such 'developing' countries as Nigeria (Maier, 2000; Jackson, 2004) appears to have been driven in part by World Bank/IMF-led initiatives for structural adjustment: for 'developing' counties to open up their economies to free trade, to downsize the public sector and make it more accountable, and to generally 'modernize' towards a Western model (Barratt Brown, 1995, provides a critique).

This has not only brought emerging countries into more direct contact with Western countries; it has also brought with it the adoption and/or the adaptation of Western concepts of managing organizations. Policies of international multilateral and bilateral agencies have driven public sector reform along Western models, and have driven the liberalization of trade, rendering local business and societies vulnerable in many instances (Barratt Brown, 1995). Activities of multinational organizations in the commercial sector have introduced management policies and practices, as well as Western management education, to countries such as China.

But these types of international interactions are not new. Hong Kong, for example, represents a complex interface of Western and Chinese culture, business practices and management processes. It is perhaps no accident that theories of cultural crossvergence have been developed by management academics focusing on Hong Kong (Ralston *et al.*, 1994; Priem *et al.*, 2000). This concept brings together opposing views of globalization, namely convergence and divergence theories.

Convergence is based on an assumption that all societies are following the same trajectory. As societies industrialize they embrace capitalism and technology and evolve towards the (Western) industrialized societies (from Kerr *et al.* 1960). Contained within this must also be noted the influence of television, Hollywood, the global reach of multinational companies, global brands such as Coca-Cola and McDonald's, conditional financial aid, structural adjustment programmes, American/Western management education programmes, migration, cosmopolitanization, and so on. These all influence a tendency towards cultural convergence.

Divergence argues that national cultures continue to be a primary influence on values, beliefs and attitudes despite globalizing forces and industrialization, and that culture is a long-lived rather than a transient phenomenon. Successive studies that focus on comparing national cultures have sought to demonstrate this (i.e. wider societal values, e.g. Inglehart *et al.* 1998, and Schwartz, 1999; and work-related values, e.g. Hofstede, 1980a/2003; Trompenaars, 1993; House *et al.*, 2004: considered in Chapter 3).

Yet both concepts, of convergence or divergence, do not appear to consider the process of what goes on during cross-cultural interactions. Rather than trying to identify the nature of a cultural entity, such as a country, it would seem more legitimate to discover the nature of intercultural interactions at different levels of analysis, and (to borrow from a phrase from Hofstede, 1980a/2003) their consequences.

A third perspective (Beals, 1953; Ralston *et al.*, 1994; Priem *et al.*, 2000) is that of cultural **crossvergence**. This suggests that culture and industrialization will interact to produce a new value system, such as in the case of Hong Kong. It is possible to go further than this in asserting, for example in relation to the way people are managed in organizations, that:

Although there may be hegemonic influences from stronger and more successful economies such as the United States that propel transitional and emerging countries to adopt inappropriate solutions, crossvergence or the interaction of different cultural influences in cultures such as South Korea and Hong Kong (Ralston, Gustafson, Terpstra and Holt, 1993; Priem, Love and Shaffer, 2000) have given rise to successful hybrid management systems. The level of industrial development of a country, its cultural values and the level and nature of cultural interactions may all play a part in the nature of people management systems and their appropriateness to the economic and cultural context within which they operate. The extent to which they prioritize stakeholders' interests and balance, for example, the potential conflicts between work and home/community life may be a function of cultural values as much as the level of industrial development of a country. (Jackson, 2002a: 456)

Crossvergence theory, when stressing the importance of interaction at different levels, may well be the key to understanding culture not as a product or characteristic of a discrete cultural entity such as a nation, but as an **interface** (Jackson and Aycan, 2006) between and among different cultural influences; between attitudes, beliefs and values, and institutions as cultural manifestations; and within relationships containing power dynamics.

It is possible therefore to think of *conduct*, the subject of this current section, as interaction at macro, meso and micro levels (see Table 2.1). Yet 'interaction' as a term is normally applied at the social psychological level of interpersonal relations. Hence the term 'interfaces' implies a broader conceptual framework whereby geopolitical dynamics at the macro level are considered, through to the meso levels of interorganizational interactions, and micro level of interpersonal interactions; and whereby these different levels further interact to produce different hybrid social forms. This is now considered in more detail.

Studying cross-cultural interfaces

Given the above discussion, how is it possible to study cross-cultural interfaces, and what is the relevance to understanding management ethics from a cross-cultural perspective? It is necessary to further unpack the concept of *interfaces*, and to provide a dynamic to the aspects shown in Table 2.1, through examining in more detail the concept of *conduct* (or, in fact, cultural interactions), and its cultural products.

The concept of *interface* for the present purpose involves a confluence of the three facets of context, content and conduct at different levels (namely macro, meso and micro: these being slightly idealized divisions which are of course overlapping). It involves a general context of globalization, within a regional or national environment, within an organizational context (e.g. Sorge, 2004). It involves the generation of sets of cultural 'rules' mainly about beliefs and actions within and towards what might be described as institutions. There is an interaction between context (institutions, rules), content (values and beliefs: internalized and externalized) through conduct (communicative interaction; or meaningful action) which means that people shape their institutions and are shaped by them.

The phenomenological view (e.g. Schutz, 1972) of this interaction appears naïve without a proper assessment of the role of power relations in shaping reality through communicative interaction. Power involves both physical and economic power that directly shapes the nature of institutions; and ideology that indirectly shapes the nature and regard toward institutions through influencing and shaping the nature of people's values, attitudes, beliefs and knowledge. For example, at the macro level hegemonic influences of empire operate through military and economic means (for example, out of 187 member states of the United Nations, the USA has a military presence in 100 of these; it was spending approximately US$50 billion in defending its interests in the Persian Gulf alone, prior to the Iraqi war: Ali, 2002: 303). Yet this also operates through ideological means: originally through religion and missionaries (e.g. Pakenham,

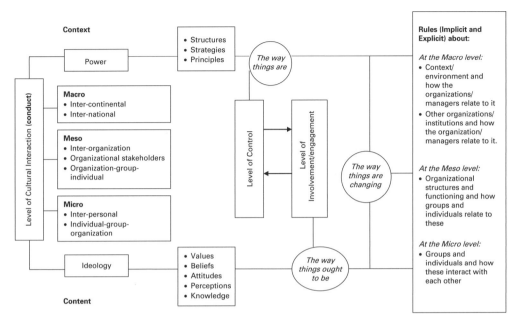

Figure 2.3   Dynamic of content–context–conduct interaction

1991, who argues, following David Livingstone, that the British Empire was founded on 'Commerce, Christianity and Civilization'), and more latterly through the media, education, literature, conditional aid, and corporate activity including corporate sponsorship. In Figure 2.3 'power' is depicted as influencing structure, strategy and principles (the 'harder' aspects of organization, or what might be regarded as 'institutions'); and ideology influencing values, beliefs, attitudes, perceptions and knowledge (the 'softer' aspects). Yet here also there is an (imperfect) interaction effect. For example, institutions might be enforced through military or economic means, but they will not be supported without affecting people's attitudes towards them. US military commanders in Iraq spoke of winning the hearts and minds of Iraqi people: introducing 'democratic' institutions in a militarily occupied country does not mean that these institutions will be accepted without some kind of ideological influence. Similarly in Africa, as noted above, Dia (1996) suggests that institutions were imposed on local societies during colonial times and still remain disconnected from these societies. Hence they are not being effective in addressing issues within African countries.

In emerging countries that have a colonial past, the influence of power within this dynamic is easily discernable (Ahluwalia, 2001). It is also an aspect that needs to be prominent in any social scientific investigation (Flyvbjerg,

Table 2.2 Cross-cultural dynamics in post-colonial societies (from Jackson, 2004)

Levels of analysis	Past	Present	Future
Intercontinental *Power dynamic*	Colonial/indigenous Economic, military and ideological	Post-colonial/Western/indigenous Economic, contractual and ideological	Future hybrid systems Contractual and obligatory
Cross-border *Power dynamic*	Restricted cross-national Political and military	Increased intra-regional Political and economic	Increased intra-continental Economic and cooperative
Interethnic *Power dynamic*	Colonial 'divide and rule' Political and military	Political/power relations Political, economic and sometimes military	Increased synergies Multiculturalism

2001), not least cross-cultural studies (Cray and Mallory, 1998). In his study of Africa Jackson (2004) provides an overview of power dynamics, within a historical perspective, focusing at the macro (intercontinental level of cross-cultural interaction), macro/meso (cross-border or international level) and meso/micro (interethnic) levels (see Table 2.2).

Interactions take place across continents (so to speak) with Western powers, both historically as former colonial countries, and through the activities of modern multinational companies and the predominance of Western education. These interactions were dominated economically, militarily and often ideologically by the colonial power (e.g. Reader, 1998). Today they are dominated economically through interactions with both multinational companies and multilateral agencies, particularly the World Bank and the IMF, and bilateral agencies of Western governments (e.g. Barratt Brown, 1995). The predominance of Western education ensures an ideological disparaging of indigenous thought/knowledge systems, although there is potential ('Future' in Table 2.2) to develop hybrid systems of management that take influences from Western and indigenous thought systems and practices.

At the cross-border level, emerging trading blocs among African countries, such as SADC, COMESA and ECOWAS, are encouraging intra-regional interaction, rather than between the African country and its former colonial master (e.g. Mulat, 1998). Colonial powers severely restricted communications among African countries. Transport infrastructure reflected this in roads and rail being built to link seaports with mineral sources, rather than to link a country with its neighbour. Trade was restricted to include only that between colony and colonial power. Trading blocs are now encouraging more interaction, although often the legacy of colonial transport infrastructure restricts this. The growing requirement to work with managers and trading partners among African countries, often within regions, introduces another level of cross-cultural interaction. It is likely that such interactions are facilitated or restricted by political/governmental considerations, and motivated by economic factors that drive competition.

Higher levels of mutual cooperation, on an intra-continental rather than just a regional basis, may well drive future interactions. Indeed, a view that many African states are not viable economic entities (Reader, 1998) may require higher levels of intra-regional and intra-continental cooperation for future economic and social prosperity.

At the interethnic level most countries in Africa (and many emerging countries in other regions) are multi-ethnic, often by virtue of the fact that successive colonial powers artificially divided up the continent, ignoring ethnic identities; and by the sheer complexity of ethnicity in any one country. For example, South Africa has eleven official languages. Cameroon, a country that was successively ruled by Germany and then partitioned and jointly administered by France and Britain, has over 250 language groups, as well as the two official languages of French and English. This type of scenario is repeated in many different forms within Africa (see www.ethnologue.com). 'Divide and rule' was a common political strategy for colonial rulers, and resentments thus created have often extended into the interethnic tensions sometimes witnessed today. Sometimes this has erupted into military action and civil war (and even genocide in the case of Rwanda and neighbouring Burundi). Yet in organizations in African countries there is potential to create synergies from multiculturalism, although this may require managing the power relationships involved among the different stakeholders (Jackson, 2004).

It may therefore be apparent that equal relations may not typify interactions at these different levels. Western multinational companies and their expatriate managers may have more power than local managers and staff. Within a particular region (say southern Africa) South African corporations, and managers, may dominate in trade or operations among SADC countries (cross-national interactions). This may also be the case in Europe where in Poland and the Czech Republic German corporations may dominate in some industrial sectors. This has created tensions in the relationships between, for example, expatriates and local managers and staff in issues such as unequal pay and influence in decision making (Gutmann, 1995; Cyr and Schneider, 1998).

White managers may dominate in a South African corporation. Managers of South Asian decent may dominate in particular organizations in Nairobi, while Kikuya managers may dominate in other organizations, in Kenya for example.

At the meso level, power relations are translated into control mechanisms within organizations (e.g. Etzioni, 1975), and reveal themselves in organizational structures and functioning. Rather than being a simple mediator where culture is the antecedent (independent variable) and the management system is the end result (dependent variable), power is an integral part of the way cross-cultural interaction gives rise to strategies, structures and principles of management, and how these are operated in an organization. In Figure 2.3 this is depicted in 'the way things are'. To provide a definition:

- *Power* can be described as the ability (militarily, economically, politically, etc.) to impose one's will on others (see for example Dahl, 1957);
- *Ideology* can be described as the hegemony of value, belief and knowledge systems created through education, media and dominant practices, which legitimize and sanction structures and practices within organizations (a thorough examination of this concept can be found in Larrain, 1979).

For example, the dominance of colonial power before independence gave rise to the disparaging of indigenous values, beliefs and knowledge systems and created education based on a Western model in post-colonial countries. Since the Second World War the dominance of American economic influence has led to a proliferation of MBA programmes and textbooks, as well as American management practices, throughout the world (see Boyacigiller and Adler, 1991). Yet global convergence (from Kerr *et al.*, 1960) of principles and practices may not be happening. That is, the acceptance, for example, of Western styles of management may not be complete. It is here that there is a strong argument to suggest that crossvergence, rather than convergence, is the dominant process within globalization as we have seen (Ralston *et al.*, 1993; Priem *et al.*, 2000). This presupposes that indigenous values, beliefs and knowledge systems are present, but modified through the hegemony of globalizing power relations, which in turn may be modified through practice. This will be related to the direct nature of foreign and post-colonial influences. This also relates to public sector organizations, under the influence of Western education, and pressures to reform from IMF/World Bank initiatives.

The judgement of 'The way things ought to be' in an organization, that is, the perception of the desirability of aspects of management systems, may well vary by 'cultural' group (be it a national group or ethnic group). However, this perception will also be influenced by the position of that group in an organization as a dominant or subordinate group, and the extent to which the dominant ideology has been accepted or not. The extent to which there is a difference between a perception of 'the way things are', and a perception of 'the way things ought to be' (Figure 2.3) reflects the level of disparity between the power of the dominant group to enforce particular strategies, structures and principles (institutions), and its legitimizing ideology in the extent to which staff in the organization accept the way things operate in the organization (values).

At the organizational and management level (the level at which this book is mainly addressed), how can organizational structures and functioning be conceptualized?

An overriding principle in the way in which organization is conceived and operated, is that of 'control' (Etzioni, 1975; Katz and Kahn, 1978). The nature of that control, and its perceived legitimacy, influence the level of involvement of staff and managers in the organization. Its perceived legitimacy may well reflect the values, beliefs and knowledge systems of a particular group, or set of individuals, and the integrity of that group in terms of acceptance or rejection of the dominant ideology.

The concept of 'control' is also fundamental to the concept of rules, and here we return to Harré *et al.*'s, (1985) hierarchy of control (Figure 2.1). They state that 'the "production" of social life is conceived to be analogous to the way actors follow a script (which is like a system of rules) to create an illusion of real life' (1985: 95). Yet, 'most people are not able immediately to formulate the rules and conventions they adhere to in social action, in solving problems, in interpreting feelings, and so on' (1985: 97). This is particularly so because 'the deep structure of mind' is bound up with the social order or macro level institutional arrangements and processes that provide control within a society. This in turn affects conscious awareness, which affects human actions. For example, Silverman (1970) as we have seen, asserts that 'action' is meaningful behaviour. Actors attribute meaning to their actions. Others also attribute meaning to these actions. These meanings attached by others in their turn influence the meaning attached by the original actor. Social reality is created through this process, although with the proviso that some individuals and groups do not have equal power with other individuals and groups. So some have more influence on the meaning of actions than others.

The subjects of social analysis, including understanding cross-cultural interfaces, are:

- the rules about how things operate around here;
- the process whereby these rules come about by focusing on 'the way things are' (the perceptions by members of different groups about the nature of control in organizations);
- the value judgements people make about the way things ought to be (the extent to which members of different groups are engaging with and involved in the organization the way it is); and
- the congruence between the way things are and the way things ought to be (the way things are changing) (Figure 2.3).

In other words, institutions lay down rules that are internalized or implicitly accepted, or explicitly conformed to and/or rejected. Explicit conformity may be achieved through forces of overt power (e.g. enactment of laws enforced through the power to impose fines or imprison). Internalization may be achieved through ideological means (instilling values, for example of Western democracy, which people accept and internalize as being the proper way to run institutions).

This, of course, is more complex than the way 'cultural values' have been conceived by cross-cultural theorists who seek to compare 'cultures' as static, concrete structures. Cultures are dynamics that involve an interaction between institutions (the ways things are) and values (the way things ought to be) within power relations. Institutions can change quite radically and quickly, as in the case with the imposition of colonial institutions in Africa, India and so on; and in the case of introducing Western democracy to Iraq after 2004.

In the latter case, 'rules' may dictate acceptance of Western-style democratic institutions. 'Values' might suggest a rejection of such rules by sections of the local population. 'Power' might be used to enforce such institutional rules, first at the level of compliance. As time goes on, and depending on the power relationship, and depending on the dominant group's ability to control the discourse about such institutions, institutional rules might become internalized and implicitly accepted by indigenous groups. When this happens, it then may become regarded as 'unethical' (that is, counter to prevailing values, or judgements about the legitimacy of such rules) to disregard or counter such Western democratic institutional rules.

Still using this example, the values of local groups may judge such institutional rules as illegitimate and contrary to traditional values, in which case the enforcement of such rules may be judged to be unethical. If such groups predominate within the power relationship, Western democratic institutional rules, motivated by Western value judgement might be eventually rejected.

The concepts of 'rules', 'values' and 'control', may therefore be the way forward in understanding culture as a dynamic, rather than a static entity. And central to this is 'power', in Foucault's (1979: 194) terms, for example: 'power produces, it makes reality; it produces domains of objects and rituals of truth'. He contends that power relations do not stand apart from other relations, but power is inherent in all relations and is the effect of divisions, inequalities and imbalances found in these relations, and at the same time are preconditions for these differentiations. In the world of business this may be in a merger, acquisition or joint venture situation; in an organization this may be in a boss–employee relationship. For Foucault power also infers the possibility of resistance, and that resistance is always part of a power relationship. From the discussion above, this may involve values coming into conflict with rules. Dominance in a power relationship has a legitimizing effect, which can generate concepts of ethical conduct.

In summary of this section, the idea of cultural *interfaces* is seen as a way of integrating different levels of interaction (macro, meso and micro: see Figure 2.3) as well as integrating *context* and *content* through the interactional processes labelled *conduct*. As can be seen in Figure 2.3, such interactions imply power dynamics through institutions (*context*: structures, strategies and principles), and ideology through culture (*content*: values, beliefs, attitudes, perceptions and knowledge): power and ideology being part of the same process, but using different means. Through these interactive dynamics, the crossvergence of cultures may be considered. In a globalized world these lead to hybrid forms of societies, organizations, values and institutions. In a postcolonial world involving such dynamics institutions were often imposed (through power dynamics) on societies (e.g. Dia, 1996). The 'rules' thus established through such institutional arrangements may be at variance to the 'values' of local culture.

Having indicated at the beginning of this chapter that ethics comprises the choices available to individuals through the influence of values, and the rules followed; the way such rules control the level and nature of choice; as well as the power relations within the different stakeholders involved and their different objectives, how can we now answer the question posed above, 'Are German managers less ethical than American managers?'

Firstly, the US Foreign Corrupt Practices Act reflects institutional arrangements within the United States that through legislation lay down a set of rules for organizations and their managers to adhere to. Following Jackson and Calafell Artola (1997) we might assert that as a result of a free-market economy in the United States proving a set of values about the way business should be conducted, there is a need to curb the excesses of a free-market economy. Not so in Germany for example, where the relationships between business, governments and financial institutions provide longer-term stability for business. Excesses in business dealings may therefore be curbed through the internalization of values. The emphasis of business ethics has not therefore been as great in Germany as it has been in the United States (this is explored in more detail in Chapters 5 and 6). There is an interface between culture and institutional arrangements in these different countries, such that the regard for ethicality may be quite different. When we then turn our attention to 'developing' countries (often the recipients of the 'bribes' that the US Foreign Corrupt Practices Act attempts to curb), the interface between institutions and culture may not be as seamless.

Closing case: are African countries more corrupt than G8 countries?

The following article appeared in Guardian Unlimited (the web pages of *The Guardian* newspaper) on Tuesday 5 July 2005.

Who pays Africa's bribes?

G8 countries are largely to blame for corruption in the developing world, says Christian Aid's Dominic Nutt

When tackling drugs crime, most British police forces know that first and foremost you have to target the dealer. The user is as much victim as criminal. This holds true for African corruption – something in which the media have rightly shown an interest in recent days. As the public lines up in increasing numbers behind Live 8 and the Make Poverty History campaign, many are asking: why should we forgive Africa's debt and give more money in aid if all Africa's leaders do is salt it away in Swiss – and British – bank accounts?

But in the case of corruption, it's the G8 nations and their rich northern neighbours who are the bribe pushers – and some (not all) African governments who are the users. It's British, American, French, German and Russian companies that pay enormous bribes to get a competitive advantage over their rivals. And it is their governments who fail to prosecute them.

In a survey by Transparency International – the field leaders in anti-corruption – domestic companies in five G8 nations (Russia, the US, Italy, Japan and France) were perceived to be among the worst bribe payers among the most industrialised countries in the world. UK law exempts British subsidiaries abroad from prosecution back home. The burden is on the government of the country in which the company is based to prosecute the bribe-giving company. But if the government itself is weak and corrupt, the company is likely never to be brought to task. In the past six years not one UK company has been prosecuted for corruption. Few are ever even investigated. Worst still, UK banks consistently facilitate corrupt governments abroad – with the tacit consent of our government. For example, in Kenya many organisations, some supported by Christian Aid, were fighting deep-seated corruption under the rotten presidency of Daniel arap Moi. Yet at the same time Moi was transferring government money out of the country – to UK bank accounts.

In October 2003 United Nations drew up the Convention Against Corruption to tackle these very problems. At least it would do, had it been ratified. But so far it has been backed by only 27 countries – 14 of them African. Not one G8 country has signed up – a fact that is unlikely to be a matter of coincidence. Far more likely a reason is that the G8 has too much to lose by ending corruption in Africa. The very genesis of African corruption is also something that the rich G8 nations must take a good deal of responsibility for. As Germany, Belgium, France, Britain and Portugal pulled out of Africa they left behind them a system of government based on elitism, patronage and power – fertile ground for the seeds of corruption.

New nations emerged blinking into the glorious light of new-found freedom and set about creating fledging democracies. Bear in mind it took Britain 700 years to establish democracy – from the signing of the Magna Carta to the 1969 Representation of the People Act which lowered the voting age to 18. It's not something that happens overnight.

But when the world's powerful countries don't like your form of democracy it becomes all but impossible. Take Zaire, as one among many painfully typical African examples. In 1960 the Belgians left Zaire and elections confirmed the Marxist Patrice Lumumba as prime minister. The country was unstable, thanks mostly to the state in which Belgian administrators had left the country. As fighting broke out in several areas and European mercenaries, hired to protect European interests, flooded in, Lumumba turned to the Soviet Union for help. This spurred the US into action who sought to replace the democratically elected prime minister. They sent in weapons and CIA personnel to support a pro-western coup. Mobuto, a man steeped in corruption, took over.

However, this was of little consequence to the west – Mobuto could be as corrupt as he liked, as long as he supported their strategic interests. It's a story that was repeated, in different forms, across the continent, from Angola to Mozambique and elsewhere. The west pumped in 'aid' and loans to buy weapons – from western arms manufacturers – to fight the proxy war against Soviet-backed rebel groups. We turned a blind eye to the fact that much aid was diverted into the pockets of the dictators we were backing.

Ironically, we are now demanding that money back – money we forced Africa to borrow, and with which we made them buy weapons to fight wars which left their countries poorer and in more need of aid than ever before. The end of the cold war didn't bring much respite. Instead, the G8 now imposes conditions on African countries when it gives aid. The G8-dominated International Monetary Fund and the World Bank make loans on condition that poor countries cut back on expenditure. Among institutions that faced the axe were schools which teach children to read and write – essential tools for the citizens in any democracy who want to hold leaders to account; the judiciary – essential to hold the corrupt to account and the police and civil servants, all of whom are needed to curtail corruption. And those who keep their jobs are often paid less than poverty wages – making them susceptible to bribery, should they wish to do anything as extravagant as feed their families.

But does this mean that African leaders are blameless? No, of course not. Africans must take their share of responsibility. But we must recognise our responsibility too. And corruption is a worldwide phenomenon – not just an African one. Italy is considered more corrupt than Botswana, Greece outranks South Africa, Poland is worse than Ghana. And remember the cashfor-questions scandal here in the UK and the mass resignation of the corrupt European commission in 2003? No one is immune.

While there are limits to whom we should give aid – Mugabe heads a regime that no one could argue should receive direct aid – we cannot wait until every African country is totally free of all corruption before we give aid. If we do, more children will die of malaria and more adults will contract HIV. And another generation will go uneducated in Africa. Illiteracy fuels corruption. To hold a government to account you need a free press and you need to be able to read, to understand and to challenge your representatives. It is not a matter of stopping aid to countries that are corrupt; it is a matter of giving the aid to stop corruption. And for our part, we must crack down on the bribe givers and the bankers who are all making a sleazy buck out of Africa's plight. The alternative is to hunt down the bribe users, while those that fuel corruption – the bribe pushers – ply their corrosive trade.

Dominic Nutt is an emergencies journalist for Christian Aid.

Accessed on 23 May 2007 at: www.guardian.co.uk/g8/story/0,13365, 1521819,00.html#article_continue

(Copyright Guardian News & Media Ltd 2005)

Implications for international managers

This chapter has mainly been concerned with the theory of why ethicality differs across countries. It has opened with a case about the way US legislators have dealt with the issue of international corruption, although the closing case has raised certain questions about its effectiveness, and indeed its seriousness. For an international manager making ethical decisions, a number of aspects are involved that were highlighted at the beginning of this chapter. Firstly, 'what choices are available?' A Western manager operating in an African country might say that if one is to get the business they have to pay the bribe. Yet it may be the case (according to our closing case) that by making this choice, Western countries are perpetuating a system that came about by colonial influences in African countries that are at variance to local cultures. Secondly, 'what values influence these choices?' The work of Transparency International (in the closing case) appears to disabuse the idea that Western countries have values that condemn corruption, and that African values support corruption. We discussed above the implementation of 'rules' in the USA in order to curb the excesses of a free-market economy. Here values (of a free-market economy) appear to be at variance to rules set down by institutions in order to curtail the effects of these free-market values.

These rules appear to be sometimes followed and sometimes not. The fact that the USA and other G8 countries still have not signed up to the UN's Convention Against Corruption may indicate a lack of effectiveness of these rules, and a lessening of choice among both bribe payers and bribe takers. Hence, in part this answers the third question, 'what rules are followed or not followed in order to make a choice?'; and in part answers the fourth question, 'how do these rules control the levels and nature of choice in a society?'

The fifth question, 'what are the power relations among the different stakeholders within the society that control rules and values that influence choice?' again indicates a power relationship between developed and developing countries that have historically introduced conditions whereby corruption can thrive, and have continued these conditions through the perpetuation of bribe paying according to the closing case. Finally, the sixth question, 'what different objectives do the different stakeholders have that influence choice in decision making?' may require an examination at macro, meso and micro levels. At macro level, what are the objectives in the G8 countries in not signing up to the UN Convention Against Corruption? At the meso level, what are the objectives of organizations from G8 countries operating in African countries and willing to pay bribes? At micro levels, what are the objectives of individual managers and their counterparts in African counties in terms of paying and receiving bribes? For the international manager these may all be questions that should be considered in their decision making.

Questions for managers
1. To what extent can German managers be seen as less ethical than Americans?
2. Under what circumstances should bribery overseas be condoned or allowed?
3. What factors would you consider in making a decision about whether or not to pay a bribe overseas?

An agenda for research

The 'why?' question in cross-cultural research is normally addressed by referring to wider societal values, such as Hofstede's (1980a/2003) cultural value dimensions. As we will see in the next chapter, these do not provide an explanation, merely a context. Hence, both Husted (1999) and Sanyal (2005) provide *Collectivism* and high *Power Distance* as explanatory cultural factors of corruption. They also discuss other correlates of corruption in countries such as level of GDP, income distribution and size of government administration. In the current text, we have interpreted the question 'why does ethicality, or the meaning of what is ethical or not, differ among countries and regions in a different way?' by referring to the interactions (or interfaces) of culture and institutions at macro, meso and micro levels, and considering the importance of power dynamics within this. In order to undertake research in this area it is necessary to investigate the different factors in the model presented in Figure 2.3. One important aspect discussed in this chapter is the disjuncture between institutions and values, or to put this another way (see Figure 2.3) the way things are, and the way they ought to be. Hence managers may see that it is necessary to pay bribes in a certain country (*context*), but may believe this is wrong and needs to change (*content*). At the micro level, the question is, what does the manager then do? (*conduct*). This constitutes interaction at the individual level, and a cultural interface also at this micro level. At this level of interaction, expectations are confirmed, created and adhered to. This may operate similarly at the organizational level, where international firms operate in a particular way creating expectations among bribe takers and givers. At the macro level of 'intercontinental' interaction and interface, expectations are created and reinforced through actions of governments and of institutions, for example in G8 countries and the failure to take action on corruption. Historic and current power relations should also be taken into account (Table 2.2) in the way rules about what constitutes ethical conduct are created through crossvergence and hybridization: also taking into account the disjuncture between what is and what ought to be. The former implies the nature and level of control of institutions, whereas the latter implies the resistance to ways of doing things, or compliance, or involvement/engagement: that is to what extent are people committed to the rules about the way things are done? Variance between the way things ought to be (values) and the way things are (rules) implies levels of change where there is resistance to the way things are.

Questions for researchers
1. Why does ethicality, or the meaning of what is ethical or not, differ among countries and regions in a different way?

2. How can the disjuncture between institutions and values, or the way things are/the way they ought to be, be investigated?
3. How can we analyse the relationships between the different levels (macro, meso and micro) of cultural interaction, in order to provide an understanding of ethicality in specific contexts?

3   Culture, values and management ethics

'Culture' in the last chapter was seen as 'that complex whole which involves knowledge, beliefs, art, morals, law, customs and other capabilities and habits acquired by man as a member of society' (Tylor, 1871); or, the 'human-made part of the environment' (Herskovits, 1948). This was distinguished, after Goody (1994), from the narrower concept of culture as being purely symbolic, or rather, excluding other 'human-made' parts of the environment and, after Sorge (2004), distinguishing between a culturalist and institutionalist position. In other words, institutions as part of 'culture' are created by sentient human beings in interaction interpersonally, interorganizationally and internationally. They are both part of the meaning systems through which people conduct their lives, as well as being created and supported by those meaning systems. Chapter 2 also discussed the relationship between 'rules' and 'values'. Again the two concepts interrelate. Rules are created out of, and supported by value systems. Yet rules also shape the values that people have. This is an essential part of comprehending the concept of 'interfaces' in cross-cultural understanding and analysis.

'Rules' (or the way we are supposed to do things around here) may be imposed on a local population, whether this be a society or an organization. This could be a management system, for example. A foreign company acquiring a local firm as its subsidiary may impose a management system comprising rules about decision making that are different to those the local staff and managers are used to. (Saying that these rules are 'more' autocratic or 'more' democratic is perhaps missing the point as this is making a value judgement about what is autocracy and the, often negative, value we place on it, and what is democracy and the, often positive, value we place upon it.)

Opening case: is participation tyrannical?

In the introduction to Bill Cooke and Uma Kothari's (2001) edited book *Participation: The New Tyranny?* the authors define from the *Collins English*

Dictionary a tyrant as 'a person who governs oppressively, unjustly, and arbitrarily' and tyranny as 'government by a tyrant or tyrants; despotism ... arbitrary, unreasonable, or despotic behaviour or use of authority'. In other words, they say 'tyranny is the illegitimate and/or unjust exercise of power' (2001: 4). How, therefore, can the introduction of participatory management be regarded as tyranny, and therefore an unjust use of power? In their book, this is treated at three levels. Firstly, asking the question 'do participatory facilitators override existing legitimate decision-making processes?' Secondly, 'do group dynamics lead to participatory decisions that reinforce the interests of the already powerful?' And, thirdly, 'have participatory methods driven out others which have advantages participation cannot provide?' In other words, in international development (which is mainly what their book is about) participatory methods that are aimed at bringing in local people and being mindful of local knowledge have largely been imposed by large international organizations as an alternative to what has been seen as autocratic, and perhaps paternalistic methods of decision making. The adoption of Western-style participation is normally conditional to providing development assistance.

In one of the chapters of the same book Taylor (2002) argues that 'participatory discourse and practices are part of a wider attempt to obscure the relations of power and influence between elite interests and less powerful groups such as ... employees of organizations' (2002: 122). Further, participator discourses serve the purpose of 'giving the "sense" and warm emotional pull of participation without its substance, and are thus an attempt to placate those without power and obscure the real levers of power inherent in the social relations of global capitalism' (2002: 125). He suggests that 'managerialism' is spreading from the private sector in industrialized countries to all kinds of organizations across the globe including state bureaucracies and NGOs in developing countries, with a technocratic view that 'management' is a universal, rational process that can be applied anywhere. Thus participatory management principles and practices developed in the West are being spread to developing countries and to different types of organization (Taylor, 2002).

Management systems comprise rules, and also imply control. Etzioni's (1975) work suggests that control systems in organizations may result in alienative, calculative or moral involvement on the part of staff. Hence, introducing a new management system, such as participatory methods in non-Western contexts, may result in staff being either initially alienated from these new systems (as in the case of colonial impositions on African societies: Dia, 1996), or having a calculative involvement with such systems (which now may be the case for Western companies in Africa: Jackson, 2004). Either way, values may come into conflict with rules. The rules imposed by a foreign multinational company may be based on the values from that foreign culture (based on a corporate or national culture or both). However, the power to impose rules is more complex than that. Ideology plays a major part in the acceptance of such rules: that is, developing a moral involvement with the organization and internalizing the values that are associated with those rules. Chapter 2 discussed how this might take place through Westernized education, television and so on (at the macro level).

Also at a meso level organizations may develop staff involvement that goes beyond what Etzioni (1975) describes as calculative involvement with the organization through remunerative control, to develop moral involvement through normative control mechanisms. Here, values are inculcated through identification with the executive goals and values of the organization. This type of management control has been successful in the 'collectivist' society of Japan (Jackson 2002b), but less so in the 'collectivist' societies of Africa and South Asia. The introduction of alien colonial management systems may be the reason why. It is also likely that in 'individualistic' societies such as in the United States, in other 'Anglo-Saxon' environments and in other Western contexts, corporations have developed successful normative control systems.

The point here is that rules are based on values, and interact with them. Values differ across cultural spaces and may come into conflict when people with different cultural values come into contact with each other. Although much of the growing literature on national cultural values relates directly to management and work values, there is a lack of connection in the literature between such values and management ethics. This connection is the subject of this chapter. Chapter 2 addressed the question '*Why* does ethicality differ across the globe?' The current chapter addresses the question '*How* does ethicality differ across the globe?'

In a way, this *how* is a descriptive *why*. Cultural values dimensions are often used to provide a rationale for why ethical values vary across cultures. But this is not an *explanatory* why, it is a *descriptive* why: that is, we describe the ethical value and then we link it with a cultural dimension. For example, the following pages will offer a connection between a justification of societal inequality (that is, it is not seen as an ethical issue) and *Power Distance* (a cultural value dimension proffered by Hofstede, 1980a/2003): we explain the ethical acceptance of social inequalities by reference to high *Power Distance*.

But this provides little explanation other than a further description of a cultural value. It is almost tautological. This is therefore a *how* explanation, rather than a *why* explanation: it explains the acceptance of inequality by the acceptance of inequality. However, what it does do is prove a wider cultural context for differences in ethical values (an ethical value becomes a subset of a cultural value), and provides further description of variance. It takes us beyond an assertion of a universal ethics that can apply anywhere in the world.

Cultural values

Among extensive cross-national studies that focus on cultural values, it is possible to distinguish between those that relate to wider societal values (Inglehart *et al.*, 1998; Schwartz, 1999) and those that relate more directly to organizations and management (Hofstede, 1980a/2003; Trompenaars, 1993; Smith *et al.*, 1996; House *et al.*, 2004). Although the former have been used to discuss issues in international management (particularly Schwartz: see for example Gatley *et al.*, 1996), they may represent values at different levels: namely macro and meso/micro. For example, Jackson (2002b) points out that Schwartz's (1994) data on values of the former West and East Germanys indicate similarities of values, suggesting that the prevailing cultural values of the two Germanys were more similar and pervasive during the Iron Curtain years than is suggested by data from studies of organizational employees and managers (such as Trompenaars, 1993). There may therefore be differences (as in the case with the former two Germanys) between values in the wider communities and those in corporations. This may also be the case in former colonial countries where work organizations may not reflect the wider values of the societies within which they exist. Yet, there are also connections between organizational values and societal values, and this is reflected in the discussion above concerning the relationship between values and rules.

The worth of studies that explore wider societal values is that they provide an indication of fit with organizational rules and values. Understanding the values of the wider (macro) society within which organizations evolve or are imposed is important. Firstly, imperialist or neo-imperialist countries such as Britain, France or the USA, do business abroad with a set of values and implicit rules that often are not manifest or explicit and are assumed to be universal. This is often one of the major quests of cross-cultural management studies, to question whether management practices used in the home country are appropriate in other countries (Hofstede, 1980b). It is important to understand the values from which management systems, or sets of rules used in organizations, are derived, and how they influence the way organizations are managed in other countries. Secondly, it is important to understand the societal values and rule systems in societies that host managers and organizations from colonial or neo-colonial countries (i.e. from multinational commercial or non-commercial organizations).

The ethical implications are, firstly, that societies give rise to (and are shaped by) values and rules, among which are judgements of right or wrong, and what is ethical or not. Judgements of ethicality are bound up with such value/rule systems and it is important to understand these. This in part is the aim of Chapters 5–9, which look at such systems in various countries or regions. Secondly, the world no longer comprises isolated communities or societies (if it ever did), and the main departure point of analysis for this book is the concept of cultural interfaces. These interfaces comprise power relations, where often hybrid management forms that arise do so as the result of one society, organization or group being able to impose its rules, and often values on another. This in itself may be an ethical issue. These interfaces are also explored in Chapters 5–9.

It is first necessary, therefore, to focus on these wider societal values, and the implications for understanding differences in ideas of ethicality, or more simply, what is right or fair or just, and what is wrong, unfair or unjust.

World Values Survey: a view from outside the corporation

Of national comparative studies of societal values, that of Inglehart and colleagues is the most extensive and, unlike other studies, takes a longitudinal perspective. However, despite Inglehart's wide publication record on the basis of his World Value Surveys (WVS), and an extensive literature that has made use of these data sets (302 journal articles and 81 books are listed as being related to this study on the website of the Inter-University Consortium for Political and Social Research (ICPSR, 2005)), little theory has been developed around these surveys that directly relates to international management, or management ethics.

The WVS has its origin in a set of surveys conducted in ten Western European countries, and now known as the European Values Surveys. The WVS, growing out of the European studies, was initiated in 1981 'to study the values and attitudes of mass publics across nations of different economic, educational, and cultural backgrounds'. Four waves of the study have been conducted: 1981–2, 1990–1, 1995–7 and 1999–2001. The most recent of these covers over sixty countries. In general terms, the Survey 'explores the hypothesis that mass belief systems are changing in ways that have important economic, political, and social consequences'. They are based on random, stratified samples of adults in the general population. Each study contains data from interviews conducted with between 300 and 4,000 respondents per nation. The areas covered include: the importance of work, family, friends, leisure time, politics and religion; attitudes towards government and religion including the frequency of participating in group activity in governmental and religious organizations; perceptions of economic, ethnic, religious and political groups and feeling of trust and closeness with these groups; assessment of relative importance of major problems facing the world and willingness to participate in solutions; assessment of self in terms of happiness and class identity (ICPSR, 2005).

Inglehart's (1997) main theory is that the shift of societies generally towards modernization and materialist values, emphasising economic and physical security, is giving way to postmodern/postmaterialist values. Core elements in the modernization trend include industrialization, increased urbanization, growing occupational specialization and higher levels of formal education. A corollary of this would normally be higher levels of mass political participation for example. Modernization might also be associated with 'cultural' changes like values conducive to economic accumulation. Postmodernization, he believes, is gradually replacing these outlooks or world views associated with modernization that have existed since the industrial revolution:

Thus, the process of economic development leads to two successive trajectories, modernization and postmodernization. Both of them are strongly linked with economic development, but postmodernization represents a later stage of development that is linked with very different beliefs from those that characterize modernization. These belief systems are not mere consequences of economic or social change, but shape socioeconomic conditions and are shaped by them, in reciprocal fashion. (Inglehart, 1997: 8)

Essentially he sees modernization as emphasizing economic efficiency, bureaucratic authority and scientific rationality; and the move towards postmodernization as moving towards 'a more human society with more room for individual autonomy, diversity and self expression' (1997: 12). Yet his conception of culture also appears to reflect a dichotomy between 'the cultural' and 'objective reality', reflecting the American tradition in cultural anthropology (see Goody, 1994, in Chapter 2 of the current text). In asserting that the move towards postmodernization is neither cultural determinism nor economic determinism he appears to separate the economic from the cultural and presents the former as 'reality'. He also appears to view modernization and postmodernization as stages in human or societal evolution with postmodernization representing 'a later stage of development' (1997: 8). One could take a cynical view of this: less industrialized societies are gradually catching up with industrialized societies and moving towards modernization; yet industrialized societies are now moving to postmodernization, so less industrialized societies have even further to go in following the path of the more advanced countries. The move also towards greater 'individual autonomy' appears to reflect a movement towards more individuality and away from collectivism and communalism (see discussion below around Hofstede's 1980a/2003 concepts).

This point is by no means an aside, or a distraction from the scientific significance of Inglehart's work. It may be an element that is endemic in what Human (1996) calls 'maximalist' studies of cultural values. It is certainly a feature of the critique of Hofstede's work (e.g. Human, 1996: 21, who states: 'the value judgements attached to the various dimensions have also rarely been explored as well as the self-fulfilling nature of the imposition of such classification on people'). Hence to say that one society is higher in *Individualism* or *Power Distance* than another, or lower in *Femininity* than another (Hofstede, 1980a/2003) may be implying a value judgement (or at least one might be inferred) that one society is better than another. Certainly when linking such cultural dimensions to measures of economic development and prosperity as indeed, for example, Hofstede (1980a/2003) and Inglehart (1997) do, there does appear to be an implied value judgement in terms of a correlation between economic and social development and cultural values. The value judgement on Inglehart's part is more than implied. He contends (as co-author with Baker: Inglehart and Baker, 2001: 16–17) that:

The World Values Survey data show us that the world views of people of rich societies differ systematically from those of low-income societies across a wide range of political, social, and religious norms and beliefs. The two most significant dimensions that emerge reflected, first, a polarization between *traditional* and *secular-rational* orientations towards authority and, second, a polarization between *survival* and *self-expression* values. By *traditional* we mean those societies that are relatively authoritarian, place strong emphasis on religion, and exhibit a mainstream version of preindustrial values such as an emphasis on male dominance in economic and political life, respect for authority, and relatively low levels of tolerance for abortion and divorce. Advanced societies, or *secular-rational*, tend to have the opposite characteristics.

A central component of the survival vs. self-expression dimension involves the polarization between materialist and postmaterialist values. Massive evidence indicates that cultural shift throughout advanced industrial society is emerging among generations who have grown up taking survival for granted. Values among this group emphasize environmental protection, the women's movement, and rising demand for participation in decision making in economic and political life. During the past 25 years, these values have become increasingly widespread in almost all advanced industrial societies for which extensive time-series evidence is available.

These dimensions are used by Inglehart to map the world in terms of modernization and postmodernization (for example see Inglehart and Baker, 2000: 35). The first dimension (Inglehart, 1997), *Traditional authority vs. Secular-Rational authority* (later simply called *Traditional vs. Secular-Rational* values: Inglehart and Baker, 2000 and 2001) is based on items that reflect an emphasis on obedience to traditional authority, often religious authority and adherence to family and communal obligations and norm sharing, versus items emphasising a secular worldview where authority is legitimized by rational-legal norms and an emphasis on economic accumulation and individual achievement. Hence items loading positively and representing the *Traditional* pole are: God is very important in respondent's life; it is more important for a child to learn obedience and religious faith than independence and determination; abortion is never justified; respondent has a strong sense of national pride; respondent favours more respect for authority. *Secular-Rational* emphasizes the opposite values: that is, provides negative scores on the above items. Inglehart and Baker (2000) also produce a list of a further twenty-four items that correlate (between .89 and .41) with this values dimension. These are mainly concerning the importance of religion, respect for parents and family including the dominance of the husband's role, importance of work and loyalty to country; with a positive correlation representing *Traditional* values.

The second dimension (Inglehart, 1997) *Survival values vs. Well-being values* (later termed *Survival vs. Self-Expression* values: Inglehart and Baker, 2000 and 2001) reflects, according to Inglehart *et al.* (1998: 14–15), 'the fact that in post-industrial society, historically unprecedented levels of wealth and the emergence of the welfare state have given rise to a shift from scarcity norms, emphasising hard work and self-denial, to postmodern values emphasising the quality of life, emancipation of women and sexual minorities and relatively postmaterialist priorities such as emphasis on self-expression.'

Items loading on the factor *Survival* are: respondent gives priority to economic and physical security over self-expression and quality of life; respondent describes self as not very happy; respondent has not signed nor would not sign a petition; homosexuality is never justifiable; you have to be very careful about trusting people. *Self-Expression* emphasizes the opposite values: that is, provides negative scores on the above items. Inglehart and Baker (2000) also produce a list of a further thirty-one items that correlate (between .86 and .42) with this values dimension. These emphasize the different role of men and women; dissatisfaction with own situation; rejection of people who are different including foreigners; favouring of technology; lack of emphasis on preserving the environment; emphasis of material wellbeing and hard work; with a positive correlation representing *Survival* values.

Countries classified under 'Protestant European' (e.g. Scandinavian countries, the two Germanys, the Netherlands and Switzerland) score highly on both the *Secular-Rational* (modernists) and *Self-Expression* (postmodernist) dimensions. They also represent countries with the highest GNP per capita (Inglehart and Baker, 2000). At the opposite extreme and representing countries with the lowest GNP per capita (Inglehart and Baker, 2001), those whose scores represent *Traditional* (pre-modern/pre-industrialized) and *Survival* (pre-postmodern) are the countries clustered in an 'Africa' group (South Africa, Nigeria, Ghana) and 'South Asia' group (Pakistan, Bangladesh, Philippines, Turkey and India).

Bordering the *Self-Expression* end of the *Survival/Self-Expression* dimension, but still representing *Traditional* values on the *traditional/secular–rational* dimension, are countries clustered in a 'Latin America' group (Peru, Venezuela, Colombia, Brazil; and bordering on the *Secular-Rational* Mexico, Argentina, Uruguay). An 'Ex-Communist/Baltic' group (Estonia, Lithuania, Latvia, Czech Republic) is clustered high on the *Secular-Rational* end of the *TraditionalSecular-Rational* dimension and at the *Survival* end of the *Survival/Self-Expression* dimension.

Bordering this group, towards the *Self-Expression* side of the dimension is a 'Confucian' group (China, South Korea, Taiwan and Japan), and towards the middle of the *traditional/secular–rational* dimension, but still at the *Survival* side of the *Survival/Self-Expression* dimension an 'Orthodox' group (Russia, Ukraine, Bulgaria and others).

An 'English Speaking' cluster (USA, Britain, Ireland, Australia, New Zealand, Canada) is grouped in the middle of the *traditional/secular–rational* dimension, and is high on *Self-Expression*. In the middle of both dimensions is a 'Catholic Europe' cluster that includes Belgium, France, Italy, Spain and Austria towards the *Self-Expression* side of the *Survival/Self-Expression* dimension, and overlapping with the 'Orthodox' group towards *Survival* is Slovenia, Croatia, Slovakia and Hungary.

Inglehart and Baker (2001) point out that America, contrary to what some modernist commentators suppose, is not the archetypal modern/postmodern or *Secular-Rational* and *Self-Expression* society that serves as the model for all other societies. In fact on Inglehart's (1997) cultural map of the world it is a 'deviant case'. Although high on *Self-Expression*, it is also high on *Traditional* values with high levels of religiosity and national pride comparable to 'developing' countries.

Inglehart and Baker (2000) also look at the movement of nations on these dimensions from the original survey to the most recent survey. The trajectory generally confirms their hypothesis that countries are moving towards *Secular-Rational* and *Self-Expression*. Yet countries such as Russia, Belarus, Bulgaria, Estonia, Lithuania and Latvia appear to be moving in the opposite direction. They assert that as a result of the collapse of the economic, social and political systems of the Soviet Union, there is an increasing emphasis on survival values, and even on traditional values. The former trend is certainly confirmed in the management literature where former Soviet countries show a bigger emphasis on what Jackson (2002b) calls *Instrumental* values where there is a perceived need for a quick move towards Western prosperity by the wholesale and uncritical importing of Western management approaches to human resource management, for example.

China shows a big shift towards more traditional values between 1990 and 1995 that is not really explained by Inglehart and Baker (2000). Also not explained is the shift of South Africa, Turkey and Brazil towards more traditional values. This could in part reflect a search for traditional approaches, and melding these with Western approaches reflected in the management literature (Jackson, 2002a, 2004). It is also interesting to note that between 1981 and 1998 Britain moved more towards *Secular-Rational* and more towards *Survival*. Perhaps this was a reflection of the Thatcher years.

Despite shortcomings in Inglehart's and his associates' theorizing, particularly the rather pejorative assumptions implied towards so-called 'developing' countries, this work is useful for descriptive theory construction in management ethics. For example, it does provide a context for the interest over the last decade or two in business ethics and corporate social responsibility, as a corollary of a move towards *Self-Expression* values and postmodernization. It may also provide a context for how countries differ in the concept and nature of ethicality, and indeed how companies from different countries working overseas may have different regard for ethical issues. It is also important as one of the few studies that provides a view over time about changing values.

WVS and implications for ethical values

There are two ways in which the WVS can be used to understand national differences regarding ethicality. The first is to draw conclusions about correlations between Inglehart's general values dimensions with specific aspects of ethicality. An example could be the relationship between *Traditional* versus *Secular-Rational* values and loyalty to one's family, group, authority and nation. We could surmise that if a society has strong *Traditional* values, being high on religiosity and deferential towards authority, then disloyalty to family, authority figures and nation could be regarded as unethical. Disloyalty to the corporation in the form of whistle-blowing, for example, could be frowned upon. Similarly, we might surmise a relationship between *Survival* values and, say, corrupt practices. With an emphasis on economic survival people might be tempted to cut corners in business and be more pragmatic about paying bribes, for example. Similarly, there may be a disregard for pollution controls as has been the case in many rapidly industrializing countries such as Eastern European countries and China. At the other end of this dimension, *Self-Expression*, we could assume that lack of democracy, low concern for the environment and disregard of women's and minorities' rights are seen as unethical.

The second way that the WVS may be used to understand national ethical values is by referring not to Inglehart's general value dimensions, but to specific aspects of findings from the WVS. For example, Moreno (2003) demonstrates a negative relationship between support for democracy and interpersonal trust, and permissiveness towards corruption.

Inglehart *et al.*'s (1998) items for environment (V12 I would give part of my income if I were certain that the money would be used to prevent environmental pollution; V13 I would agree to an increase in taxes if the extra money is used to prevent environmental pollution; and negatively, V17 Protecting the environment and fighting pollution is less urgent than often suggested) may indicate attitudes in the wider society that would condemn organizations as unethical if they did not undertake to protect the environment. If we consider that out of the countries surveyed China was ranked highest in percentage positive response to item V13 at 83% of respondents agreeing that they would be prepared to pay higher taxes, United States ranked 25th with 64% of respondents agreeing, and former West Germany ranked 37th with only 49% agreeing, then this may indicate differences in general attitudes towards pollution controls if a German or US company operated in China. However, this response from a country such as China may indicate that with late and heavy industrialization, pollution is a major issue, whereas in Germany it may not be. Care should be taken therefore on how such values or concerns are interpreted. In fact, can this be regarded as indicating a societal value, or is it merely a current concern?

There are a number of items that relate to individuals' membership and involvement in social and civil organizations and community; regard for government; attitudes to business ownership and regard for wealth accumulation; regard for trade unions; centrality of work and family. Many of these individual items may provide an indication of wider societal values that can be used both in the formulation of *a priori* assumptions about differences in ethical attitudes in organizational settings and *post hoc* explanations of such differences. Some of these explanations will be examined after considering other concepts derived from empirical study of values that have been used more specifically in management studies.

Schwartz's value dimensions: a view from the custodians of culture

Schwartz (1999) argues that there are three basic issues that confront all societies. The first issue is the relation between the individual and the group; the second is the way it is possible to guarantee responsible behaviour to maintain the social fabric; the third is the relationship between humankind and the natural and social world within which they exist.

The way the first issue is addressed, he reminds us, is reflected in the large body of literature on individual-collectivism. Much of this literature is contained within management and organizational studies, and is reviewed later in this chapter. Schwartz (1999) also explains that this concept is reflected in a wider literature and described as individualism-communalism, independence-interdependence, autonomy-relatedness and separateness-interdependence (see Schwartz, 1999, for a bibliography). He suggests that inherent within this issue are two themes: the extent to which the individual's or the group's interests should take precedence; and the extent to which persons are autonomous versus their embeddedness in their group. He believes that the latter is more fundamental as the extent to which a person is embedded in their group determines the extent to which conflicts of interests are unlikely to be experienced. One pole of this dimension reflects cultural values that see a person as being embedded in the collectivity, finding meaning in life mainly through social relationships and identifying with the group through participation in a shared way of life. This set of values is encompassed in Schwartz's empirical derived value type *Conservatism*, or 'a cultural emphasis on maintenance of the status quo, propriety, and restraint of actions or inclinations that might disrupt the solidary group or the traditional order (social order, respect for tradition, family security, wisdom)' (Schwartz, 1999: 27). The other pole reflects individual autonomy. He distinguishes between two types of autonomy. These are *Intellectual Autonomy*: 'A cultural emphasis on the desirability of individuals independently pursuing their ideas and intellectual directions (curiosity, broadmindedness, creativity)'; and *Affective Autonomy*: 'A cultural emphasis on the desirability of individuals independently pursuing affectively positive experiences (pleasure, exciting life, varied life)'.

The second issue seeks to address the way it is possible to guarantee responsible behaviour to maintain the social fabric, and gives rise to two polar resolutions. From Schwartz's (1999: 27) empirical work, one resolution involves using power differences, and the other involves voluntary responses to promoting the welfare of others. He terms the first *Hierarchy*: 'A cultural emphasis on the legitimacy of an unequal distribution of power, roles and resources (social power, authority, humility, wealth)'. The second Schwartz (1999: 28) terms *Egalitarianism*: 'A cultural emphasis on transcendence of selfish interests in favour of voluntary commitment to promoting the welfare of others (equality, social justice, freedom, responsibility, honesty)'.

The third issue that addresses the relationship between humankind and the natural and social world is resolved again through two possible responses. The first seeks to master, change and exploit the outside world out of personal or group interests; the second seeks to fit into the natural world and to accept it as it is. From his empirical study Schwartz (1999: 28) defines these two value types as *Mastery*: 'A cultural emphasis on getting ahead through active self-assertion (ambition, success, daring, competence)'; and *Harmony*: 'A cultural emphasis on fitting harmoniously into the environment (unity with nature, protecting the environment, world of beauty)'.[1]

So, for each of the three issues, there is a bipolar dimension that represents alternative resolutions of the issue that can be found in different cultural groups: 1. relation of individual and group (*Conservatism* versus *Autonomy*);

---

[1] Single values in brackets that relate to each pole of each value dimension are examples from his values questionnaire that Schwartz (1999) provides in the original.

2. preservation of the social fabric (*Hierarchy* versus *Egalitarianism*); and 3. relation to nature (*Mastery* versus *Harmony*).

Schwartz's (1994) samples are from teachers and students. He argues that the former are good representatives of the cultures as they are custodians of cultures and it is they who pass this on to the next generation. The samples of university students generally corroborate results from school teachers. It is likely that because of the way the constructs and the variables comprising them have been tested among various cultural groups in some forty-four countries, at both individual and group level, that they may be claimed to be universally representative of values which may occur anywhere in the world. They also reflect societal values (rather than those in corporate settings) because of the populations from which Schwartz took his samples.

There also appears to be some overlap with Inglehart and colleagues' theory concerning modernization/postmodernization trends and associated societal values, suggested in Table 3.1. Hence, we could postulate that *Conservatism* and *Hierarchy* may prevail in Inglehart's 'traditional' cultures (reflecting 'developing' countries) as well as in 'secular-rational'/'survival' cultures (such as in rapidly industrialized or 'emerging' countries, e.g. Eastern European countries); *Autonomy* in 'secular-rational'/'self-expressive' cultures (such as Western European and Anglo-Saxon countries); *Egalitarianism* in 'secular-rational'/'self-expression' cultures; *Mastery* in 'secular-rational'/'survival' cultures (such as the Eastern European and rapidly industrialized countries); and *Harmony* in both 'traditional' and 'self-expression' cultures (Table 3.1).

Schwartz's value dimensions and implications for ethical values

Previously noted has been the reluctance of those theorists who postulate about cultural values to extend their theories and empirical findings to a consideration of ethical values and decision making. Schwartz (1999: 26) is almost there when he says:

I postulate that cultural dimensions of values reflect the basic issues or problems that societies must confront in order to regulate human activity. Societal members, especially decision-makers, recognize and communicate about these problems, plan responses to them, and motivate one another to cope with them. Values (e.g. success, justice, freedom, social order, tradition) are the vocabulary of socially approved goals used to motivate action, and to express and justify the solutions chosen.

His view indicates a direct relationship between the types of cultural values he is investigating to what is believed in a society to constitute ethical decision

Table 3.1 Conceptual associations of value dimensions with Inglehart's modernization and postmodernization trends

WVS Trends	Modernization		Postmodernization	
	Traditional	Secular-Rational	Survival	Self-expression
Schwartz's issues/values				
Individual & group: Conservatism–autonomy	Conservatism	Conservatism/Autonomy	Conservatism	Autonomy
Social fabric: Hierarchy-Egalitarianism	Hierarchy	Hierarchy/Egalitarianism	Hierarchy	Egalitarianism
Relation to natural and social world: Mastery–harmony	Harmony	Mastery	Mastery	Harmony
Smith, Dugan and Trompenaars' broad values dimensions				
Conservatism–egalitarian commitment	Conservatism	Egalitarian commitment	Conservatism	
Utilitarian involvement – Loyal involvement	Loyal involvement	Utilitarian involvement		Utilitarian involvement
Hofstede's cultural dimensions				
Power Distance	High Power Distance	Medium to High Power Distance	High Power Distance	Low to Medium Power Distance
Uncertainty Avoidance	Low to Medium Uncertainty Avoidance	Medium to High Uncertainty Avoidance	High Uncertainty Avoidance	Low Uncertainty Avoidance
Individualism–collectivism	Collectivism	Individualism	Collectivism	Individualism
Masculinity–femininity	Femininity	Masculinity	Masculinity	Femininity

GLOBE dimensions

	High Power Distance	Medium to High Power Distance	High Power Distance	Low to Medium Power Distance
Power Distance	High Power Distance	Medium to High Power Distance	High Power Distance	Low to Medium Power Distance
Uncertainty Avoidance	?	?	High Power Distance	Low Power Distance
Humane Orientation	?	?	?	?
Institutional Collectivism	High Institutional Collectivism	Low Institutional Collectivism	Medium to high Institutional Collectivism	Low Institutional Collectivism
In-group Collectivism	High In-group Collectivism	Low In-group Collectivism	Medium to high In-group Collectivism	Low In-group Collectivism
Assertiveness	Low Assertiveness	High Assertiveness	High Assertiveness	Low Assertiveness
Gender Egalitarianism	High Gender Egalitarianism	Low Gender Egalitarianism	Low Gender Egalitarianism	High Gender Egalitarianism
Future Orientation	?	?	?	?
Performance Orientation	Possibly Low Performance Orientation	Possibly High Performance Orientation	Possibly High Performance Orientation	Possibly Low Performance Orientation

making. Yet he appears not to make this connection. The way that societies define the relationship between individual and group has implications for solidarity and loyalty issues, depending on the nature of the group: family, community, corporation, nation. Work on collectivism that is reviewed below suggests issues with out-group members (Triandis, 1990), and the difference in treatment of in-group and out-group members in the work place, for example. This has implications for the ethicality of aspects such as nepotism, including recruitment, promotion and job security. It is more likely that in a *Conservatism* culture 'nepotism' is not an ethical issue, but in an *Autonomy* culture it is. Similarly, what is acceptable in terms of inequalities and autocratic or paternalistic management styles in a *Hierarchy* culture may not be acceptable in an *Egalitarianism* culture. Also the acceptability of 'conquering nature' would be far less in a culture that reflects *Harmony* values. Similarly in a *Mastery* culture socially assertive behaviour that could reflect an aggressive business style may be more acceptable.

Inglehart's and Schwatz's work together provides a view of cultural values across a number of countries. The values dimensions, as well as individual items from the WVS, provide information from which conclusions may be drawn about the wider society within which corporations exist. Other cultural values studies are more specific to corporate life. It is to these studies that we now turn. These include the work of Hofstede (1980a/2003), Trompenaars (1993) and Smith *et al.* (1996), and the more recent GLOBE project (House *et al.*, 2004).

Smith's reinterpretation of Trompenaars' work: a view from within the corporation

The work of Trompenaars (1993) has severe limitations in methodology and academic rigour. Yet it has been used extensively, particularly in connection with cross-cultural management development activities. It is interesting to consider its conceptual relevance to understanding differences in ethical values, although here the reanalysis of Trompenaars' extensive database led by Peter Smith (Smith *et al.*, 1996) is discussed, as its concepts are partly related to those of Schwartz and, as we see below, to those of Hofstede.

Trompenaars' (1993) work was conceptually built on Parsons and Shils (1951) and Kluckhohn and Strodtbeck's (1961) formulations of cultural differences, and other dimensions drawn from Rotter (1966) and Hall (1959). These are: regard for rules or relations (universalism–particularism);

individualism–collectivism; neutral–affective expression of emotions; low and high context societies (specific-diffuse); and the way status is accorded (achievement–ascription). Trompenaars (1993) also considers attitudes to time (synchronic-sequential) and relation to nature (external-internal locus of control). His results are presented in terms of the percentage of positive (or negative) responses to each of several questions for each of some fifty different nationalities. His information was gathered through administering a questionnaire to attendees of management seminars in the various countries surveyed (Trompenaars, 1993).

Smith *et al.* (1996) then undertook a rigorous statistical reanalysis of Trompenaars' extensive international database. This provides two major value dimensions (through multidimensional scaling). It is still useful to refer back to Trompanaars' original 'dimensions' to describe these larger values dimensions that in part correlate with Schwartz's dimensions, and those of Hofstede. Smith *et al.*'s (1996) dimensions are as follows.

- **Conservatism**: comprises items that represent ascribed status, particularist/paternalistic employers and formalized hierarchies, and represents an external locus of control. It correlates with Hofstede's *Collectivism* and *Power Distance* (see below) and falls just short of a significant correlation with Schwartz's *Conservatism*.
- **Egalitarian commitment**: comprises achieved status, universalistic and non-paternalistic values, as well as functional hierarchy and internal locus of control. It correlates with Hofstede's *Individualism* and low *Power Distance*. It also correlates with Schwartz's *Egalitarianism*.
- **Utilitarian involvement**: comprises aspects of individualism that emphasize individual credit and responsibility. It correlates with Hofstede's *Individualism* and low *Power Distance*.
- **Loyal involvement**: comprises aspects of collectivism that stress loyalty and obligation to the group, as well as corporate loyalty and obligation. It correlates with Hofstede's *Collectivism* and high *Power Distance*.

Smith's reinterpretation of Trompenaars' work and implications for ethical values

Conservatism–egalitarian commitment

Of Trompenaars' (1993) dimensions referred to above, *universalism–particularism, achievement–ascription* and *Locus of Control* are the most relevant to our present discussion. In some cultures people see rules and regulations as applying universally to everyone, regardless of who they are. In cultures which are more particularist, people see relationships as more important than applying rules the same for everyone. There is an inclination to apply the rules according to friendship and kinship relations. This has implications for recruitment and promotion policies in organizations in, for example, some Asian countries which may be at variance to practices in countries such as the United States and Britain where this might be termed 'nepotism', and be regarded as an ethical issue. However, there are differences in European countries. Greece, Spain and France are seen as more particularist, and Sweden, former West Germany and Britain as more universalist. One of Trompenaars' (1993) questionnaire items asks respondents to assume they are a passenger in a car which a friend is driving in an urban area above the speed limit. He hits a pedestrian. His lawyer says that it will help him considerably if you swear in court that he was driving below the legal speed limit. Helping your friend indicates particularism; not helping him indicates universalism.

Yet this might have implications beyond a regard for treating people differently. On the one hand it is concerned with rules about how we relate to others and to institutions. It is concerned on the other hand with rules about rules (see Figure 2.3 in Chapter 2). This has implications for the discussion in Chapter 2 about the relationship between values and rules in society (or 'cultural' aspects and 'institutional' aspects).

Also within the *conservatism–egalitarian commitment* construct is Trompenaars' concept of achievement–ascription. Status is accorded to people on the basis of what they achieve in their jobs and their lives (achievement) or who they are and where they come from such as family background, their school or some other prior factor (ascription). Quite often more traditional societies attribute status according to the latter precept. Again, this may influence recruitment and promotion policies which may be at variance to practices in some (but not all) Western cultures, and again may raise ethical issues. On some measures Austria, Belgium, Spain and Italy are more ascription oriented, and Denmark, Britain and Sweden more achievement oriented.

Locus of Control is another concept that is subsumed within the *conservatism–egalitarian commitment* construct. People tend to believe that what happens to them in life is their own doing (internal locus of control), or they have no or little control over what happens to them (external locus of control), the causes of which are external to them. Although a connection has not been made directly to Schwartz's (1994) *Harmony-Mastery* construct (Smith *et al.*, 1996), locus of control does raise issues about how people relate to their environment, and the level of control they believe they have over the natural world. This may have implications for the nature of interaction with the natural and social world, and raise ethical questions about power (in the social sphere) and environment controls (in the natural sphere). It also may have implications regarding the nature of management control in organizations. For example, setting targets may be inappropriate as a form of management control in a society that culturally has an external locus of control.

Paternalism is also an important concept in cross-cultural management research and is captured in part by Trompenaars' concept of specific-diffuse which contains questionnaire items such as 'should the company provide housing' and involves the extent to which relationships at work, particularly with the boss, are carried through to other aspects of one's life. It is subsumed within the construct of *Conservatism*, and may have ethical implications for the regard for interference/protection in one's life by the corporation. Paternalism is however more thoroughly investigated elsewhere (see for example Aycan *et al*. 1999, who define it as 'people in authority assuming the role of parent and considering it an obligation to provide support and protection to others under their care').

Utilitarian involvement–loyal involvement

This dimension is most allied to Hofstede's *Individualism–Collectivism* and *Power Distance* (see below), but reflects the nature of loyalty of the individual to the group and corporation. While individuals may have a contractual relationship with the organization within the Utilitarian Involvement construct, members of a group or corporation have relations with the wider collective that involve obligation and reciprocity. This may reflect on the extent to which loyalty issues are regarded ethically. For example, whistle-blowing may be regarded quite differently by societies whose culture is at two different poles of this dimension. A lack of loyalty (as well as what constitutes loyalty) may be an ethical issue in a society that reflects more the Loyal Involvement side of the pole.

Hofstede's cultural values: a view from within one corporation

Geert Hofstede (originally in 1980a, and later revised in 2003) was one of the first to attempt to develop a universal framework for understanding cultural differences in managers' and employees' values based on a worldwide survey within the company that employed him at the time: IBM. Hofstede's work focuses on 'value systems' of national cultures which are represented by four dimensions (the following is well rehearsed in the literature, so please do skip to the next section if you are familiar with Hofstede's work):

- *Power Distance.* This is the extent to which inequalities among people are seen as normal. This dimension stretches from equal relations being seen as normal to wide inequalities being viewed as normal. For example, the former West Germany scored (scores are nominally between 100 and 0) a relatively low 35, USA a relatively low to medium 40, Britain 35 and France a relatively high 68. Brazil scored 69 and Mexico 81. China was not included in the study. Hong Kong scored 68 and Taiwan 58. Eastern European countries were also not included in the study. An all-white South African sample scored 49. Schwartz's (1994) concept of Hierarchy equates with *Power Distance.*

- *Uncertainty Avoidance.* This refers to a preference for structured situations versus unstructured situations. This dimension runs from being comfortable with flexibility and ambiguity to a need for extreme rigidity and situations with a high degree of certainty. For example, the former West Germany scored a medium 65, France a high 86 on a level with Spain. The USA scored a relatively low 46, with Britain at 35. Brazil scored 76 and Mexico 82. Hong Kong scored 29 and Taiwan 69. The all-white South African sample scored 49.

- *Individualism–collectivism.* This looks at whether individuals are used to acting as individuals or as part of cohesive groups, which may be based on the family (which is more the case with Chinese societies) or the corporation (as may be the case in Japan). This dimension ranges from collectivism (0) to individualism (100). The USA is the highest (91). France scores 71 and Britain 89. The former West Germany scored 67. Brazil scored 38 and Mexico 30 (Guatemala was the most collectivist at 6). Hong Kong scored 25, and Taiwan 17. The all-white South African sample scored 65. Schwartz's (1994) concept of *conservatism–autonomy* has similarities with this dimension.

- *Masculinity–femininity.* Hofstede distinguishes 'hard values' such as assertiveness and competition, and the 'soft' or 'feminine' values of personal relations, quality of life and caring about others, where in a masculine society gender role differentiation is emphasized. The USA scored a medium to high (masculinity) 62, with the former West Germany at 66. Britain scored 66 and France 43. Brazil scored 49 and Mexico 69. Taiwan scored 45 and Hong Kong 56. The all-white South African sample scored 63. Aspects of Schwartz's (1994) concept of *mastery–harmony* have similarities with this dimension.

Hofstede (1980a/2003; 1991) conceptually extrapolates from these dimensions derived from factor analysis of items on his questionnaire, to infer wider descriptions of the nature and implications of cultural values both within and outside the corporate setting, as follows.

Power Distance is polarized into small and large *Power Distance* and comprises attitudes which people within the culture have about the acceptable inequalities between people in the society or organization. In small *Power Distance* cultures there is a belief that inequalities among people should be minimized, that parents should treat children as equals and that teachers expect student initiative in the classroom. Hierarchies in work organizations are established as a convenience only to manage inequality of roles. Decentralization is popular, subordinates expect to be consulted and privileges are frowned upon in a small *Power Distance* society. Conversely, in a large *Power Distance* culture, inequalities are expected and desired; parents teach children obedience; and teachers are expected to take the initiative in the classroom. Hierarchies in organizations reflect the natural order of inequalities between the higher-ups and the lower-downs; centralization is popular; and subordinates expect that they are told what to do. Privilege and status symbols are expected.

Weak *Uncertainty Avoidance* cultures accept uncertainty as a feature of everyday life; there is generally low stress and people feel comfortable in ambiguous situations. People are curious with what is different. Students are happy with open-ended learning situations, and teachers can say 'I don't know'. Rules should only be for what is necessary. People may be lazy, and work hard only when needed. Punctuality has to be learned, and people are motivated by achievement and esteem or belonging to a group.

Strong *Uncertainty Avoidance* is characterized by the threat of uncertainty which is always present but must be fought. It is characterized by high stress and a fear of ambiguous situations and unfamiliar risk. There is a feeling that what is different must be dangerous. Students are more comfortable in a structured learning situation and like to be told the right answer: teachers are supposed to know the answers. There is an emotional need for rules, even when these may not work. There is a need to be busy, and a feeling that time is money: an inner urge to work hard. Punctuality is natural, and people are motivated by security, esteem or belongingness.

In societies where *Individualism* describes cultural values people look after themselves and the immediate nuclear family. A person's identity is based on him or her as an individual. Speaking one's mind is respected. Education is aimed at learning to learn, and academic and professional diplomas increase self-respect and potential economic worth. The employer-employee contract is assumed to be based on mutual advantage, and hiring decisions are supposed to be based on individual competence. Managers manage individuals, and tasks are more important than relationships.

In *Collectivistic* societies people are born into and protected by extended families, to which they exchange loyalty. One's identity is based in the belongingness to a social group or network. Children are taught to think of 'we' not 'I'. Rather than speaking one's mind, harmony should be maintained and direct confrontation avoided. The purpose of education is to learn how to do, and diplomas provide an entry into higher status groups. Rather than purely a contract, the employer-employee relationship is seen as a moral one such as a family relationship, and when hiring or firing the employee's in-group is considered. Managers manage groups, and relationships are more important than tasks.

In a *Masculine* society values are based on material success, money and possessions. Men are expected to be assertive and ambitious, and women tender and concerned with relationships. The father deals with facts and the mother with feelings. There is sympathy for the strong and the best student is the norm: failing in school is seen as a disaster. People live in order to work. Managers are expected to be decisive and assertive, and there is a stress on competition, performance and resolution of conflict by fighting them out.

In contrast, the *Feminine* society has values of caring for others and preservation rather than progress. People and good relationships are more important than money and things, and people are expected to be modest. Both men and women are expected to be concerned with relationships, and both mother and father should deal with feelings and facts. There is sympathy for the weak, and the average student is the norm. Failing in school is a minor accident. People work in order to live. Managers use intuition and try to gain consensus. There is a stress on equality, solidarity and quality of work life. Conflicts are resolved by compromise and negotiation.

A fifth dimensions was added by Hofstede to the original four. This was developed through the Chinese Cultural Connection study (CCC, 1987) and in part justified by Hofstede's warning of the dangers of developing constructs from a Western point of view. The Chinese Cultural Connection was an attempt to counter this by introducing an Eastern perspective and values. The study reinforced three out of the four dimensions in Hofstede's original study: the Chinese dimension of 'human-heartedness', which incorporates values such as kindness, courtesy and social consciousness, correlates negatively with masculinity; 'integration' which encompasses the cultivation of trust, tolerance and friendship correlates negatively with *Power Distance*; 'moral discipline' including values of group responsiveness, moderation, adaptability and prudent behaviour correlates negatively with individualism.

None of the new dimensions correlated with *Uncertainty Avoidance*, but a new dimension was developed from the data termed *Confucian Dynamism* and later referred to by Hofstede as *Long Term Orientation*, with values of persistence and perseverance, ordering relationships by status and observing order, thrift and having a sense of shame. *Uncertainty Avoidance* is concerned with absolute *truth* which may not be a relevant value in Chinese society and other Eastern cultures which are more concerned with *virtue*. Of particular relevance is the virtue of working hard and acquiring skills, thrift, being patient and persevering: these are all values connected with this fifth dimension that may replace *Uncertainty Avoidance* as a relevant Eastern concept. On a scale from a minimum score of 0 to a maximum 118, Pakistan scores 0 and China 118. The Chinese societies of Hong Kong (96) and Taiwan (87) are towards the top of the scale with Japan (80) and South Korea (75) next. Brazil scores 65, Singapore 48 and the Netherlands 44. Sweden (33), Poland (32) and the former West Germany (31) follow. The USA scores a relatively low 29, with Britain at 25. Of African countries, Zimbabwe (25) scores the same as Britain, and Nigeria is second from bottom with 16. This seems to bear out an assumption that the Eastern 'tiger' countries which have done well economically are high on this dimension, with the Anglo-Saxon countries relatively low, and African countries with a short-term economic perspective scoring very low.

Hofstede's value dimensions and implications for ethical values and institutional arrangements

Hofstede's work has been widely cited in the international management literature, especially when it comes to providing (descriptive) explanations for cultural variation across countries. This also applies to the management and business ethics literature. This makes it possible to postulate connections between Hofstede's value dimensions and ethicality far more readily than was possible with WVS and Schwartz's work. It also makes it possible to surmise relations between values and institutions, and the place of rules within society.

Two cultural dimensions are of particular interest for that reason: *Uncertainty Avoidance* in the areas of economic and social regulation, and *individualism–collectivism* in the area of relations with the corporation and relations with significant others in one's social or work group (Hofstede, 1980a/2003, 1991), and these are discussed in more detail in Chapter 4. Cultural variations in these areas may help to explain the perceived ethicality of management actions within organizations. *Power Distance* also offers some explanation for the justification of autocratic management styles and high hierarchies in organizations as well as inequalities of wealth in the wider society. *Masculinity–femininity* offers justification for gender inequalities, but may also be connected with the levels of achievement orientation in society affecting issues such as work centrality, and work-life balances that have implications for levels of women in the workforce, childcare provision and imposition of corporations on wider life-space of individuals. However, relying on Hofstede's dimension may result in oversimplification of explanations about cultural variance in concepts of ethicality, and this is taken up in more detail in Chapter 4.

GLOBE culture constructs

The GLOBE project (Global Leadership and Organizational Behavior Effectiveness Research Program) is a more recent cross-national study undertaken by Robert House and a team of 170 researchers across 62 societies (House *et al.*, 2004). Its main focus is the relationship between culture and leadership characteristics. In some ways the study is disappointing because it did little to break out of the conceptual framework of cultural dimensions set by Hofstede in the early 1980s, and it mirrors many of Hofstede's cultural dimensions. Yet this, for our current purpose, is useful as it provides a more up-to-date view of these cultural dimensions and, like the other studies examined above, provides a basis for considering *how* ethicality may differ across nations, rather than *why*. It also purports to investigate both 'values' (e.g. 'Followers *should be* expected to obey their leaders without question') and 'practices' (e.g. 'Followers *are* expected to obey their leaders without question').[2]

The cultural value dimensions proffered by the GLOBE project are as follows (Javidan *et al.*, 2004: 30).

---

[2] As an example of an item given for Power Distance this could be interpreted as 'should be' (value), 'are' (rule, rather than what people actually do). A third alternative could be written 'Followers *do* obey their leaders without questions' (practices). This reflects the framework provided in the current text, Chapter 2: Context (institutional rules), Content (values), Conduct (behaviour).

- Power Distance: 'The degree to which members of a collective expect power to be distributed equally.' This ('practices' only, not 'values') correlates positively with Hofstede's *Power Distance* and Schwartz's *Hierarchy*.
- Uncertainty Avoidance: 'The extent to which a society, organization or group relies on social norms, rules, and procedures to alleviate unpredictability of future events.' Curiously 'values' correlates positively and 'practices' negatively with Hofstede's *Uncertainty Avoidance*. It correlates positively with Schwartz's *Embeddedness* (this is Schwartz 1994's dimension at the individual level, and equates with *Conservatism* at the group level).
- Humane Orientation: 'The degree to which a collective encourages and rewards individuals for being fair, altruistic, generous, caring and kind to others.' This does not appear to correlate with Hofstede's or Schwartz's dimensions.
- Collectivism I (Institutional Collectivism): 'The degree to which organizational and societal institutional practices encourage and reward collective distribution of resources and collective action.' 'Values' correlates negatively with Hofstede's *Individualism*, but not with any of Schwartz's dimensions.
- Collectivism II (In-Group Collectivism): 'The degree to which individuals express pride, loyalty, and cohesiveness in their organizations or families.' 'Practices' correlates negatively with Hofstede's *Individualism*, but not with any of Schwartz's dimensions.
- Assertiveness: 'The degree to which individuals are assertive, confrontational, and aggressive in their relationships with others.' 'Practices' correlates positively with Hofstede's *Masculinity* and negatively with Schwartz's *Egalitarianism*.
- Gender Egalitarianism: 'The degree to which a collective minimizes gender inequalities.' This does not correlate with any of Hofstede's dimensions, but correlates positively with Schwartz's *Egalitarianism*.
- Future Orientation: 'The extent to which individuals engage in future-oriented behaviours such as delaying gratification, planning, and investing in the future.' This does not appear to correlate with any of Hofstede's or Schwartz's dimensions.
- Performance Orientation: 'The degree to which a collective encourages and rewards group members for performance improvement and excellence.' Again this appears not to correlate with Hofstede's or Schwartz's dimensions.

Implications of the GLOBE Study for Ethical Values

The GLOBE project findings reflect many of the cultural dimensions proffered in earlier studies, and as such do not add conceptually to our descriptive understanding of ethical values across cultures. They do, however, provide current information that is perhaps more rigorously validated and covers more countries than previous studies. For example, it covers some six African countries and six post-communist countries.

Locus of human value: instrumentalism–humanism

Jackson (2002a, 2002b) was concerned about an assumption in the literature of the universal application of 'human resources' and the implication for the management of people in different countries, particularly those in non-Western countries where the concept or value of a person may be different. He undertook a study (Jackson, 2002a) across seven national cultures to ascertain the nature and variance of an *instrumental* and *humanistic* view of people in organizations. The former refers to a view of the utilitarian value of people, that is managing people as a resource, whereby people are seen as a means to an end. Hence human resources are used to meet the executive objectives of the organization. The concept (or at least the phrase) of human resource management is met with across the globe and suggests a universalism that is the subject of Chapter 5 in the current text.

Yet this can be challenged by an alternative *humanistic* view of the intrinsic value of people in their own right. People are seen as having a value for who they are, rather than what they can do for the organization. This concept has some antecedence in the literature (Koopman, 1991; Lessem, 1994; Saunders, 1998; Jackson, 1999), although had not been directly studied empirically. Jackson's (2002a) study suggests that these are not straightforward, orthogonally related dimensions: it is possible to score high on instrumentalism and high on humanism (such as Russian managers), or low on instrumentalism and low on humanism (such as American managers), or low on instrumentalism and high on humanism (such as Japanese managers). Although none of the managers in this study scored high on instrumentalism and low on humanism, this is theoretically possible, and could figure in a more extensive geographical study.

Implication of the locus of human value for ethical values

There are a number of reasons why the instrumentalism–humanism concept could be important. The first is that it provides a critique of the concept of human resource management as a set of policies, principles and practices that can be employed universally, and indeed challenges the ethicality of doing so. It relates HRM to a Western concept of the value of human beings in an organization, where the ethicality of regarding a person purely as a resource may be problematic. Secondly in a global context of cultural crossvergence, it does cast doubts on whether it is possible to construe 'value dimensions' as simple opposites, such as femininity-masculinity or individualism–collectivism. Often these are derived from the same question: for example, a high score equals individualism; a low score equals collectivism. Managers may score high for both individualism and collectivism if these constructs are derived from two different scales. In fact, if one assumes the reality of 'cultures' today, that they are a mix of local and global, it is highly likely that such a method would return similar results to Jackson's (2002a).

Closing case: the tyranny of participation revisited

In the same book introduced in the opening case (Cooke and Kothari, 2001), John Hailey, following a study of nine successful South Asian non-governmental organizations in Bangladesh, India and Pakistan, writes about, and criticizes the introduction of 'formulaic' participatory approaches by Western NGOs in South Asia, saying that this is so often done on the basis of how organizations should be run and how they should make decisions on Western perceptions of good practice. He writes Hailey (2002: 96):

Cultural researchers have noted that South Asian cultures are marked by their collective nature and a general acceptance of innate social differential. Hofstede (1991) suggests that South Asian societies have 'high power distance' levels, with the implication that less powerful members of an organization expect and accept that power is distributed unequally. His findings also suggest that these societies are highly 'collectivist', with the implication that people are integrated into strong, cohesive social groups from birth. Trompenaars (1993) also identified the highly collectivist nature of South Asian society, and the importance of 'ascription' in South Asian cultures. He sees this as the extent to which position and power is ascribed by virtue of birth, kinship, education, networks and connections.

Hailey (2002: 96) then goes on:

Thus we have a cultural context in which cohesive group relations are paramount, and where it is accepted that the power and status of key decision-makers is dependent on kinship ties, personal relationships and connections. This is seen as alien to the highly individualistic, 'low power distance', achievement-oriented meritocracies of Western Europe and North America ... These are cultures that depend on a network of highly personal relationships. Consequently, it is no surprise to find in many South Asian NGOs that informal, highly personal relationships are at the heart of the decision making and planning process.

To what extent do we assume in the individualistic West that our form of participation is right and fair and appropriate universally? Hailey (2002: 97) suggests that the process of participation is contingent on different cultural norms or assumptions. A value judgement that Western participation is better than South Asian forms of personal and consultative and/ or paternalistic management must be questioned in light of the discussion above on value differences. In addition, the imposition of Western participation in non-Western cultures should be questioned not only in terms of its appropriateness and desirability, but also its ethicality. This leads back to the question that Cooke and Kothari (2001) pose: 'Participation: The New Tyranny?'

Implications for international managers

For the international manager, an awareness of cultural values dimensions is a good start to understanding possible differences in the regard for ethicality across the world. We have seen that the nature of participation may be an issue across cultures when a Western organization imposes participatory methods on a local organization at variance to local culture. In simple terms this can be understood by reference to Hofstede's dimension of *Power Distance*. The oversimplification of this construct may also be a problem, however. The reasons for introducing limited and perhaps tactical forms of participation may be far from altruistic, and merely a means for an international organization to maintain control by asking local managers and staff to take ownership of the implementation of strategic decisions or policies. While such decisions are taken at the foreign headquarters, local teams may implement them in any way they like (Jackson, 2004). The work of Hofstede and others suggest that 'developing' countries are higher in *Power Distance* than 'developed' countries. This may well be the case. Evidence also suggests that societies in 'developing' countries may also be consensus seeking, with forms of participation far exceeding Western models of democratic decision making (Jackson, 2004).

International managers have to take decisions. So it is not sufficient for them to be aware that cultural differences imply differences in regard for ethicality. Do they go along with local culture, or do they impose principles from their own culture, or do they try to meld the two? These are issues that will be taken up later in this text.

Questions for managers

1. Is it possible, and desirable, to introduce participatory management practices into high *Power Distance* cultures? What are the ethical implications, if any?
2. Is the introduction of corporate social responsibility programmes a luxury that can only be achieved and is only relevant to organizations in societies that have achieved a level of *self-expression* in Inglehart's postmodernization dimension?
3. Is nepotism justifiable in societies that Schwartz would consider high in *conservatism*?

An agenda for research

The first aspect a research agenda should focus upon is the adequacy of cultural dimensions research. In Chapter 2, a number of issues with this conceptual framework were touched upon. There are two main areas for this: the adequacy of specific theories such as that of Hofstede; and the adequacy of the cultural dimensions approach itself. For the former, Hofstede's theory has come under much criticism for its methods (e.g. Berry *et al.*, 1992), conceptual approach (e.g. McSweeney, 2002) and specific dimensions (e.g. Fang, 2003). The conceptual criticism can certainly extend to the other cultural dimensions theories discussed in this chapter. It is the view within the current text that this type of research, per se, has now met a dead end. Looking at current or new ways of comparing discrete nations is no longer productive, yet existing studies may serve to contextualize ethical values across nations. As pointed out in this chapter, cultural values research does not provide an explanation of variation in perceptions of ethicality, but merely provides a wider descriptive context. Chapter 4 provides an overview of research into ethical variation across nations. The question asked at the end of this current chapter is, what is the value of this type of cross-national cultural research in understanding more about management ethics? The answer must be that it raises the issue of appropriateness. For example, how appropriate are Western participatory management practices in organizations in non-Western societies? From a management perspective there are two types of interconnected issues when transferring management techniques from one country to another: How effective is it? and How appropriate is it? This raises the question of effective or appropriate to whom? The way, say, a US health care product company is run in South Africa may be effective for shareholders because of the return on investment. But to what extent is it appropriate to employees, or the local community? To what extent do local employees feel alienated from their work, because of the Western management practices employed in the factory? Cultural dimensions research may help us understand this better, while remaining quite a blunt instrument for doing so. This type of research also does not tell us what to do: persist with Western practices, adapt, or adopt local approaches? The appropriateness of transferring Western practices may constitute an ethical question, as may the way the issues are resolved.

While not proposing any new research in this area, existing cultural dimensions research may provide a first stage in any cross-cultural ethical research in terms of the likelihood of the appropriateness of transferring management practices, as well as transferring any concepts of ethicality. For example, it may be useful in assessing first the reasons for 'nepotism', or 'corruption' in a particular society, and then the appropriateness of management responses to these issues. Table 4.1 (Chapter 4) provides a starting point for contextualizing ethical issues within broader cultural dimensions that could be useful in future initial research in this area, and this provides the subject area for the next chapter.

Questions for researchers
1. How can the appropriateness of participatory management practices be analysed cross-culturally?
2. How can 'nepotism' be analysed cross-culturally?
3. How can 'corruption' be analysed cross-culturally?

4 Comparing management ethics across cultures

In the last chapter differences in cultural values, and their possible connections with ethical values, were discussed. This was premised on such differences in cultural values not providing an explanation for differences in
ethical values, but ethics being a subset of values. Hence national cultural
values provide a context for discussing ethics and ethicality, but not an
explanation of why there are differences in ethical values, as many studies
try to argue (Jackson, 2001).

The decision of a multinational company to lay off considerable numbers of
employees in a subsidiary may be judged differently from culture to culture.
Higher levels of loyalty expected of a company for its employees in collectivist countries such as Japan and Korea (Bae and Chung, 1997) may provide
the context for such differences. Similarly the degree of loyalty expected from
employees to their company may differ across cultures on the basis of the
degree to which collectivism is focused on the corporation (Hui, 1990), or the
extent to which individualism prevails in a culture (Hofstede, 1980a/2003)
and employees have a calculative or instrumental regard towards their
organizations. Also, the extent to which group members may rally around
a disadvantaged colleague when threatened with dismissal and the degree
to which a manager should go along with this could differ according to the
extent to which collectivism is focused on the group (Hui, 1990) or on the
level of egalitarian commitment (Schwartz, 1994) which is evident in an individualistic society (see Table 4.1).

If we assume that there are differences in values across cultures (e.g.
Hofstede, 1980a/2003), we must also assume that there are differences in ethical values across cultures. This chapter focuses on those differences by reference to the national context of cultural values discussed in Chapter 3. These
differences may be in terms of ethical values including the criteria used for
making ethical decisions or the structure of ethical decisions. They could also
be in the content of ethical decision making, or what is regarded as ethical or
unethical. What should not be focused upon in international management is

Table 4.1 Description of possible associations of values and ethical judgements

Judgements about management actions involving:	Exemplified by:	Examples of which are:	Values that may contextualize decisions:
Interactions with external stakeholders	Regard for environment	Environmental awareness Pollution controls Waste management and recycling Compliance with international/ national laws and conventions	Survival-Self Expression (Inglehart) Mastery–harmony (Schwartz)
	Regard for community	Strategic involvement of international, national and local community Employment of locals and skills/job creation Funding of local projects Managing relationship between employees' work and home/ community life	Traditional-Secular-rational/ Survival-Self-Expression (Inglehart) Collectivism–individualism (Hofstede and correlates)
	Regard for government	Local and national government involvement in organizational decision making Compliance to legislation Lobbying of government Payment of bribes and involvement in corruption	Conservatism–autonomy/ Egalitarian commitment (Schwartz/Smith *et al.*) Institutional Collectivism (GLOBE)
	Regard for suppliers	Receiving of gifts/bribes Involvement in corruption Fair treatment/competition of suppliers Involvement of suppliers in corporate decision making	Survival-Self-Expression (Inglehart) Collectivism–individualism (Hofstede and correlates)

Regard for customers	Payment of gifts/bribes Involvement in corruption Fair treatment of customers Involvement of customers in corporate decision making	Survival-Self-Expression (Inglehart) Humane orientation (GLOBE)
Regard for trades unions	Involvement of trade union in decision making Encouragement/discouragement of TU membership Accommodations with TU officials/corrupt practices	Institutional Collectivism (GLOBE)
Regard for shareholders	Providing a return on investment	Traditional-Secular-rational/ Survival-Self-Expression (Inglehart) Loyal involvement-Utilitarian involvement (Smith *et al.*)
Relationships with internal stakeholders		
Loyalty and commitment to organization (the executive)	Adherence to confidentiality involving third parties Commitment to work Commitment to corporate goals and vision	Loyal involvement- Utilitarian Involvement (Smith *et al.*) Institutional Collectivism (GLOBE)
Loyalty and commitment of organization	Involvement of internal stakeholders in decision making Commitment to work security Fair treatment of staff Management of relation between work and community/home life	Loyal involvement- Utilitarian Involvement (Smith *et al.*) Institutional and In-group Collectivism (GLOBE)

Table 4.1 *(cont.)*

Judgements about management actions involving:	Exemplified by:	Examples of which are:	Values that may contextualize decisions:
	Relationships with group	Loyalty to group Favouring group members Pursuing group objectives Discriminating against non-group members	In-group Collectivism (GLOBE) Conservatism–autonomy (Schwartz)
	Conflicts between self/group/ organizational interests	Pursuing group interests in contradiction to organizational (executive) interest Not reporting group members' violations of corporate policies Favouring group members in contradiction to organizational policies or objectives	In-group Collectivism (GLOBE) Loyal-involvement-Utilitarian Involvement
	Conflicts between self and organizational or group interests	Pursuing own objectives in contradiction to group or organizational goals Concealing one's errors	Collectivism–individualism (Hofstede and correlates) Traditional-Secular-rational (Inglehart)
	Conflicts between organization (executive) interests and external stakeholder interests (or laws)	Whistle-blowing	Survival-Self-Expression (Inglehart) Conservatism–autonomy (Schwartz)

the extent to which managers from one country are more or less ethical than another. Many cross-national studies imply this, or explicitly express it. The approach taken here is in understanding why managers from one country may have a different way of making a decision about whether one course of action is more or less ethical; and may have a different opinion from managers in other countries about what constitutes ethicality.

The other assumption, and approach, taken here is that ethical decisions are all about relationships, and the way people interact with others, in different situations, and the way they regard those interactions. Ethical decisions have antecedents and consequences, not in an abstract sense, but often in terms of impact on others and the general context and environment within which people and organizations act. Understanding how and why managers and other staff in organizations take decisions is a first stage in understanding how to interact and take decisions across cultures. This chapter does not purport to provide guidelines as to what to do when you understand that someone has a different regard for ethicality than you. That will come later. This chapter focuses on:

First, the structure of ethical decision making across cultures;

Then, on the different regard for ethicality and what constitutes an ethical decision;

And, finally, on relationships between people.

Opening case: Johnny Mbeke

Johnny Mbeke is employed as a warehouseman at a stationery factory. He was recruited two years ago by his present supervisor who is from the same village and a family friend. He earns one-twentieth of the amount his manager earns. He has ten dependants. His manager has only two. He wouldn't dare question an order from his supervisor or manager and, like his colleagues, has no say in any decisions the company makes. Johnny has a lame leg and is very slow at his work and not very good at it. He has been given several warnings. He is often late for work. His work group has told the manager that they are happy to cover for Johnny. Often the employees where Johnny works will steal items of stationery from the warehouse for personal use. The senior management at the company where Johnny works often pays bribes in order to win contracts.

What is regarded as ethical or unethical within the above situation, and how this decision is made, may be dependent on what country this case is situated within. This is the subject of the current chapter.

The structure of ethical decision making

The 'structure' of ethical decision making can be thought of as comprising those aspects which contribute to the making of a judgement as to whether or not a decision is ethical. This we now consider. This can be contrasted with the 'content' or the extent to which a decision is seen to be ethical or unethical, and the extent to which this varies across national cultures. This will be considered in the next section.

In the literature the basis for ethical judgements seems logically to fit into two broad dimensions:
1. Judgements based on consequential considerations (teleology); and
2. Judgements based on non-consequential considerations (deontology) (Brady, 1990; Tsalikis and LaTour, 1995).

Hence consequential judgements may be based on their having a result which on balance is good for the majority of stakeholders (utilitarianism) or in the overall interests of the person making the decision or those with whom he or she identifies, such as the company (egoism). Non-consequential judgements are based on prior considerations of an explicit or implicit set of rules or principles which guides conduct. Judgements are based on these 'universal' moral principles which do not anticipate the results of a decision (deontology).

However, it is unlikely that the bases for these different types of judgement are 'pure' (Hunt and Vitell, 1986) or that we solely rely on one to the exclusion of the other (Brady, 1990). Hence we may make a judgement on prior considerations of what we believe to be 'fair' to all concerned (justice). Ideas of fairness may be based on perceptions of the outcome of a decision providing to each the greatest amount of liberty which is compatible with a like liberty for all, but also implies judgements of the extent to which such liberty should be distributed unequally according to principles of difference (Rawls, 1971) such as Hofstede's (1980a/2003) concept of *Power Distance*. We may also make ethical judgements based on what we believe is acceptable to us as a member of a family, to other groups which influence us, and as a member of a cultural group or society (ethical relativism).

It is also unlikely that these principles are invariable across cultures and across different contexts. Ethical relativism is the only theory which addresses this issue, not by explaining it, but simply by acknowledging it.

Although the cross-cultural literature focuses more on the content of ethical decisions, there is some evidence that the way judgements are made, or the 'structure' of ethical judgements, may vary among different cultural groups, although this has mainly focused on differences between Asian and non-Asian cultures. Ralston *et al.* (1994) for example discuss differences between the apparent self-serving attitudes of Hong Kong Chinese managers compared with American managers as being explained by differences in the Western view of ethical behaviour as an absolute that applies universally. In the East 'face' is important and ethical behaviour depends on the situation. As long as 'face' is intact it is not a concern. This situationalism is also seen in Dolecheck and Dolecheck's (1987) study which found that Hong Kong managers equate ethics to acting within the law, compared with American managers who see ethics as going beyond keeping to the letter of the law. Singhapakdi *et al.* (1994) also found that Thai managers rely more on the nature of the ethical issue or circumstance and less on universal moral principles when making ethical judgements, compared with their American counterparts. This may provide a basis for assuming that Asian ethical judgement may be more relativistic in structure, and that the way judgements are made may vary from one situation to the other. Ethical judgements of Western managers may be based more on the application of universal principles of ethical behaviour.

More specifically, a study by McDonald and Pak (1997) set out to investigate cross-cultural differences in 'cognitive philosophies' among managers from Hong Kong, Malaysia, New Zealand and Canada. Their findings suggest that self-interest is important in ethical decision making for Hong Kong managers, but that 'duty' (a deontological consideration) is important to all these national groups. Justice, or considerations of fairness, is also important to all national groups. Utilitarian considerations are shown to be less important, but more important relatively for the Malaysian group. This study, as others which focus on the way ethical judgements are made (Reidenbach and Robin, 1988, 1990), indicate that judgements are made using multiple criteria rather than relying on one specific basis of ethical decision making. It is the combination of multiple criteria which constitutes the 'structure' of ethical judgements.

Specific studies of management ethics in Japan suggest that Japanese managers' ethical decisions tend to be situational (Nakano, 1997), although the development of Japanese 'moralogy' (Taka and Dunfee, 1997) may be indicative of a deontological emphasis in ethical decision making. American managers may look to industrial norms and what their company expects when making an ethical decision (Posner and Schmidt, 1987).

Consequential considerations of organizational efficiency figure lower for American than for Australian and Hong Kong managers in a comparative study of organizational values by Westwood and Posner (1997). In this study organizational stability is seen as significantly more important by the American than by the Australian and Hong Kong managers. A comparative study by Elenkov (1997) of managers in the United States and Russia suggests that Russian managers display higher levels of Machiavellianism than those in the United States, as well as being as competitively oriented as the American group and equally not dogmatic. This may indicate a tendency to employ self-seeking criteria in ethical decision making, or at least employing utilitarian criteria among Russian managers.

However, Neimanis (1997) suggests that the Soviet system militated against people making their own decisions, but justifying the interests of the state, the corporation or the party as superseding that of ethical considerations. This may have encouraged an egoism based on best interests of the corporation, and more latterly based on self-interest with a move towards a free-market economy (see also Apressyan, 1997). However, it may also have encouraged a reference to rules and principles in order to avoid the consequences (punishment) of making a wrong decision. Principle-based decision making of managers and negotiators in the former Soviet Union is well documented (see for example Glenn *et al.*, 1977, in relation to negotiation style), and the more recent Russian (and other post-Soviet countries) ethical judgement structure may be a complexity of historical and current influences (Apressyan, 1997).

Jackson (2001) set out to study these possible differences in the structure of ethical decision making using the Reidenbach-Robin multidimensional scale (Reidenbach and Robin, 1988, 1990). This is well established in the management ethics literature, and in the cross-cultural literature (Tsalikis and Nwachukwu, 1991; Hansen, 1992; Tsalikis and LaTour, 1995). It provides an instrument which is purported to measure the ethical decision-making process by anchoring items to ethical philosophies, namely: justice, relativism, egoism, utilitarianism, deontology (Reidenbach and Robin, 1990). Jackson's (2001) study focused on internal stakeholders, concerning corporate loyalty to employees, loyalty to company and loyalty to one's group, and uses three vignettes that represent each of these aspects.

Hence corporate loyalty to employees was represented by the scenario:

In a time of economic recession, profits have been significantly reduced. The company could struggle on for another year, but this would mean greatly depleting financial reserves to a dangerous level. Unemployment in the local community is now very high. The company decides to make redundant (lay off) up to a third of the workforce as necessary.

Loyalty to company was represented as follows:

You know that when your colleague goes on business trips he sometimes inflates the amount of expenses he can claim back from the company by about 50 per cent. You speak to him about it and he says that he gives a lot of his time to the company on these trips, and this is just fair recompense. You decide to report this to a superior.

Loyalty to group was represented as follows.

An employee has been late on a number of occasions and his productivity has gone down significantly over the last six months. You know that the employee financially supports an extended family. Members of his work team have said they will work harder to compensate for the employee's deficiencies. You accept this.

The study included managers in the Anglo-Saxon countries of the United States and Australia; the East Asian 'tiger' countries of Japan, Korea and economic region of Hong Kong; and managers in the 'transitional' countries of Russia (albeit in the Asiatic region) and Poland.

Findings from this study suggest that American managers base their judgements not on reference to prior principles (for example, as contained in the many codes of ethics published by American companies) but on consequential considerations. This is an indication that corporate codes may not be effective in intervening in management decision making in the country that has most propagated them. The indication also in this study that American managers may employ relativistic criteria in a judgement on the ethicality of retaining an inefficient employee out of consideration of group solidarity may suggest a social influence on this type of dilemma.

Like the Americans in this study, Australian managers indicated little use of deontological criteria in their ethical judgements. This may be more expected in the absence of wide-scale corporate emphasis on codes of ethics and educational programmes on business ethics in Australia. However, there is an indication in the study of a strong emphasis on the social referencing of ethical judgements by Australian managers who employ relativistic criteria. The collegiality contained within Schwartz's (1994) concept of egalitarian commitment discussed in Chapter 3 may provide the cultural context for this as Australians score relatively highly on this dimension. However, the ethical judgement regarding the decision to keep on the unproductive employee is based on utilitarian considerations, and is judged by the Australians, as well as the Americans, as being in the interests of the company.

A situational regard for ethical judgements by East Asian managers is supported in this study by findings indicating an emphasis on consequential considerations for the Japanese, Korean and Hong Kong managers. Relativistic criteria is important for the Japanese managers for their ethical judgement of the decision to lay off employees, for the Hong Kong managers in their judgement about the decision to support the inefficient employee, but only being used marginally by the Korean managers in their judgement about the decision to lay off employees. Although the study suggests that deontological considerations do figure in their ethical judgements, this is only marginally so. The decision to lay off employees is seen as less ethical than other national groups by the Japanese and Hong Kong managers, but not the Koreans. It supports an assumption that Korean and Japanese managers will be more ethically concerned with loyalty of the corporation to employees than the Anglo-Saxon managers. The Korean position on this may reflect Bae and Chung's (1997) finding that co-worker solidarity is less well developed in Korean industry than in Japan. So, even though the expectation of corporate loyalty to employees may be high, because it is not happening to them, they may put corporate interests first. The Hong Kong managers' position on this may reflect both a calculative relationship with the company and a higher level of solidarity with co-workers.

The Japanese managers in the study display an element of loyalty to the corporation by viewing the decision ethically to report the colleague for inflating the expense claim. This is seen as being less acceptable to their culture by the Koreans, while remaining neutral on the related criteria of being ethical or not. This may well reflect a general collectivism in Korean society with elements of social solidarity which militates against reporting co-workers (Korea is high on collectivism on Hofstede's 1980a/2003 index). This is also apparent in this study by the Korean managers' judgement that the decision to support the inefficient employee is more ethical than the American and Japanese managers believe.

In the study (Jackson, 2000) the Russian and Polish managers base their ethical judgements on multiple criteria. The ethical judgement on the decision of the company to make employees redundant is based on deontological and consequential considerations for the Russians and the Poles. The Russians see this decision as being less ethical in contrast to the Polish managers. This may indicate that the Russian managers expect a higher level of loyalty from the company to its employees than the Poles, and a lower level of employee solidarity from the Poles (the Polish managers see this in the best interests of the company, a criterion which is highly associated with an ethical judgement in this case). This may be an indication of the results of a faster move towards a free-market economy and the adoption of Western concepts on the part of the Poles. On the judgement of the decision to report one's colleague for inflating expenses claims, the Russians in this study use a combination of deontological and consequential criteria and the Poles a combination of relativistic and consequential criteria. They both see this as less of an ethical decision than the Japanese and American managers. This may indicate a lower level of loyalty to the corporation and a higher level of co-worker solidarity. However, it may also indicate a reluctance to report one's colleague for wrong doing, where in recent times, the consequences of doing this may have been dire for the colleague. The argument that this may indicate higher levels of solidarity is supported in the Polish and Russian managers' judgement that the decision to support an inefficient employee is more acceptable in their culture than in the Japanese managers' culture. This judgement also is multifaceted in that it is based on relativistic, deontological and consequential criteria for the Russian and Polish managers. The importance of referencing this judgement to one's culture, family and significant others is also indicative of the importance of social influences and solidarity in these societies.

The multidimensional nature of the structure of ethical judgements for managers in the two 'transitional' economies surveyed is indicative of the historical and current influences on ethical decision making (Jackson, 2000).

The study draws the following conclusions:

- Managers from the 'Anglo-Saxon' countries seem to look more to the consequences of their decisions in order to judge whether a decision is ethical, while managers from East Asian countries employ a social referencing to guide their judgements, and Russian managers employ more principled or deontological considerations. Although all groups tend to use multiple criteria, the study indicates differences in emphasis among different cultures or countries.

- This different emphasis on different decision criteria across cultures has implications for the way organizations attempt to influence the ethical decision making of its managers. There is little direct relevance of employee codes of ethics if managers are employing predominantly consequential criteria, as in the case of the managers from Anglo-Saxon countries. This may be more directly relevant to managers in Russia to whom deontological considerations are more relevant. Intervention in group processes may be more applicable to East Asian managers, and to a certain extent Australian managers who employ socially referenced criteria alongside consequential considerations. For those managers such as the Americans, who employ predominantly consequential considerations, discussion groups in organizations which address the issues of the consequences of management decisions may be more applicable in guiding ethical decision making.

- The study also points to differences in the content of ethical decision making (which is discussed in more detail in the next section): that is, judging the extent to which a decision is ethical or not. The findings indicate that the Australian and American managers saw a decision to lay off workers as being relatively ethical, and the Russian and Hong Kong managers saw this decision as relatively unethical. For the decision to report a colleague for falsifying his expenses account, the Japanese and American managers saw this as relatively unethical and the Polish and Russian managers relatively ethical. For the decision to support the poorly performing colleague the Korean managers saw this as relatively ethical and the American and Japanese managers saw this as relatively unethical.

Such differences in ethical content provide the subject for the next section of this chapter.

The content of ethical decision making

The cross-cultural literature is mainly concerned with differences in the 'content' of ethical judgement, or what managers regard as ethical or not ethical, although sometimes this is framed in a consideration of which country is more or less ethical than another.

The growing cross-cultural literature on management ethics provides evidence that there are differences among national groups in the perceptions of what constitutes ethical decision making among European countries (Becker and Fritzche, 1987; Jackson and Calafell Artola, 1997), among Anglo countries (Alderson and Kakabadse, 1994), between Anglo and European countries (Lyonski and Gaidis, 1991), between American and other nationalities (Hegarty and Sims, 1978, 1979; Izraeli, 1988; White and Rhodeback, 1992; Schlegelmilch and Robertson, 1995; Okleshen and Hoyt, 1996), and between Asian and non-Asian countries (Dolecheck and Dolecheck, 1987; Ralston *et al.*, 1994; McDonald and Pak, 1997).

This literature suggests that for issues concerning relations with external stakeholders such as customers and suppliers (see Table 3.1 in Chapter 3), managers from Anglo countries have a higher ethical concern than European and Asian managers, and that Americans show a greater concern than their other Anglo counterparts (Becker and Fritzche, 1987;

Lyonski and Gaidis, 1991; White and Rhodeback, 1992; Okleshen and Hoyt, 1996; McDonald and Pak, 1997). However, for issues involving loyalty relationships with the organization, Americans have a lower ethical concern than European managers (Izraeli, 1988; Alderson and Kakabadse, 1994) with some indication of variation among European groups (Jackson and Calafell Artola, 1997). There is some suggestion that Americans are more ethically concerned with issues of group loyalty (Izraeli, 1988) and that American managers may not put the organization first when it comes to conflicts with either group- or self-interests (Izraeli, 1988; Alderson and Kakabadse, 1994).

Studies undertaken which focus on management ethics in specific countries also indicate that for Japanese managers, company interests are more likely to take precedence over personal ethical considerations (Nakano, 1997), and that Japanese corporations instil a reciprocal loyalty with employees (Pickens, 1987) with high levels of commitment of Japanese employees to the organization (Bae and Chung, 1997). As noted above, the study by Bae and Chung (1997) which compares Korean employees with Japanese and American employees, shows a higher level of solidarity of Korean employees with the corporation compared with Japan and the United States, and indicates that Koreans expect the corporation to show the same degree of loyalty to them. However, in the same study they show a lower level of solidarity with co-workers compared with the USA and Japan. McDonald and Pak's (1997) study of Hong Kong managers compared with (Anglo) expatriates in Hong Kong shows a lower ethicality for Hong Kong managers, including a lower ethical concern for the manipulation of expenses (an indication of the level of loyalty to the corporation). In a study which compares the work values of Australian, Hong Kong and American managers, Westwood and Posner (1997) indicate that US and Australian managers place more importance on employees and co-workers as organizational stakeholders than their Hong Kong counterparts.

Ethical content and value dimensions

Following on from this work, Jackson (2001) undertook a study of ten diverse countries with a premise that ethical regard for such issues would vary according to the levels of two of Hofstede's cultural value dimensions, *Uncertainty Avoidance* and *individualism–collectivism*. It is worth first revisiting these concepts, introduced in Chapter 3, in order to look at their possible ethical implications, before discussing the results of Jackson's (2001) study.

First, *Uncertainty Avoidance* (Hofstede, 1980a/2003) is an important consideration in the areas of economic and social regulation, and *individualism–collectivism* in the area of relations with the corporation and relations with significant others in one's social or work group. Cultural variations in these areas are important in explaining the perceived ethicality of management actions within organizations. However, these dimensions in themselves have limitations.

Individualism–collectivism in particular comprises a number of complex factors. This construct may represent an oversimplification through which it may be difficult to interpret differences in ethical importance attributed to issues concerning group and organizational loyalty. Other cultural studies that were discussed in Chapter 3 (Schwartz, 1994; Smith *et al.*, 1996) may also serve to clarify some of the oversimplifications inherent in Hofstede's (1980a/2003, 1991) treatment of *individualism–collectivism*. We now look more specifically at what these dimensions might tell us about perceived ethicality, and their limitations.

Individualism–collectivism and ethicality

This dimension is well substantiated in the literature (from Tönnies', 1887, *gesellschaft* and *gemeinschaft* to Hofstede, 1980a/2003, and Triandis, 1995). Hofstede (1980a/2003) defines individualism as 'pertaining to societies in which the ties between individuals are loose: everyone is expected to look after himself or herself and his immediate family', and collectivism as 'pertaining to societies in which people from birth onwards are integrated into strong, cohesive in-groups, which throughout people's lifetime continue to protect them in exchange for unquestioning loyalty' (1991: 51). This may well have implications for ethical issues concerned with company loyalty. For example, it has been argued that collectivism engenders organizational commitment (Boyacigiller and Adler, 1991).

Individualism may engender a calculative relationship with one's organization and colleagues based upon a concern for individual achievement within an individualist culture. Collectivist societies engender an obligation-oriented concern or moral involvement through patterns of duty towards one's organization (Hofstede, 1991). Schwartz (1994) explores this aspect further in his value dimension of 'conservatism' (which is negatively correlated with Hofstede's individualism, as we saw in Chapter 3). He opposes this to 'intellectual autonomy' (which is positively correlated with Hofstede's individualism). Conservatism represents values that support the status quo and is associated with societies based on close-knit harmonious relations.

Interests of the person are the same as the group. Values stress security, conformity, tradition and relations of obligations. In contrast, intellectual autonomy stresses values that favour the individual's pursuit of own interests and desires.

In a collectivist culture, therefore, the nature of the relationship of individuals to organizations is likely to be based on obligation and moral duty. In an individualist culture it is likely to be calculative, and based contractually on self-interest. This is supported in the cross-cultural ethics literature which suggests that American managers, comparatively, do not attribute a high ethical importance to issues relating to corporate loyalty (Izraeli, 1988; Alderson and Kakabadse, 1994).

Yet Hui (1990) argues that Hofstede's view is oversimplistic because collectivism is target specific: individuals feel solidarity with some people (ingroup) but not others (out-group). Also, different collectivist cultures differ in their locus of concern with Japanese men being more psychologically involved with their organizations and workplace, and Chinese more psychologically involved with their families, but at the expense of those outside the collective.

In Hong Kong there is evidence in the literature to suggest that relationships based traditionally on kinship ties are waning, and voluntary and instrumental relationships are in the ascendancy (Ho and Chiu, 1994). In the People's Republic of China there is evidence that there are high levels of obligatory commitment to one's work organization and group. Over the last fifty years these units have taken care of their people's welfare and even marriages. Through such state influence as emulation campaigns they have instilled loyalty into workers of state-owned enterprises (Jackson and Bak, 1998). This may also change with large-scale layoffs from state-owned enterprises.

Schwartz (1994) is also concerned with the oversimplification of the collectivism–individualism concept. As we saw in Chapter 3, results from his empirical study contrast 'conservatism' with 'egalitarian commitment'. In the latter, selfish interests are transcended and there is a voluntary commitment to promoting the welfare of other people. This contrasts with obligation and kinship ties that would be found in a society representing 'conservative' values. Contained within the egalitarian commitment construct are individual values such as loyalty, social justice, responsibility and equality. Egalitarian commitment is also contrasted with Schwartz's (1994) dimension of 'hierarchy' which correlates negatively with Hofstede's individualism. Egalitarian commitment correlates positively with Hofstede's individualism, and somewhat confounds a simplistic view of individualism–collectivism.

Within Jackson's (2001) ten-country study, Hong Kong and China are relatively low on egalitarian commitment; and Spain, France, Germany, Switzerland and the United States are relatively high. Australia is in the middle of this dimension. India and Britain are not represented in Schwartz's (1994, 1999) study, but on Smith *et al.*'s (1996) associated dimension of conservatism–egalitarian commitment, India is in the middle of the dimension, with Britain relatively high on egalitarian commitment, grouped together with the United States and Australia. In collectivist cultures, therefore, the relationship that the individual has with the peer group or work team is likely to be based on an obligatory commitment to promote the interests of the group as a collective entity: possibly at the expense of out-group individuals. In an individualist culture this relationship is based on an egalitarian commitment to voluntarily promote the welfare of others. Izraeli's (1988) study supports this in that American managers attribute a high ethical importance to issues of 'collegiality'.

Smith *et al.*'s (1996) reanalysis of Trompenaars' (1993) database on cultural values provides a first factor 'conservatism–egalitarian commitment' as was noted in Chapter 3. This is associated with collectivism–individualism. Items from Trompenaars's (1993) questionnaire relating to a concept of 'universalism–particularism' load highly on this factor. This cultural dimension, which has antecedents in the literature (see Smith *et al.*, 1996 and Trompenaars, 1993), concerns the extent to which rules and principles are seen as applying universally to everyone in a society (universalism); or seen as applying differently to different significant others and circumstances (particularism). This cross-cultural concept relates to the situationalism discussed in the work of Ralston *et al.*, (1994), Dolecheck and Dolecheck (1987) and Singhapakdi *et al.* (1994), as was mentioned above. They propose that the Western view of ethical behaviour is as an absolute which applies universally (universalism). The Eastern view is that ethical behaviour depends on the situation and is not concerned with absolute truths or principles (particularism).

In collectivist cultures, therefore, it is likely that ethical decision making will be based on the contingencies of the situation and of maintaining 'face'. In individualist cultures it is likely to be based on concepts of universal principles of what is right and wrong. As we saw above, the illicit pursuit of self-interest in collectivist societies is well documented in the cross-cultural ethics literature, as is the lack of reference to universal principles of morality (Ralston *et al.*, 1994; Singhapakdi *et al.*, 1994).

Let us now turn more specifically to *Uncertainty Avoidance*, and see how this might inform ideas about perceived ethicality.

Uncertainty Avoidance and ethicality

Hofstede's (1980a/2003) value dimension of *Uncertainty Avoidance* has conceptual roots in such work as Peltro's (1968) dimension of tight-loose cultures. Triandis (1990) also uses a general construct to describe differences between cultures that adhere to rules and those that 'play it by ear'. This is essentially a measure of the tolerance of ambiguity in a society. In Hofstede's dimension this combines questionnaire items on the desirability of breaking company rules, the intention of staying with one's company and the degree to which managers feel nervous or tense at work. It is therefore concerned with the level of regulation that is deemed comfortable in order to manage the potential ambiguity in a situation. Generally, the higher the degree of *Uncertainty Avoidance* in a society, logically, the higher the level of regulation should be in such areas as the economy or business life.

In high *Uncertainty Avoidance* cultures, therefore, the level of economic and social regulation is likely to be high and internalized within the community. In low *Uncertainty Avoidance* cultures this acceptance of regulation is likely to be low. However, there may be legislation that attempts to regulate the excesses of a free-market economy such as in the United States, as well as responding to public indignation against such excesses, as we discussed in Chapter 2. There is strong evidence from the cross-cultural ethics literature that managers from 'Anglo-Saxon' countries (which are low in *Uncertainty Avoidance*) attribute more ethical importance to issues involving business dealings with external stakeholders. This is in contrast to managers from higher *Uncertainty Avoidance* countries such as Germany and France, which have a higher social and economic regulation (Becker and Fritzche, 1987; Lyonski and Gaidis, 1991; Hegarty and Sims, 1978, 1979; White and Rhodeback, 1992; Okleshen and Hoyt, 1996; McDonald and Pak, 1997).

Hofstede (1991: 113) defines *Uncertainty Avoidance* as 'the extent to which the members of a culture feel threatened by uncertainty or unknown situations'. There is therefore a tendency to shun ambiguous situations. People look for rules and regulations in a situation in order to avoid ambiguity. So, along with the internalization of and adherence to social and economic regulation within a community, the bases of decision making may be different from high to low *Uncertainty Avoidance* cultures. In high *Uncertainty Avoidance* cultures, the ethical decision-making process and criteria are likely to be based on the implicit adherence to rules. In low *Uncertainty Avoidance* cultures they are likely to be based on the interpretation of rules and a consideration of possible outcomes. Apart from individualism, low *Uncertainty Avoidance* may provide some explanation for Alderson and

Kakabadse's (1994) and Izraeli's (1988) findings that American managers have a more pragmatic attitude towards conflicts of self and organizational interests.

If we focus on these two cultural dimensions, *Uncertainty Avoidance* and *individualism–collectivism*, it is then possible to infer national variation in the attribution of ethical importance to particular types of organizational relations: interaction with external stakeholders, loyalty to one's organization and loyalty to one's group. Other explanations such as religiosity and level of economic development seem less convincing when applied to present day societies (Hofstede, 1991; Schwartz, 1994).

By combining these two dimensions in interaction (e.g. individualism with low *Uncertainty Avoidance*, collectivism with high *Uncertainty Avoidance*) Jackson (2001) shows how ethical perceptions may be framed in terms of cultural attributes in different groups of countries. The ten countries investigated are divided into four groups, as follows.

Group 1 countries fall into an *Individualism* and low *Uncertainty Avoidance* quadrant comprising Britain, the United States and Australia. The literature suggests that there is low implicit control of economic relations within low *Uncertainty Avoidance* countries (typically Anglo-Saxon countries). There may therefore be a need for explicit legislation to control excesses. This may sensitize managers to the ethical importance of issues concerning relations with external stakeholders. Becker and Fritzche's (1987) study of American, French and German managers indicated that Americans were less pragmatic towards ethical decision making than their French and German counterparts. Lyonski and Gaidis (1991) undertook a replication of this study with American, New Zealand and Danish business students. They concluded that respondents from the two Anglo-Saxon countries judged more unethical the paying of bribes, divulging propriety information about their previous employer and releasing pollution, compared with their Danish counterparts. White and Rhodeback (1992) also found that American managers were more likely to judge such actions as unethical compared with Taiwanese managers. Okleshen and Hoyt (1996) found differences between two Anglo-Saxon groups in a study of American and New Zealand business students. This indicated that American respondents judged actions involving fraud, coercion and self-interest as more unethical than their New Zealand counterparts. Yet Whipple and Swords (1992) found no significant differences between American and British business students, and Abratt *et al.* (1992) found no differences in the responses between Australian and South African (presumably white) managers in judgements of ethicality.

A study by McDonald and Pak (1997) also found that American and British managers judge issues concerning external stakeholders as having a higher ethical importance than Hong Kong managers. Their finding also indicated that Anglo-Saxon expatriates living in Hong Kong judge such issues as having more ethical importance than ethnic Chinese managers. Yet they found no significant differences between Hong Kong managers and those from the People's Republic of China and Macau. The literature therefore suggests that managers from the Anglo-Saxon countries attribute a higher ethical importance to relations with external stakeholders concerning issues such as gift giving and receiving. They are more likely to rate actions such as paying or accepting bribes as more unethical than their counterparts from the other countries discussed above. As noted from the literature on cultural value dimensions, this may be because of the low implicit control of economic relations and the need for explicit legislation to control excesses in a low *Uncertainty Avoidance* culture.

The literature on cultural values reviewed in Chapter 3 also suggests that a high calculative relationship with the organization in an individualistic culture may diminish the ethical importance placed on loyalty relations with one's organization. Alderson and Kakabadse (1994) in their study of American, Irish and British managers found that the Americans attached less ethical importance to decisions concerning such relations with the organization (judging kickbacks and expense account fraud as more ethically acceptable than their counterparts in the other two countries). Similarly a study by Izraeli (1988) indicated that American managers place less ethical importance than Israelis on issues concerning loyalty to the organization (rating significantly more ethical 'taking extra personal time such as breaks' and 'doing personal business in the organization's time').

The literature on collectivism–individualism discussed above and in Chapter 3 also suggests that a higher level of 'egalitarian commitment' in individualistic cultures may lead to a higher level of collegiality and concern for one's immediate colleagues. There is only some support for this in the cross-cultural ethics literature. For example, in the study by Izraeli (1988) American managers indicated a higher level of collegiality, rating as more unethical than their Israeli counterparts actions involving 'passing blame for errors to innocent co-workers'; and 'claiming credit for someone else's work'. Israel appears higher in *Uncertainty Avoidance* and lower in *Individualism* than the Anglo-Saxons.

This led to the assumption that managers from this group (individualistic/low *Uncertainty Avoidance*) would place a higher ethical importance on external stakeholder relations, a lower ethical importance on loyalty relationships with the organization, and a higher ethical importance on loyalty relations within their group, which were largely borne out by the results of the empirical study (Jackson, 2001), where a higher level of egalitarian commitment (Schwartz, 1994) may explain managers' attributions of a higher ethical importance to loyalty to the group in an individualistic culture.

Group 2 countries in this study (Germany, Switzerland and France) fall into the *Individualism* and high *Uncertainty Avoidance* quadrant. Of relevance here is the evidence in the literature on cultural values discussed above, that in countries with higher *Uncertainty Avoidance* cultures, the higher levels of shared regulative norms in business practices and higher levels of social and economic regulation may lead managers to place a lower ethical importance on issues involving external stakeholders (such as customers or suppliers). Such behaviour as gift accepting and giving in exchange for favours may therefore be rated as more ethically acceptable. This may be because internalized norms make this less of an ethical issue than for managers in the Anglo-Saxon group. This has some support in the cross-cultural ethics literature. Hence Becker and Fritzche's (1987) study indicated that French and German managers have a more pragmatic attitude to such issues than Americans. Some support is also found in a study by Schlegelmilch and Robertson (1995) which indicated that European managers (German and Austrian, but also including British) are likely to place a lower ethical importance on issues associated with controlling employees' use of corporate information in respect of external stakeholders. The ensuing assumption that managers in this group will place a lower ethical importance on issues of relationships with external stakeholders was largely supported by the results of Jackson's (2001) study.

Higher *Uncertainty Avoidance* may also be associated with a higher commitment to one's organization. However, the calculative nature of the relationship with organizations, which may be associated with individualistic cultures, may moderate this. This may indicate that managers will judge issues relating to loyalty to the organization as having a moderate ethical importance. The literature on cross-cultural management ethics only tentatively supports this. The findings of Izraeli (1988) suggest that Israeli managers (who would also fall into group 2) judge issues concerning loyalty to the corporation as having a lower ethical importance compared with their American counterparts. There are, however, also differences between German and French managers in the study by Jackson and Calafell Artola (1997) in this area. Schlegelmilch and Robertson's (1995) findings indicate that German and Austrian managers judge issues involving loyalty to the corporation (use of corporate information) as having a lower ethical importance than American managers, but the same importance as British managers.

An assumption may also be made from the literature that managers would place a higher level of ethical importance on issues involving relations with the group through the need to reduce uncertainty by having stable relations with one's group in a high uncertainty culture. The higher level of egalitarian commitment in an individualistic culture may also contribute to this attribution of a higher ethical importance. They would therefore judge as unethical actions that may be detrimental to this relationship. Prior studies of this aspect of management ethics are limited. Jackson and Calafell Artola (1997) provide a comparison between their results for Germany and France, and the studies by Newstrom and Ruch (1975) and Ferrell and Weaver (1978) on American managers, and by Izraeli (1988) on Israeli managers. This is on the same questionnaire items as the Jackson (2001) study, measuring ethical attitudes to group loyalty. This shows uniformly low ratings (seeing as unethical 'passing blame for errors onto an innocent co-worker', and 'claiming credit for someone else's work') for this cultural group. Results from Jackson's (2001) empirical study supported the assumption that managers from this group (individualistic/high *Uncertainty Avoidance*) will place a higher ethical importance on issues involving loyalty relations with their group.

Group 3 countries in Jackson's (2001) study fall into the *Collectivism* and high *Uncertainty Avoidance* cultures, and comprise Spain and China. A higher obligation-based culture (Hofstede's, 1991, *Collectivism*; Schwartz's, 1994, and Smith *et al.*'s, 1996, *Conservatism*) together with higher levels of regulation (Hofstede's, 1991, *Uncertainty Avoidance*) would suggest that managers from this loose grouping would judge issues involving relations with external stakeholders, organization and group as having a higher ethical importance. However, there is a lack of reported comparative findings on Spanish and Peoples' Republic of China managers in connection with such ethical issues. A comparable country which would appear in group 3 is Thailand, which is both high in *Uncertainty Avoidance* and *Collectivism* (Hofstede, 1991, Singhapakdi *et al.*, 1994). Singhapakti *et al.*'s (1994) findings suggest that in relations with external stakeholders, Thai marketers (in comparison with Americans) are more idealistic and adhere to 'moral absolutes' which represent a reduction in uncertainty.

This finding may seem contradictory to those studies reported above which suggest that American managers also judge issues involving external stakeholders as having a higher ethical importance. However, this may represent the difference between what Paine (1994) has called a compliance attitude, and an integrity-based attitude to ethical issues. In the American situation (low *Uncertainty Avoidance, Individualism*) a compliance attitude may prevail. Laws and rules are needed to curb excesses of a highly individualistic and competitive free market, but are not internalized. In a Thai situation (high uncertainty, collectivism) idealism, and an integrity-based attitude, may prevail to reduce uncertainty. The difference also between the countries in group 3 and group 2 (high *Uncertainty Avoidance* and individualistic) is the extent to which collectivism through networks of reciprocal and obligatory relations may encourage such practices as giving and receiving gifts in exchange for favours.

The proposal (largely from this Thai study) that managers from collectivist and high *Uncertainty Avoidance* cultures will place a higher ethical importance on issues involving relations with external stakeholders, was supported by the finding of the Jackson (2001) study, with managers from China and Spain.

The growing literature on other aspects of corporate life in China (explored in more detail in Chapter 9) indicates higher levels of loyalty to the corporation than may be expected in countries in the Anglo-Saxon group (Jackson and Bak, 1998). This appears also to be the case for Korea and Japan (Bae and Chung, 1997) which also could be included in group 3. Hence the proposition that managers from collectivist and high *Uncertainty Avoidance* cultures will place a higher ethical importance on issues involving loyalty relations with the organization was borne out by the Jackson (2001) finding, with differences between Spanish and Chinese managers, as might be expected, with Chinese managers placing a higher ethical importance on organizational loyalty (which may reflect a higher collectivism and *Uncertainty Avoidance* than Spain). The proposition that managers in this group will place a higher ethical importance on issues involving loyalty relations with their group, is supported by the results of the Chinese managers, but is inconclusive with the Spanish managers.

Group 4 countries (Hong Kong, India) in Jackson's (2001) study are both collectivist and low in *Uncertainty Avoidance*. Because this group has low *Uncertainty Avoidance* (as distinct from group 3), higher levels of social and economic control may not therefore counter higher levels of obligatory relations that encourage practices such as gift giving and accepting. Hence, as reported above, in comparison with Anglo-Saxon managers Ralston *et al.*'s (1994) and McDonald and Pak's (1997) findings suggest that ethnic Chinese managers from Hong Kong place a lower ethical importance on issues concerning external stakeholders. Lee's (1982) earlier study which found no significant differences in ethical standards in marketing practices between ethnic Chinese and British expatriates in Hong Kong may urge caution. However, Lee (1982) believes that this may simply be a function of the high levels of acculturation of the British managers. Given this, Jackson (2001) proposed that managers from this group will place a lower ethical importance on issues involving relations with external stakeholders. The fact that his results support this suggests that an attribution of a lower ethical importance is due to a higher obligation-based relationship with such stakeholders. This may favour reciprocity and thus gift giving and receiving as expressing mutual obligation. The lower regulatory framework makes it difficult to exert sanctions on this.

Lower levels of *Uncertainty Avoidance* and a low dependence on one's organization may give rise to a more instrumental view of one's organization. Hence managers may judge issues involving loyalty to their organization as having a lower ethical importance. There is little direct support of this assumption in the ethics literature. However, in Chinese cultures outside China the literature suggests that collectivism is targeted towards the family rather than the corporation (Hui, 1990), and that in Hong Kong, instrumental relationships in corporate life are becoming more prevalent (Ho and Chiu, 1994). Gupta (1991) also provides evidence of a lack of identification with the organization of Indians, and a tendency to draw meaning from familial relations. It is therefore possible, Jackson (2001) surmises, that managers from group 4 will place a lower ethical importance on issues involving loyalty relations with the organization. Although the results from the study are ambivalent, they do suggest a view from managers from both countries (Hong Kong and India) that the relationship with the organization is somewhat instrumental, yet a desire on the part of the Indian managers that it were less so.

As collectivism may be directed more towards the family, rather than the organization, in the countries within this group, managers' in-group may well be their family members rather than work colleagues. This may suggest that managers judge issues involving loyalty relations with their work colleagues as having a low ethical importance (unless they are within their family groups). Some evidence of this in the ethics literature suggests that Hong Kong managers judge the use of self-serving behaviour, such as spreading rumours about others, as more ethically acceptable than their American counterparts (Ralston *et al.*, 1994). Hence, in comparison with managers from other groups, managers from collectivist and low *Uncertainty Avoidance* cultures (group 4) may place a lower ethical importance on issues involving loyalty relations with their group. This is supported by results of the study in terms of managers' perception of the judgements of others, but not in terms of self-judgements. This may reflect a perception that despite people regarding organizations instrumentally, and loyalty being directed towards the family rather than the work group, there is a need to change (that is, other people see these issues as not so ethically important, but my view is that they are).

Relationships: the value of people

In the opening case a number of different types of relationships have been alluded to. Following the discussion above on the structure and content of ethical decision making, we are now in a better position to analysis these relationships, and the antecedence and consequences of ethical decision making. For this we will also need to refer to Table 4.1, although this provides indicative types of relationships, is not exhaustive, nor does it try to cover all of these relationships in the above discussion and in the opening case study. Hence relations with the environment have not been considered, yet value dimensions such as Inglehart's *Survival* versus *Self-Expression* may have a bearing on how managers related to environmental issues where the former values may drive industrialization in countries that see a need to catch up quickly with industrialized countries at the expense of pollution controls. Schwartz's *mastery* versus *harmony* values dimension may provide clues about a manager's relationship with nature and implications for minimizing human encroachment on natural environments.

Opening case revisited

The fact that Johnny Mbeke was recruited by his present supervisor who is from the same village and a family friend may not raise too many eyebrows in a collectivist (Hofstede, 1980a/2003) and a particularistic rather than a universalistic (Trompenaars, 1993) culture. Though this may be regarded as nepotistic in an individualistic/universalistic culture, the recruitment of a complete stranger on the basis of an abstract job specification, and often brief assessments of a candidate's abilities, for example in a job interview, may be considered most unwise in a particularistic culture. Someone that you know, and whose family you know and through which pressure can be imposed if the employee does not perform to expectations, might seem the wisest option. In addition, providing work directly to the local community, through having and maintaining good contacts, and benefiting directly the local community through job opportunities may be seen as the normal course of events in a collectivist and *traditional* as opposed to a *secular* culture in Inglehart's terms.

That Johnny earns one-twentieth of the amount his manager earns may be an indication of a higher *Power Distance* (Hofstede, 1980a/2003) although it could be argued that an achievement-oriented society may reward higher performance and may differentiate more between different levels in the organization. If reward is simply based on seniority, and the differentials are great, it is likely to reflect values of a higher *Power Distance* culture. The fact that Johnny would not question an order from his supervisor or manager and, like his colleagues, has no say in any decisions the company makes, provides further clues that this is a high *Power Distance* culture, where such inequalities in terms of income as well as decision making in the organization is not seen as an ethical question. Such disparities of income and authority could be challenged in a low *Power Distance* culture as unethical.

The way employees where Johnny works relate to the organization is reflected in their stealing items of stationery from the warehouse for personal use. This might indicate a particular orientation to loyalty to the organization. Table 4.1 provides other possible indicators that were not explored above (such as adherence to confidentiality and general commitment to work). Noted above was the connection between attitudes to loyalty and Smith *et al.*'s constructs of *loyal involvement* versus *utilitarian involvement,* and the GLOBE study's institutional collectivism (discussed in Chapter 3). That taking personal supplies from the company is not seen as an ethical issue by employees might indicate utilitarian involvement. Blunt and Jones (1992), for example, note the instrumental approach that employees take to their organization in African countries, often using a job as a way of resourcing other affairs such as a business either directly or indirectly.

We also know that the senior management at the company where Johnny works often pays bribes in order to win contracts. The ethical attitudes towards this in any given society might be indicative either of *Survival* versus *Self-Expression* in Inglehart's terms where in the former it is seen as expedient, or of collectivism where gift giving and taking may be regarded as building relationships.

We have already seen that Johnny is paid twenty times less than his boss, yet he has ten dependants, whereas his manager has only two. Could this be considered unethical, or at least be seen to need some kind of ethical questioning? Clearly in an individualistic and achievement society this would not be questioned as unethical. Yet what about in a collectivist and feminine (Hofstede, 1980a/2003) society where looking after one's own and a nurturing attitude are fostered? Yet can these cultural values that have already been discussed really explain the differences here?

Similarly, it was noted that Johnny has a lame leg and is very slow at his work and not very good at it; that he has been given several warnings, but despite this is often late for work. What values can be referred to that account for his work group telling the manager that they are happy to cover for Johnny? Certainly group solidarity reflecting *in-group collectivism* (GLOBE) and *conservatism* as opposed to *autonomy* (Schwartz) as discussed above and in Chapter 3 could be referred to. The concept of instrumentalism–humanism introduced in Chapter 3 may shed more light on this. If Johnny is seen purely as a 'human resource' then clearly he should be sacked. Similarly, the fact that he is supporting ten dependants is not a concern of the management where he works. A humanistic view of employee relations may suggest at least taking a more sympathetic approach. It could even suggest taking a paternalistic approach. This latter is much maligned in the Western literature (Aycan, 2006; Jackson *et al.*, 2008), but does indicate a concern for staff over and above their being a resource.

Implications for international managers

This chapter has sought to show a relationship between culture, or more specifically cultural values dimensions, and regard for ethicality. In other words, what is regarded as ethical in one country may be construed as unethical by another. This may cause problems for the international manager from one country working in another. This chapter does not seek to instruct, or even suggest ways that managers should deal with this other than in very broad terms, but purely to understand it. There are a number of approaches that managers can take when trying to deal with such differences, and most relate to what we have termed above the structure of ethical decisions: that is, how ethical decisions are made. Hence a manager can take a relativist position: what happens in one country is okay according to the local culture and therefore one goes along with it. For example, if bribes are generally asked for and paid, then this is what one should do. A manager can also take a universalistic approach: bribery is generally (from a certain Western perspective, perhaps) regarded as unethical and therefore should not be accepted. This position might be taken by the manager's company and formulated in the company's code of ethics. He might take a pragmatic or utilitarian approach: what will be the consequences if I pay the bribe? These will be discussed over the next five chapters in the form of what might happen in different regions or countries. For the time being we can focus on some of the issues pointed to at the beginning of the current chapter.

The decision of a multinational company to lay off considerable numbers of employees in a subsidiary may be judged differently from culture to culture. Similarly the aspects of the opening case may be judged differently by managers from different cultural backgrounds. Perhaps the job of the international manager is to first understand the cultural context: how can differences be accounted for in attitudes towards what is ethical and what is not ethical? Being critical about assumptions that a manager takes from one culture into another is an important step in understanding how to manage differences that may arise.

This chapter also takes an important step further than the last in focusing on research undertaken specifically on ethical structure and content across cultures. The best research provides some explanation or context for differences, rather than simply stating that there are differences. It is an international manager's job to understand what these differences are, and why.

Questions for managers
1. Think of three reasons why paying gifts in some countries might be acceptable practice. For the same countries, think of three reasons why this practice is not acceptable. On balance, what would you do?
2. Should Johnny Mbeke be given the sack?
3. How do you make ethical decisions? Is this different among the various stakeholder relationships you are involved in (external stakeholders: customers, suppliers, etc; internal stakeholders: employees, the company)? Do you predominantly use deontological or teleological thinking?

An agenda for research

Much of the detail within Table 4.1 has not been systematically researched. Here assumptions are made about differences in ethical decision making regarding different types of stakeholders. Although some of this has been the subject of the research studies discussed in this chapter, there is still need for detailed research about differences among managers from different country cultural backgrounds, and the differences in decision making involving different types of stakeholders, although purely comparative studies have several limitations. Table 4.1 presents the basis for a research agenda for investigating these differences. However, as discussed above, care should be taken in two regards: (1) implying that managers from one country are more or less ethical than managers from another; and (2) assuming that cultural values are independent variables or cultural antecedents that explain ethical differences.

The current author has attempted to overcome the problems inherent in the first, in his own work by firstly concentrating on the regard for ethicality, or differences in what managers regard as ethical or not ethical, and the basis upon which they make these assumptions: the structure of decision making. Secondly, he has insisted that any differences be placed in cultural context: what cultural factors can include regarding giving gifts as acceptable ethically? This takes us to the point (2) above, that cultural is not an independent variable, because ethical values are subsumed under cultural values, which are part of 'culture'. It is therefore difficult to say that collectivism predicts the employment of friends and family (nepotism). More logically we should say that collectivism includes taking care of those within one's in-group. This may seem to be a small and rather pedantic point. Yet it has major implications for the way ethics is conceptualized cross-culturally and how it is researched. These issues were taken up in Chapters 2 and 3.

The purpose of the current chapter has been to explore the research undertaken on cross-cultural differences in ethical decision making in terms of how decisions are made (structure) and what those decisions are (content). These may be areas suitable for further research, and should go beyond simply describing ethical content and structure.

Questions for researchers
1. Why does the structure of ethical decision making across cultures appear to be hybrid? Can this be attributed to cultural crossvergence, or do we need to develop different concepts and tools to analyse this aspect of cross-cultural management ethics?
2. Beyond culture, how can we explain differences in the content of ethical decision making across nations?
3. What are the ethical issues of researching differences in ethical attitudes and behaviour across cultures?

Part II

Understanding values and ethics within and among cultural spaces

5 Geopolitics and cultural invisibility: the United States

In part, an assumption has been made in the previous chapters, especially Chapter 2, that we live in a global world that can be characterized as post-colonial and neo-colonial. Although management theory, and cross-cultural management theory, have largely ignored geopolitical factors, the nature of the type of power dynamics involved in globalization and its influences on social and organization characteristics worldwide is significant. This does not simply involve, for example, the exploitation of human and natural resources in 'developing' countries. There are also major implications for population mobility and, as discussed in Chapter 2, for cultural crossvergence and hybridization of organizational and other human forms (such as the family and religious institutions). Not only has Britain's empire, for example, had the consequence of large numbers of Britons distributed around the world in what used to be her colonies (including the United States), the UK is now a multiculturally diverse nation. This is not simply a consequence of its own empire, and its subsequent breakdown, but more recently a result of the breakdown of the Soviet Empire, and new additions to the European Union. Britain can no longer be regarded as a cultural monolith.

This of course applies to the United States. Starting its modern history as a destination for European and other immigrants, its international activities have greatly increased its reach and attraction for immigration. China may also be a future magnet for immigration. With trade and other interests developing in Africa and other 'developing' countries, with an estimated one million Chinese in Africa, the Chinese government is increasingly encouraging the take-up of studentships for foreigners in Chinese universities. Since the 1980s China has been seen by the West as a huge market. International joint ventures there have boomed and direct investment is increasing. These activities have increasingly encouraged inward as well as outward mobility.

One of the implications of this level of international mobility (which perhaps is nothing new if one looks at intra-continental emigration patterns in Europe and Africa for example, yet the levels of multiculturalism appear to be a phenomenon of the late twentieth and early twenty-first centuries) is the difficulty of speaking about 'a culture'. Much of the discussion in Chapter 4 involved comparisons of ethical values among nation states, yet cross-cultural national comparisons are becoming less feasible and less relevant. It is becoming more relevant to focus on cross-cultural dynamics, and Chapter 2 suggested that cultural interfaces should be the focus of our attention. In this regard it is appropriate to take as a starting point the United States, to situate it within its geopolitical context, and to focus on the nature of its cultural interfaces.

Despite its leading economic role following World War II, and its resultant pre-eminence in the field of organization management, as pointed out a number of years ago by Boyacigiller and Adler (1991), or perhaps because of it, little attention has been given overtly to the cultural attributes of the United States in the cross-cultural management literature, other than the numerous studies that compare it with some other country or countries with merely a superficial analysis. A notable exception is Martin J. Gannon's work (Gannon and associates, 1994; Carroll and Gannon, 1997), examined shortly, which in part draws on the work of Stewart and Bennett, 1991. Yet coming back to the point: if seeing the USA as a cultural monolith is problematic, so looking at the United States outside its geopolitical role is really missing the point. This actually touches on another point: that doing social science is a political activity, and by implication an ethical one. Flyvbjerg (2001) makes the point quite strongly that normal social science attempts to take a 'view from nowhere'. Studying management ethics, in particular, is difficult to do from a position of value-neutrality (who on this Earth, literally, is able to do this?). The relevance of this assumption when studying 'universals' in management ethics across the globe, is that universals are generated through a geopolitical power dynamic, with the United States being largely at the centre of this.

Opening case: the universalism of human rights[1]

There are three main issues concerning the universal nature of universal human rights. The first is the extent to which those countries which are in the best position to influence the nature of 'universalism', are the most flagrant ignorers of the human rights that are declared to be universal. The

---

[1] I am indebted to the work of Schech and Haggis (2000, ch. 6).

second issue is whether or not human rights are indeed universal, or whether their universal nature is dictated by cultural norms that are asserted through world power relations. The third issue, in part connected to the second, is what happens when the exercising of these (individual) human rights are at variance to the interests of wider groups or nations, for example longer-term development plans. The following landmarks in recent history appear to be relevant to these points.

- The 'Declaration by United Nations' was signed by the Allies to unite them during the Second World War in 1942, and is considered to be a pre-runner of the concept of the UN.
- The Second World War ended in 1945.
- The Universal Declaration of Human Rights was proclaimed by the General Assembly of the UN in 1948, prefaced by the statement that the 'disregard and contempt for human rights have resulted in barbarous acts which have outraged the conscience of mankind'. Article 2 affirms that: 'Everyone is entitled to all the rights and freedoms set forth in this Declaration, without distinction of any kind, such as race, color, sex, language, religion, political and other opinion, national or social origin, property, birth or other status.' Eleanor Roosevelt was chair of the Commission which drafted the Declaration.
- Other Articles provide for: basic civil rights, such as Article 4 'No one shall be held in slavery or servitude,' Article 13 'Everyone has the right to freedom of movement' and Article 1 'All human beings are born free and equal in dignity and rights'; for political rights such as Article 21 'Everyone has the right to take part in the Government of his [sic] country'; for rule of law such as Article 9 'No one shall be subjected to arbitrary arrest, detention or exile' and Article 10 'Everyone is entitled to full equality to a fair and public hearing'; and for material well-being such as Article 17 'Everyone has the right to own property.'
- In 1957 Ghana became the first country in Africa to gain its independence. Zimbabwe gained its independence as late as 1980, with South Africa attaining democracy in 1994.
- In 1960 the Belgian Congo obtained its independence. Patrice Lumumba became its first democratically elected leader. He was very outspoken against the West, believing that political independence was not enough, but only through economic liberation could the continent cease to be an economic colony. Belgian, British and American corporations by then had large investments in the Congo with its vast resources of copper, cobalt, diamonds, gold, tin, manganese and zinc. Lumumba, with his

increasing influence in the area, was setting off alarm bells in Western capitals. In addition, he could not be bought, but, finding no friend in the West, turned to the Soviet Union for help. It is now a matter of public record that the US National Security Council subcommittee on covert operations, which included CIA Chief Allen Dulles, authorized Lumumba's assassination. The democratically elected Prime Minister of the newly independent nation of the Congo was arrested, beaten and finally shot in Elizabethville in January 1961, with a CIA agent driving around the city with Lumumba in the boot of his car trying to find somewhere to dispose of the body. Following a US-supported coup in 1965 Mobutu Sese Seko remained as dictator for thirty years, with US military help in repelling several attempts to overthrow him. The United States provided over US$1 billion in military and civilian aid during this time, with France contributing even more to what was regarded as a brutal and corrupt regime, with Mobutu salting away in foreign banks far in excess of the total national debt, his personal fortune put at US$4 billion, while driving his country into bankruptcy (adapted from Hochschild, 1998).

• In 1989 the World Bank published a document arguing that 'underlying the litany of Africa's development problems is a crisis of governance'. This led to the advent of conditionality in development aid in order to introduce liberal democratic government, and Structural Adjustment Programmes (SAPs) with an emphasis on reductions in government spending. This policy is fully endorsed by one of the most influential donors, the US Agency for International Development, holding that 'there is growing evidence that open societies that value individual rights, respect the rule of law, and have open and accountable governments, provide better opportunities for sustained economic development than do closed systems which stifle individual initiative' (Decalo, 1992: 23 cited in Ahluwalia, 2001). Yet Agbese (1994, and cited in Ahluwalia, 2001) asserts that SAPs require a repressive regime to implement, and tend to reflect imperial interests rather than those of the country's citizens.

• In 1980 the African Charter of Human and Peoples' Rights was adopted by the Organization of African Unity, to 'reflect the African conception of human rights, [and] should take as a pattern the African philosophy and law to meet the needs of Africa' (Amnesty International, 1991, cited in Ahluwalia, 2001). The main difference to the UN Declaration is the stress on community: 'collective rights to national sovereignty free from external influence' (Paul, 1990, cited in Ahluwalia, 2001).

- In 1981 the Iranian representative to the UN criticized the Universal Declaration of Human Rights as 'a secular understanding of the Judeo-Christian tradition'.
- In 1990 the Cairo Declaration of Human Rights in Islam was adopted by forty-five foreign ministers of the Organisation of the Islamic Conference. The predominance of Shar'ia Law can be understood by Article 1(a) 'All human beings form one family whose members are united by their sub-ordination to Allah and descent from Adam. All men are equal in terms of basic human dignity and basic obligations and responsibilities, without any discrimination on the basis of race, colour, language, belief, sex, religion, political affiliation, social status or other considerations. The true religion is the guarantee for enhancing such dignity along the path to human integrity.'
- Since 2002 Guantanamo Bay Naval Base in Cuba has been used by the Americans as a detention camp for detainees from Afghanistan and around the world believed to be al-Qaeda or Taliban fighters. President George W. Bush asserted that detainees were not entitled to protection under the Geneva Convention. Operations and conditions at the camp have been internationally criticized, often as infringements of basic human rights. In 2009 the new US President Barack Obama declared that the camp be closed. It should also be noted that the American occupation of Guantanamo Bay is considered illegal by the Cuban government, asserting that the 1903 American–Cuban Treaty was agreed to by threat of force, in violation of international law.
- Although an original signatory to the UN Declaration China has long con-tested its principles and application, particularly in contradistinction to the USA, and in its trade-off with national and economic development. Schech and Haggis (2000) provide a useful illustration of this by reference to an article in the *Guardian Weekly*, outlining, from official reports from the US State Department and from China, how the two countries view each other's human rights (Table 5.1)

Studying America's role in international management ethics

It is not the intention to convey, by this opening case, that universal human rights are purely a product of a dominant economy in a post-World War world order. As An-Na'im and Deng (1990) argue, non-dominant countries have considerably added to the debate on human rights, that they should be

Table 5.1 Perceptions of human rights: China–USA, USA–China (adapted from Schech and Haggis, 2000: 161)

The USA sees China as follows	China sees the USA as follows
Rights deteriorated with a crackdown on political dissent	Human rights abuses of the poor and blacks
Harsh prison conditions, often with executions following summary trials	Prison population is huge, and includes around 200,000 mental patients
Blocked websites and foreign broadcasts	Texas death row cells have unbearably high temperatures
Compulsory abortions and sterilization	Lowest voter turnout among developed world
Crackdown on Muslim activity in Xingjian	One per cent of Americans own 90 per cent of the wealth
Sex workers number up to 10 million in China	No medical insurance for 41.7 million Americans
Female infanticides are reported	Racial discrimination, particularly in the jobs market place, abounds
Outlawing of independent trade unions, often with union activists being jailed	Females comprise only10 per cent of US Congress members
Tibetan monasteries are under tight control and schools closed down	

considered within the context of particular cultures, yet should attain legitimacy by obtaining international recognition of the logic of cultural variation, and that cultural difference should not be used as a justification for violations against basic human rights. The purpose here is to locate this debate within its geopolitical context, and indeed to locate the context of management ethics, what is regarded as ethical, and what is significantly seen as an ethical question (such as gender or financial inequality), in its context. Yet an overriding issue is that the way we study these issues, our orientation or starting point as scholars or policy makers or managers, contain value judgements.

In order to examine the political and ethical implications of doing social science, and why this is important to understanding the role of the United States in international management ethics, it is useful to draw on the work of Flyvbjerg (2001) who argues for a return to a consideration of *phronesis*, which Aristotle expounds in his *Nicomachean Ethics* (Aristotle, 1953 translation). Among other important aspects of this work, Flyvbjerg (2001) reminds us that social scientists cannot take a 'view from nowhere'. This brings us back to the problem of many cross-cultural studies in management ethics which perhaps typifies what Flyvbjerg (2001) suggests is still a problem within the social sciences: positivism and its emulation of the natural sciences, particularly its tendency towards rationalism, reductionism and propensity towards establishing context-free prediction; and its inability to incorporate context, values, power and intuitive action. Flyvbjerg (2001: 166) holds that 'scientism' or 'the tendency to believe that science holds a reliable method of reaching the truth about the nature of things' still continues to dominate thinking in the social sciences, and this unfortunately is an issue in (predominantly American) approaches to management and cross-cultural management.

What is regarded as 'science' or 'knowledge' or 'ethics' is a product of geopolitical power dynamics. It is relevant to start on a quest to understand the 'universal' nature of ethics by focusing on the main centre of this power relationship: the USA.

Flyvbjerg (2001) asserts that epistemic science and predictive theory derive from an Aristotelian concept of *episteme*: based on analytical rationality, this is universal, context-independent knowledge. Aristotle contrasted this with *techne*, or pragmatic, variable and context-dependent know-how. Yet forgotten in the depths of time, he suggests, is Aristotle's concept of *phronesis*, or the analysis of values or 'things that are good or bad for man' as a point of departure for action. It is based on praxis, on context. It is 'practical value-rationality'. Yet it has little to do with comparing nations in terms of their ethicality, on the basis of a limited number of universally applied value dimensions in the modern Hofstedian tradition. Flyvbjerg (2001: 167) contends that 'the purpose of social science is not to develop theory, but to contribute to society's practical rationality in elucidating where we are, where we want to go, and what is desirable according to diverse sets of values and interests' and therefore, 'The goal of the phronetic approach becomes one of contributing to society's capacity for value-rational deliberation and action.'

The relevance for cross-cultural management theory is the need to incorporate context-specific insight in a multicultural and globalized world. Elucidating the capacity for action through a value-rational approach is more important, intellectually more stimulating, and more likely to progress the subject area than merely comparing nations or 'cultures' along reductionist lines, or trying to predict on this same basis.

Hence the current book is less about comparisons across 'cultures' and more about what we can learn, as international scholars or managers, from focusing our attention at particular cultural intersections.

For the purpose of this book, we can call these intersections 'countries' or 'regions' out of convenience. Yet these intersections could equally be organizations or individuals. As noted above, it is becoming more difficult to describe these intersections as a 'culture' (although 'cultural space' might be applied). The implication, for example, for studying management ethics of the United States, is that this country should be seen as an important (dominant) intersection, which interfaces with other such cultural intersections through power relationships. In order to elucidate this, a number of theoretical positions need to be drawn together:

- The modern interpretation of *phronesis* in the social sciences (Flyvbjerg, 2001) combines a concept of value-rationality and power in deciding whose value-rationality. This approach to social science appears to have great potential in the understanding of the importance of cultural values for both the researcher as subject and researched as object (assuming a relationship between researcher and the object of study in the syntactic structure 'I [subject] study the organization [object]', rather than the normal mode of thought of the behavioural/social scientist studying her 'subjects'); and to balance between universal and particular, while aiming social science at a meaningful social contribution.
- A geopolitical view of the context of the perception of value-rationality combining both dependency theory (Frank, 1969) and postcolonial theory (Said, 1978/1995; Bhabha, 1994) to provide a comprehensive, hopefully not eclectic, view of power dynamics in a post/neo-colonial globalized world.
- A concept of cultural crossvergence (Ralston *et al.*, 1993; 1994) in a globalized world, with its products – hybrid social, institutional and organizational forms, as well as hybrid knowledge and values.
- An integrating theory of cultural intersections/interfaces that brings these other theories together.
- A clear understanding of the post-WWII, post/neo-colonial, post-Soviet, post-9/11 (and possibly post-financial meltdown of 2008/9) role of the United States and implications for international management ethics.

This chapter, and the understanding of the role of the United States, is also key in understanding subsequent chapters and the international management of ethics in other regions. Hence Europe, China and East Asia, South Asia, the Arab world, Latin America and sub-Saharan Africa intersect/interface with the United States in a power dynamic in a globalized world. Rather than studying these as comprising isolated countries, cultural values and management ethics should be seen as a result of a dynamic of cultural crossvergence, and varying forms of hybrid management and organization.

Phronetic social science and management ethics

Chapter 2 outlined the basic elements in ethical decision making, namely: choice; values; rules; power; control; culture; institutions; objectives; and stakeholders. This led to the outlining of specific questions about:

1. What *choices* are available to individuals and organizations in the decisions they make?
2. What *values* influence or govern these choices?
3. What *rules* are followed (or not followed) in order to make such choices?
4. How do these rules *control* the levels and nature of choice in a society or an organization?
5. What are the *power* relations among the different stakeholders within the organization or society that control the rules and the values that influence choice?
6. What different *objectives* do the different *stakeholders* have that influence choice in decision making?

Flyvbjerg (2001) proposes a similar set of questions in his explanation of doing *phronetic* social science. He states (2001: 60):

the principal objective for social science with a phronetic approach is to carry out analysis and interpretations of the status of values and interests in society aimed at social commentary and social action, i.e, praxis.

Later he adds (2001: 130):

By definition phronetic researchers focus on values; for example by taking their point of departure in the classic value-rational questions: where are we going? Is it desirable? What should be done? ... the objective is to balance instrumental rationality with value-rationality by increasing the capacity of individuals, organizations, and societies to think and act in value-rational terms. Focusing on values, the phronetic researcher is forced to face the question of foundationalism versus relativism, that is, the view that central values exist that can be rationally and universally grounded, versus the view that one set of values is just as good as another.

He adds that such researchers reject both these '-isms' and focus on contextualism or 'situational ethics' (2001: 130).

Flyvbjerg (2001: 131) goes on to discuss the place of power in *phronetic* analysis:

Besides focusing on the three value-rational questions ... a contemporary reading of *phronesis* also poses questions about power and outcomes: Who gains, and who loses? Through what kinds of power relations? What possibilities are available to change existing power relations? And is it desirable to do so? Of what kind of power relations are those asking these questions themselves a part? Phronetic research poses these questions with the intention of avoiding the voluntarism and idealism typical of so much ethical thinking.

His four principal questions, that distinguish *phronetic* analysis, therefore become:

1. Where are we going?
2. Who gains, and who loses, by which mechanisms of power?
3. Is it desirable?
4. What should be done?

The general implications are that social science itself is an ethical/political activity: ethical because (explicit or not) it is concerned with values and their application; and politically because '[K]nowledge and power, truth and power, rationality and power are analytically inseparable from each other; power produces knowledge, and knowledge produces power' (Flyvbjerg, 2001: 132). The specific implication of this is that to study the United States and the global role of the United States in the formulation of ethical values and action, is to focus on power relations, its desirability and implication for action. This takes us on to a consideration of how we might conceptualize those value/power relations.

Geopolitical relations

If power and knowledge are intertwined, then unless we consider the nature of this relationship, and the implications of this in terms of the researcher/ scholar/manager's (as subject), and the regions/countries/institutions/organizations/individual's (as object) understanding of (ethical/value) knowledge, we are in trouble. One of the necessities of cross-cultural management as a field of study is that scholars should be able to reflect on themselves, on their theories and on their objects of study, as a product of an international dynamic. This is best explained in terms of postcolonial theory.

Postcolonial theory has provided an elaboration and critique of these more subtle power dynamics within literary studies (Said's *Orientalism* (1978/1995) is the landmark study), in development studies (e.g. Mohan, 2002, provides an outline) and more recently in organization studies (Prasad, 2003). Mohan (2002: 157), for example, puts it rather sharply when saying 'Postcolonial studies alert us to the epistemic violence of Eurocentric discourses of the non-West and the possibilities of recovering the voices of the marginalized'.

Postcolonial theory (Said, 1978/1995; Bhabha, 1994; Spivak, 1996) proposes that the 'developing' world is represented in the eyes of the 'developed' world. Western imperialism, through Western culture, has developed a systematic 'body of theory and practice' that constructs or represents the 'Orient' (in Said's terms, 1978/1995: 49). In colonial times, this has portrayed images of the 'noble savage' or the 'wily oriental', where Westerners are regarded as 'rational, peaceful, liberal, logical … without natural suspicion and Easterners as irrational, degenerate, primitive, mystical, suspicious, sexually depraved'.

These representations are carried over to Western intellectual and cultural production including research and management studies (for example Jackson, 2004, points to the derogatory light in which 'African' management is seen in the literature). The acceptance and internalization of such representations by the developing world itself can mean two things. Firstly, there is both an acceptance and challenging of these representations that constitute hybrid forms of presentation of the nature of people of the Third World. Secondly, because this challenging itself grows out of the cultural and intellectual representations of Western discourse, this 'contamination' of the colonized means that they can never refer back to an 'authentic' identity of pre-colonial times. Any conceptualization of this identity would be by definition seen through the eyes of the colonizer's representations (Kapoor, 2002).

This is similar to the dependency theory critique of modernity theory: that the 'developing' world was created by imperialism (as a form of globalization) and does not exist apart from a developing-developed world dependency.

Dependency theory (Frank, 1969) suggests that today's Third World underdevelopment is the underside of the same globalizing conditions that led to the First World being developed. The latter's development is dependent on the former's underdevelopment. The prime mover in this is capital seeking profits, and this is easiest in countries where labour and resources are cheap and governments are weak. The structural consequence of this is to reproduce the process, and to block local initiatives pursuing their own development paths (Schech and Haggis, 2000). This represents an economic or institutional theory, originally based on Marxist critique of modernity theory. Modernity theorists see the Third World as originally underdeveloped or untouched, and whose trajectory, and the aim of international development, was to modernize in the same direction as the First World. In a way modernity theory can be seen as a justification for globalization (or imperialism), and is reflected in many international management and international business texts. In fact, modernity theory appears to be tacitly accepted in international management studies, and has not been specifically critiqued in the manner it has, for example, in sociology and development studies.

The 'culturalist' view, represented by postcolonial theory, brings us to the same point as dependency theory: a concept of purity of local or indigenous thought or practice in the Third World (and perhaps the Second World) does not exist apart from thought or practice in the First World. This causes problems when studying values and knowledge across cultures because rather than looking at 'indigenous' knowledge, we are really looking at a reflection of dominant ideologies, and often this dominant knowledge denigrates 'local' knowledge in whatever form this may still exist. Escobar (1995) sees the dominance of Western knowledge not through a privileged proximity to the truth but as a result of historical and geographic conditions coupled with the geopolitics of power.

The debate extends, particularly within development studies, to whether the West wants to hear indigenous voices. For example hooks (1990: spelt with a small h), from an autobiographic position in the Third World (cited in Briggs and Sharpe, 2004) asserts that Western researchers want only to know about her experiences. They do not want to hear her explanations. This would require them to relinquish their position as experts. There is also a debate about whether the 'subaltern' (in the language of postcolonial theory) can ever really speak in terms of a true 'indigenous' knowledge (Spivak, 1988).

The first issue is whether that voice will be heard, unless it is expressed in the language, and within the experience, of the West. That is, it may be dismissed as unscientific, unless it can be expressed in the language of formal science. There appears to be a lack of tolerance of indigenous knowledge and value systems challenging dominant world views or criticizing existing terms of debate and proposing different agendas. Certainly in the development sector (international aid and development) the aim appears to be simply adding to the existing ways of doing things (Briggs and Sharpe, 2004). The second issue is whether an indigenous voice can ever truly be indigenous, and know itself as such in a globalized world where the perceptions of the Third World by the West have been adopted and internalized by 'indigenous' people in the Third World. An example is the extent to which indigenous management practices (such as *Ubuntu* in South Africa: Mbigi, 1997) can be articulated and used given the dominance of Western management practices through universalized management training and education.

Yet in a post-WWII world, this does not simply apply to the Third World. Japanese management practices have been lauded in the West, particularly in the United States since the publication of Pascale and Athos' (1981) *The Art of Japanese Management*, and similar texts. Yet the view that there is something intriguingly (and exotically) unique about Japanese management has been disabused in the more critical literature, for example:

most of the characteristics of the Japanese management style were formed relatively recently, after the Second World War. Japanese management was a product of rational thinking; some of it introduced from America during the Occupation, some developed from earlier imports, such as Taylorism, moulded to the paternalism and cooperative traditions already established in Japan (Tsutsui, 1998). Many theories and business practices, such as management committees and quality controls, later to be seen as uniquely Japanese in application, were transplanted from the US or Europe. (Clegg and Kono, 2002: 271)

Major world events and processes, such as world wars, imperialism and financial crises, change things. Much as management studies, organizational behaviour, industrial psychology and management and business ethics would like to remain in their own microcosm, they cannot.

To what extent is it possible to study 'Japanese' management ethics, before first considering the influences on this, including the contribution from America after WWII? The same argument is applied to all subsequent chapters in this book. The argument, however, goes deeper if we consider this from a postcolonial theory perspective: dominant geopolitical influences disparage local contributions, and this disparaging is internalized by local people. What we end up with may be a lack of articulation of a local view. Hybridity, through a process of cultural crossvergence, is not the result of a cosy dialogue, or a reasoned and equal negotiation. It occurs through a process involving 'the epistemic violence of Eurocentric discourses of the non-West' as we saw above (Mohan, 2002: 157). This brings us to the next part of the puzzle: cultural crossvergence and hybridization.

Cultural crossvergence and hybridization

Concepts of crossvergence, as discussed in management studies, and already outlined in Chapter 2, are inadequate in the way they treat this process as one of equal negotiation. The concept of cultural crossvergence is implicit within postcolonial theory. Bhabha's (1994) elucidation of 'mimicry' applies predominantly to a colonizing power's ability to get the colonized to mimic the colonizer, in order to better control the unfamiliar, and to gain acceptance of transferred-in knowledge. Yet as Frenkel (2008) points out this is also a function of the acceptance that the colonizers are the natural repository of (technical, management, medical) knowledge, and the colonized need this knowledge. This could equally be applied to what appears to be happening in post-Soviet countries such as Russia: a perceived need to catch up and to emulate the West, adopting Western management methods in the extreme, often (as Jackson, 2002b points out) the hard aspects of HRM, for example. The large-scale adoption of private enterprise and a free-market economy seems to be evidence of this.

In Bhabha's (1994) view the process of mimicry leads to hybrid cultures as an ongoing process of colonial imposition and resistance from the colonized. It is never possible therefore to speak about an authentic or innate culture, and is an ongoing product of a conflictual process between the powerful and less powerful. For Bhabha (1994) the result is the Third Space. Frenkel (2008: 928) puts it well, as follows:

With the change of the centuries, argues Bhabha, we are all located on intercultural boundaries and are exposed to a wide range of cultures that are perpetually created in the innumerable intercultural encounters that are themselves occasioned by an ongoing historical process. Within this metaphoric space we construct our identities in relation to these varied and often contradictory systems of meaning.

When we focus on management ethics around the world, we are predominantly looking at this 'Third Space' or, more accurately, 'Third Spaces'. The argument in this chapter is that the United States is a powerful contributor to those Third Spaces, through the processes and factors already outlined in this chapter. To study a Third Space implies a need to enter a political/value debate that can be addressed by a *phronetic* methodology.

Cultural interfaces: an integration

If, as Frenkel (2008) suggests above, we are all located on intercultural boundaries, the concept of cultural intersections/interfaces is useful in encapsulating much of what this chapter has said so far.

Flyvbjerg (2001: 61) asserts that *phronetic* researchers 'can see no neutral ground, no "view from nowhere" for their work'. Both the perspective of 'a view from nowhere', that is the assumption that there is a 'universal' truth or ethic or values, can be explained by postcolonial theory, as can where the view might come from if we accept that it must come from somewhere.

An assumption, like the Universal Declaration of Human Rights, that truth or ethical values are universal must surely come from globalization. In some respects, the Declaration (as some kind of statement of a global ethic) was a reaction against imperial ambitions (for example the atrocities of WWII), yet can also be seen as part of this (the imposition by more economically dominant nations of a universal truth, subsequent resistance to that imposition; and apparent ignoring of such 'global' human rights when inconvenient to a dominant nation's 'imperial' ambitions). Certainly this is only one example. Another example might be the nature of scholarship. This is particularly the case in management studies (Boyacigiller and Adler, 1991 explain why), but this may also apply in other social scientific areas, and this is what Flyvbjerg (2001) speaks out against. If, as discussed above, knowledge and power are inexorably intertwined, this may certainly apply to all types of scientific and technical knowledge. Yet the whole notion of ethics, as a subject of study, is value driven, subjective and laden with 'value-rationality'. Our concepts and means of studying this must come from somewhere.

A 'view from somewhere' is connected to the concept of interfaces in cross-cultural research. Views come from somewhere, can be understood by postcolonial analysis, but exist in various forms at various cross-cultural interfaces. Put another way, if our focus is now directed towards where and how cultural influences intersect we are interested in the nature of value-rationality that operates at that interface, the reasons why that value-rationality exists, including the different influences that have shaped that value-rationality and processes of power involved, and the consequences, such as the solutions that are provided to questions posed by Flyvbjerg (2001) as representing the essence of *phronetic* research: (1) Where are we going? (2) Is this desirable? (3) What should be done?

Now, taking this approach could simply result in relativism. The contrast made between *episteme* and *phronesis* could simply be equated with a contrast between universalism and relativism, the latter being dependent on context and the former on establishing a universal instrumental rationalism. As Nonaka and Toyama (2007, who also cite Flyvbjerg) point out, the relativist view that everything is subjective with no universality is of little practical use. Indeed, they site the interactions of different subjectivities within the realm of knowledge creation: 'What is "truth" depends on who we are (values) and from where we look at it (context). And it is the differences in our values and contexts that create new knowledge' (Nonaka and Toyama, 2007: 374).

The objective of studying cultural interfaces is not merely to learn about the influences (antecedents) of hybrid cultural forms. It is also about studying what knowledge is created from this and how; and what use is this and to whom: the appropriateness of the knowledge created to the context in which it is applied: e.g. management principles and practices that are created through interaction between powerful Western organizations and weaker African/Latin American/South Asian/Eastern European organizations or individual managers, and their appropriateness to, for example, communities and staffs. In Bhabha's (1994) terms, as scholars, or managers, we are looking from one Third Space to another.

The role of the United States and implications for international management ethics

Clearly, within this formulation of cross-cultural analysis, which encompasses largely phronetic (value-rational) analysis, and postcolonial theory which attempts to explain power from a culturalist perspective, America must play a significant global role in the way management ethics is seen internationally. Major world events have shaped and consolidated this role. These include:

- The outcome of WWII and the consolidation of America as a dominant economic, then military, then cultural power in the world.
- Its more recent consolidation of its neo-colonial role in the world through extensive activities of multinational corporations, conditional aid, military and political involvement in the internal affairs of nations in Latin America, Africa, but rarely direct military occupation such as Iraq and Afghanistan; as well as more subtle cultural influence through Hollywood and television.
- The demise of the Soviet Empire and the loss of influence of Russia as a world power, and as an example of an alternative to capitalism, with the discrediting of communism, with profound effects on some African and Latin American countries (which may again be changing with a left-wing swing in Latin America, and the increasing influence of China in Latin America and Africa). This has also contributed to more influence on post-Soviet countries in Eastern and Central Europe, along with the dynamics of the EU and its relationship with the USA.
- Post-9/11 and the 'war on terror' has seen a shift in global dynamics through a new alignment (following the previous alignment of the Cold War), with implications for the way many people in the West see people from the Middle East and Muslims, with sometimes effects on relations with immigrant populations in the West.

It could also be argued that these events have not just had implications for America's role and influence in the world, but also internally within the shores of the United States. In Bhabha's terms, America should also be examined as a Third Space: the result of historical and current interaction within a global power dynamic. By understanding this Third Space, we can then begin to understand the 'view from somewhere' of the universal nature and applicability of management and business ethics, and the way management scholars in a dominant economy may view ethicality in other Third Spaces.

American cultural identity and management ethics

There are very few American studies of American culture, values or ethics that are specifically introspective. That is, quite often the 'American culture' is taken for granted in management studies of organizations in America, with an assumption that this is what is done everywhere. As cross-cultural management has grown, particularly in the United States as a subdiscipline of management studies, these views may be questioned by studies that investigate if particular theories, principles or practices work in other countries. Yet 'American-ness' is still very much taken for granted. Explanations in cross-cultural management studies put more weight on why the situation in other countries may be different. When 'different to what?' (i.e. the USA) is considered, it would be usual to refer to Hofstede's (1980a/2003) work which designated the USA as an *Individualistic* rather than a *Collectivist*, medium *Power Distance*, fairly high *Feminine* rather than *Masculine*, and reasonably low *Uncertainty Avoidance* society. Similarly, there are few contemporary studies by management scholars from other countries that specifically examine American management from a (cross)cultural perspective. In other words, American culture is largely 'invisible'. It reinforces a 'view from nowhere' methodologically criticized by Flyvbjerg (2001).

The task here, which appears to be daunting, is to present the United States as a Third Space (and likely different Third Spaces within the county) vis-à-vis other Third Spaces. Its history is firstly as a collection of small nations comprising native populations relatively undisturbed by outside interference for many centuries; as a colony and aggressor towards the indigenous populations; as a refuge from persecution from European countries and an independent country; as a magnet for immigrants attracted by the 'American dream'; as a 'melting pot' for different national and religious cultures; as a mostly economically successful nation based on a free-market economy; as a one-time reluctant and then relatively aggressive economic and military world superpower; as an often socially and culturally divisive society from time to time accentuated by economic recessions.

Of course this is a wildly sweeping summary of a nation's history, and also from an author who himself occupies another 'Third Space'. Yet the point is that the United States has had influences and pressures on it, in a relatively short history, from both inside and outside. It has been shaped by, first, the apparent need of a disparate population to take aggressive action against the indigenes as well as other (immigrant) groups and individuals to defend assumed private property rights; its need to defend itself and take aggressive action against British colonialism, not least in defending economic self-determination; and then from perceived enemies including the Soviet Union and al-Qaida. It has been shaped by almost continuous immigration, first mainly from Britain (also heralding enforced immigrants from Africa), then other European countries (the 1924 Immigration Act favoured immigrants from Northern Europe), then from other parts of the world. The metaphor of a 'melting pot' to describe an assumed integration of immigrants to the United States appears also to shape self-identity. Certainly Stewart and Bennett (1991) feel able to describe American culture as an entity. Typically this takes the form of:

The American self-concept is the integral assumption of the culture. Americans naturally assume that each person is not only a separate biological entity, but also a unique psychological being and a singular member of the social order. Deeply ingrained and seldom questioned, the dominant American self, in the form of individualism, pervades action and intrudes into each domain of activity. (1991: 129)

Again, this appears to be a case of an 'invisible' culture or an assumption of cultural homogeneity (or universalism) where none exists. This assumption has been criticized more recently in the area of whiteness studies. Hence McDermott and Samson (2005) write:

Much of the research on white racial identity during the past ten years has focused on how whiteness, and the privileges associated with whiteness, remain invisible to many whites, especially those with limited interracial contact ... Instead, whiteness is normative ... an unexamined default racial category. Although many nonwhites, especially African Americans, are confronted with their race on a daily basis ... many whites do not think of themselves as really having a race at all. In this respect, white is an unmarked identity, such as heterosexual or middle-aged. (2005: 248. Original authors' extensive references in this quotation have been removed)

The connection between being white and privilege is one that often is not made by many whites. McDermott and Samson (2005) contend that this lack of connection is due to non-obvious legacies of structural advantage, or in some cases from a desire to accentuate individual achievement.

It is interesting to note that Stewart and Bennett (1991), originally writing in 1972 and revising their work in 1991, are likely to be from white middle-class backgrounds, and although Stewart states he is from a bicultural family, he, like his co-author Bennett, with experience of living abroad, is likely to be aware of his cultural identities vis-à-vis non-American cultures, rather than in interface with other American (e.g. black) cultural groups.

Frankenberg (2001) accentuates the situational nature of whiteness, noting that changes in American society have brought racial groups more into contact with each other, urging that the idea of whiteness as invisible should be changed. Historically, what has been regarded as white has changed from a position where certain European groups (Jews, Italian, Irish) were not identified with American whiteness. Currently Arab Americans are regarded as white under the US Consensus, although as McDermott and Samson (2005) point out, they often have stronger identification with their countries of origin than with a white racial identity. Perhaps, if Stewart and Bennett had been writing as recent Irish immigrants in the early twentieth century, or as a white working-class youth growing up in a multicultural neighbourhood, their perceptions (and their Third Space) would have been different.

Indeed, America, like Britain and countries in Western Europe, has changed significantly over the last few decades, rendering both the concept of one American identity, and the basis of cross-cultural studies such as Hofstede's, GLOBE and others almost facile. It is interesting that in the more recent GLOBE study, South African samples are taken of both whites and blacks, and in Canada samples are taken from English and French speakers, yet the much larger USA is taken as one sample (House *et al.*, 2004). In the 2000 US census, out of a total population of nearly 249 million, 75.1% said they were white or Caucasian, 21.36% (60 million) claimed German descent, 12.3% said they were black or of African American descent, 12.5% were Hispanic and 3.6% were Asian (US Census Bureau, 2000).

Perhaps it was (and is) true as Carroll and Gannon (1997) claimed, that there is far less diversity in the ranks of management at the top of organizations than there is at lower levels. Surely this is an indictment of the lack of success of both the American Dream and melting pot metaphors (or myths). Yet Carroll and Gannon are not simply claiming a racial homogeneity for managers, but a homogeneity through socialization through the education system and American literature, and through recruitment and selection processes which favour such traits as 'decisiveness, persistence, social dominance, emotional stability/stress tolerance, self-confidence, dependability and assertiveness [which] have often been identified as important to managerial success' (1997: 148). Performance appraisal and compensation systems further reinforce these types of traits. However, from the US 2000 census results it does appear to be the case that more blacks and Hispanics live in poverty than whites, fewer graduate from high school and fewer hold bachelors degrees (US Census Bureau, 2000).

Schildkraut (2007) suggests that multidimensional studies of American identity are lacking, and are only focused on two components: 'liberalism (America as a land of freedom and opportunity) and ethnoculturalism (America as a nation of white Protestants)' (2007: 597). Through an empirical study she seeks to focus on the importance of four aspects of American identity, as follows (2007: 599):

- Liberalism: 'stresses minimal government intervention in private life and promotes economic and political freedoms along with equality of opportunity. ... The normative boundaries liberalism places on membership in the American community are that group members endorse liberal principles, that they not infringe upon the political and economic rights and freedoms of others, and that they try to achieve the American Dream through hard work.'
- Ethnoculturalism: 'is an ascriptivist tradition that sets rigid boundaries on group membership. In its extreme, ethnoculturalism maintains that Americans are white, English-speaking Protestants of northern European ancestry.' Although this tradition has been discredited 'it is far from breathing its last breath. Since 9/11, elites and masses have endorsed restricting the full range of citizenship rights to people of certain ethnic and religious backgrounds.'
- Civic republicanism: 'emphasizes the responsibilities, rather than the rights of citizenship. It advances the notion that the well-being of the community is more than just the sum of individualistic pursuits of private gain. Rather, a vibrant self governing community needs individual members to act on its behalf ... In this view, we should all be involved in social and political life and pursue ends that serve the public good.'
- Incorporationism: 'America's unique identity is grounded in its immigrant legacy and in its ability to convert the challenges immigration brings into thriving strengths.' Yet 'The simplicity of incorporationism – the idea that the United States is a nation of immigrants – belies complex beliefs about the balance between unity and diversity ... Incorporationism celebrates our ability both to assimilate and maintain difference.' Diversity and assimilation are sometimes seen at opposite ends 'yet many Americans believe that in the ideal, a balance between the two can be reached, and it is this ability that forms the core of this view of what uniquely distinguishes the United States from other countries.'

When focusing on differences among racial groups surveyed, blacks and Latinos appear more likely than whites or Asians to endorse ethnoculturalism (this appears counter-intuitive, yet may be a reflection on what they see, rather than what they agree with). Schildkraut (2007) distinguishes between action-oriented civic republicanism (based on actual membership of civic organizations) and identity-oriented civic republicanism (based on expressions of opinion). Latinos are more likely than whites to endorse the former, but less likely to endorse the latter. Whites are less likely than the other three groups to endorse the divergence facet of incorporationism of carrying on the cultural traditions of one's ancestors, although more than 60 per cent of white respondents endorsed this particular facet (less than the other groups but still a majority of the white sample).

Yet despite these apparent differences between black (n=300), white (n=1633), Latino (n=441) and Asian (n=299) groups Schildkraut (2007) adds that no majority of one racial group comes to a different substantive conclusion than another about what constitutes the norms of American identity. This study, undertaken by telephone interviews, is therefore interesting as it points to a high level of shared identity norms among different racial groups in America, and appears to support the melting pot thesis.

However, of course this is just one study. Other studies point to substantive differences in the perception of American versus minority group identity. Massey and Sanchez (2007) for example point to differences in the perception towards American and Latino identity. Latin American immigrants appeared to see a great contrast in the content of the two identities. They viewed American identity as involving bigness and power and saw (white) Americans as being in constant motion and in a hurry, competitive, commercial, cold, distant and impersonal. They saw Latino (American) identity as focused on people and on intimate social relationships. They saw the building blocks of Latino identity as work, home and Latin American symbols.

Acculturation is a complex process that Schwartz *et al.* (2007) claim has changed over time due to the sheer numbers of immigrants to the USA post-1965. This has resulted in ethnic enclaves in most large cities. This lack of integration may also have been influenced by the ease with which immigrants can keep in contact with people back home, due to technology such as the Internet and emails (that is, tools of globalization have given rise to the maintenance of diversity rather than diminishing it). They define *assimilation* as adopting the receiving culture while discarding the heritage culture; *integration* as adopting the receiving culture and retaining the heritage culture; *separation* as retaining the heritage culture while resisting the receiving culture; and, *marginalization* as neither retaining the heritage culture nor adopting the receiving culture. They assert that ethnic identity is a subjective experience of acculturation, involving both exploring the subjective meaning of one's own ethnicity and valuing one's ethnic group positively. This helps immigrants to retain ideas and practices from their heritage culture and resist influences from their peers in the receiving culture and media influences.

As in the whiteness studies explored above, Schwartz *et al.* (2007) report that research confirms ethnic minorities are more likely to have higher levels of ethnic identity than white Americans, because American culture is synonymous with white culture; although this does appear to be changing through white Americans' proximity to other groups both within and outside America. Their study among university students through factor analysis yielded three dimensions of cultural identity: America-culture identity, heritage-culture identity and biculturalism. The factor structure was consistent across ethnic groups (white, black, Hispanic and Asian) but ethnic differences emerged in their association with familial ethnic socialization, acculturative stress and perceived ethnic discrimination. This appears again to support the situational nature of cultural identity in the American context. It is not a matter of which ethnic group one belongs to, but the situational factors involved in upbringing, neighbourhood and life experiences. Yet it does seem extremely likely demographically that you will suffer discrimination if you are black, or from another minority, have problems adapting to normative (white) culture and gain support for retaining heritage culture from one's familial group. For example, James (2000) reported a slower promotion rate for black managers in a survey in a Fortune 500 service firm.

The commonalities that Carroll and Gannon (1997) suggest, arise from the US educational process that emphasizes individual performance and competitive performance against one's peers. They suggest that there is not the stress on cooperation and sharing as may be found in the Japanese educational system. Further, they assert (1997: 144), American students are taught 'about the superiority of Americans as a people and America as a nation of destiny, compared to most others in the world. This seems to have produced a marked ethnocentrism. It has been said that this gives Americans a certain arrogance toward other peoples and their ideas.' Gannon and associates (1994) assert that this is reinforced by constant depressing news of other countries as being volatile, violent and miserable with few positive features being constantly highlighted by the media.

In Gannon's work on cultural metaphors (Gannon and associates, 1994) he applies the metaphor of the American football game to explain American culture. A high level of individualism and competitive specialization is combined with 'huddling' and the ceremonial celebration of perfection. American culture celebrates the high-achieving individual and denigrates failure, but it also appears to favour collegiality. This is quite different from the collectivism or communalism (Hofstede, 1980a/2003; Triandis, 1990) described in the literature and is akin to Schwartz's (1994) egalitarian commitment (see Chapter 3). Although as in American football 'huddling' or team play is important, one only comes together (on a voluntary basis) to solve particular problems, and then goes away again to compete on one's own initiative. Huddling is quite unlike the Japanese sense of community within the corporation. It is often seen as a necessity but not an obligation. Hence cooperation, rather than working as a loner, is sought. As a result of a short-term perspective and always in a hurry to get things done ('time is money') these associations can be superficial and not lasting.

The values that are repeated in the literature and appear to typify American cultures are those described by Gannon and associates (1994) as equality of opportunity, independence, initiative and self-reliance. Yet competitive specialization can be taken to the extremes of emotional intensity and aggression with the United States having one of the highest rates of incarceration in the world, and some well-publicized gun atrocities with a Federal law that sanctifies the ownership of guns. American football rules seek to enhance competition on the field and the league, so does US legislation such as antitrust laws. Technology, which is developed at a fantastic rate in the United States, plays a key role in competitive specialization (both on the field and in corporate life). The team in American football is divided into squads to which players identify more readily, as they do to the nuclear family rather than to the extended family. Children are raised in the nuclear family to believe that they can achieve anything if they avail themselves of the opportunities offered.

A short-term perspective may also lead to standardization of work processes (such as Taylorism) and the quick-fix approach (the 'one-minute manager'). An emphasis on the 'bottom line' and the achievement of results often leads to the standardized ranking of individuals and teams (students against their classmates, ranking of quarterbacks and teams in the league). Judgements are therefore standardized and objective and this is often reflected in corporate practices such as management by objectives and identification of competences of managers and key workers, as well as codes of ethics.

A form of solidarity is seen in the celebration of perfection. Ceremonies around the football match include celebration of the team and the country, and often include a religious input: hence more than half of Americans are estimated to be regular church-goers (Gannon and associates, 1994).

Religiosity may be a real feature of American culture(s) that ultimately influences ethical values (although the relationship between religiosity and ethicality is vexed within the literature: Weaver and Agle, 2002). Yet religion may offer yet another main influence on any Third Space, and indeed may be another reference group (such as race or ethnic group). Hence Weaver and Agle (2002: 80) contend that 'religions offer role expectations that, when internalized through repeated social interaction, contribute to a person's self identity as an adherent of a specific religion. Yet a religious identity need not have the same salience for each member of a particular religion, thus leading to individual differences in religiously influenced behavior.' Indeed, identity salience is an important issue when considering aspects of American cultural identity: the importance to an individual, or a group, at any one time of being 'an American', 'a Hispanic', 'a Christian'. The more salient an identity, the more likely the failure of adherence to that identity is to create cognitive dissonance and emotional discomfort (Weaver and Agle, 2002). Referring to Symbolic Interactionist theory, Weaver and Agle (2002) suggest that identity salience is dependent on the number and importance of interpersonal commitments. This is based on the network of relationships based on one's various role identities. This may then bring us back to the previous discussion on the Third Space at the macro level, but applied to the micro level of human interaction: that identity salience (from Symbolic Interactionism) may well be based on power.

Hence one's nation, work organization, religious groups and so on, may all engender degrees of conformity due to social pressure from particular institutions. In postcolonial countries this may be quite complex, as international hegemonic institutions such as educational systems, the movie industry, the influence of multinational corporations and religion, as well as one's nationhood and community affiliations, may provide conflicting pressures for conformity to values and ethicality. In the United States, conflicts may arise through influences to conform to American nationhood, country of origin links or community affiliations. The influence of such institutions may change sharply in such situations as 9/11 (American nationhood increasing in salience), or the delay in the government response to Hurricane Katrina in 2005 and its destruction in New Orleans, which must have had a profound effect on the hierarchy of identity salience, particularly of the mostly black residents living through this tragedy (American nationhood decreasing in salience).

Identity salience will influence an individual's behaviour within a role, including ethical behaviour. For example, a manager may sublimate personal values and conform to the moral ethos of the work organization (Weaver and Agle, 2002). Jackson (2000) found that one of the main influences on managers' reported ethical values and behaviour was their perceptions of those of their peers within the organization. This was over and above what the corporation purported to espouse via codes of ethics.

Cultural identity is therefore far more complex than exponents of cross-national cultural values study would lead us to believe. The 'national' culture that such studies attempt to capture by reducing this to four, five, or even several measureable dimensions, may well be one aspect of cultural identity salience hierarchy. Indeed, the main popular aspects of what is projected to be American culture both within the USA (the American dream) and outside (by Hollywood) may be called into serious question and directly challenged, at particular junctions in history, or by particular groups or institutions. The individualism and achievement nature of American culture projected by studies such as Hofstede (1980a/2003) may be challenged by looking further into ethnic and racial diversity in American society, and by events such as the flooding of New Orleans which may bring tighter collectivist responses from the black and other local communities, and alienation from the achievement society of the American dream.

Yet little research has been undertaken on ethical attitudes between different racial groups in the United States. Tsalikis and Nwachukwu (1988) found no significant differences in attitudes between white and black American students in a rather small-scale study. Perhaps since, this has been regarded as an unfruitful area of study.

American management ethics abroad

Having examined some of the complexities of American cultural identity, and the apparent 'invisibility' of the white normative culture that underlines value structures and ethical attitudes, what can now be said about the nature of American management ethics? Certainly, as Carlin and Strong (1995: 387) remind us, 'American discourse on business ethics is steeped in the traditional ethical theories of Western philosophies, specifically the Greek classics, Kant, and the British Utilitarians'. Certainly one of the main discourses coming out of the United States is that of the dichotomy between teleological ethical decision making, based primarily on Bentham's concept of utilitarianism, and deontological approaches based largely on Kant and his Categorical Imperative (Brady, 1990). Yet as we saw in Chapter 4, cross-national studies using this distinction do not always make sense. This construct perhaps does not travel well when we start to look at non-Western cultures. For example, we saw in Chapter 4 that Ralston *et al.* (1994) note the apparent self-serving attitudes of Hong Kong Chinese managers compared with American managers. They explain this by differences in the Western view of ethical behaviour as an absolute that applies universally. They assert that in the East 'face' is important and ethical behaviour depends on the situation. 'Face' is more important than any supposed universalistic rules or principles that may be applied. A study by Dolecheck and Dolecheck (1987) found that Hong Kong managers equate ethics to acting within the law, compared with American managers who see ethics as going beyond keeping to the letter of the law. Similarly, Singhapakdi *et al.* (1994) found that Thai managers rely more on the nature of the ethical issue or circumstance and less on universal moral principles when making ethical judgements, compared with their American counterparts. This situationalism is far removed from the assumption that one can base ethical judgements on either an assessment of the outcomes, such as in utilitarianism, or on predefined rules: perhaps typically enshrined in a corporate code of ethics.

Indeed Langlois and Schlegelmilch (1990) pointed to the movement in Europe of introducing corporate codes of ethics as mainly due to the activities of American multinational corporations in Europe. They also pointed to the movement in US academia at the time, in the late 1980s, to set up courses and research centres in business ethics, in marked contrast to the lack of interest in Europe. This also reflected the initial lack of interest by the corporate sector in Britain and continental Europe in adopting codes of ethics and other measures in sharp contrast to US corporates. So is 'business ethics' an American invention and construct? As an area of study, and of more general corporate interest, it does seem to be.

In partial answer to the question, Why should there be more interest in business ethics in the United States? Jackson (2000) points to studies which contrast American and European countries, such as Germany and France. They always appear to indicate that American managers are more ethical than their counterparts elsewhere. A possible explanation is that:

societies differ in the way market forces are regulated, where the United States may be characterized as having a low regulation of market forces (yet strong ethical legislation) and Germany and France as having governmental policies which curtail the extremes of an unabated free market economy (yet little emphasis on legislating for ethical conduct of organizations). It may therefore be necessary for companies to have a visible policy aimed at guiding managerial decision making which may otherwise try to 'bend the rules' or sail close to the ethically unacceptable in a less regulated economy. This may be to satisfy the company's stakeholders, such as customers, that the company is concerned with a high standard of business and managerial conduct, or in the case of the United States, to reduce possible financial liability under the Federal Sentencing Guidelines. Hence companies in less regulated economies (United States, Britain, and perhaps Spain) are more likely to have clear policies on ethical issues than those in more regulated economies (France with a more centralized and nationalized industrial base; and Germany with strong consultative provision). (Jackson, 2000: 355)

This in part may explain why ethics has been towards the top of the academic and corporate agenda in the United States. American managers certainly appear more conscious of ethical issues than their counterparts in other parts of the world. However, it would appear that business ethics, and perhaps its slightly younger cousin, corporate social responsibility, is another academic and corporate export to the rest of the world. Certainly, back in 1990 Langlois and Schlegelmilch were reporting that as European firms took up codes of ethics, their contents were different to US equivalents. European codes addressed the question of employee conduct far more than American codes, with the latter dealing more explicitly with customer relations. US codes also were far more concerned with relations with government, whereas this aspect was not widely included in European codes. It is likely that codes of ethics, as an example of the concern given to ethical issues in the Western Judeo-Christian tradition, may be propagated by US corporates around the world. It is less likely that any such initiatives come from corporates in non-Western countries.

Jackson (2000) found that there was no significant correlation between codes of ethics and managers' attitudes or behaviour, and that perceptions of what peers thought and did were far more important. Codes may yet be an extension of public relations operations for largely American corporations. They do indicate to us the formal regard for business ethics emanating from both corporate and academic America.

As Palazzo (2002) points out, the explicit way that American corporations have dealt with this is through 'business ethics programs'. These typically include a written *code of ethics* and *ethics committees of the board of directors*, to integrate ethics at the top level and 'communicate their concern for ethics to the outside world' (2002: 196). This committee is then supported by the *ethics office* which handles the day-to-day management of the 'program' and runs the company's *ethics training*, as well as controlling and enforcing the process. It also communicates the ethics code to employees and answers their questions, with some companies also operating a telephone *ethics hotline*. Typically the *ethics officer* will head the ethics office and act as an ombudsperson to investigate violations of the code and report to the board. The office will also be responsible for running an *ethics audit*, which monitors employees' knowledge of the code and their ability to deal with issues and any adjustments needed. It is highly likely that the implementation of such 'programs' are influenced by legislation and legal incentives such as the Federal Sentencing Guidelines which provides for the substantial ameliorating of sentences for criminal infringement by corporates if they have such programs in place.

Palazzo (2002) contrasts this with the situation in Germany where corporates are unlikely to have such programmes in place, but might be relying on inculcating a shared vision of corporate norms and values. They are unlikely to address such questions publicly. They are also likely to rely on implicit means, and more formally on corporate mission statements that rarely mention words such as 'ethics' or 'integrity'. At the time of writing though, Palazzo (2002) did indicate the increasing trend of German corporates to explicitly address the issue. However, Chapter 6 of the current text deals more explicitly with German approaches.

In the meantime, it is worth staying with Bettina Palazzo (2002). She provides a useful analysis of American culture, including areas where it diverges, as it relates to ethical attitudes and practices. Specifically she asks why are business ethics so explicitly dealt with, in contrast for example with Germany, and why do American companies believe that ethics is something that can be 'managed', again in sharp contrast to German attitudes which might be that ethics is something private, complex and philosophical. She remarks that the American attitude is one of 'just do it'. Certainly, this has been an approach that has previously been criticized by Jackson (1993b), and typified in quick-fix approaches rather reminiscent of *The One Minute Manager*, a book authored by Kenneth Blanchard who also co-wrote *The Power of Ethical Management* (Blanchard and Peale, 1988). Hence a belief that the complex relationship between ethics and economics can be effectively managed by a set of tools, without examining the fundamental theoretical underpinning and implications, and that in so doing there will be a pay-off, and benefit to the bottom line (Jackson, 1993b). It may well be that one of these tools may be the corporate code of ethics, together with the full 'ethics program' discussed by Palazzo (2002). That an apparent deontological 'tool', such as a written set of ethical roles, may have stemmed from a teleologically pragmatic/utilitarian approach may seem contradictory, but could also simply be the lack of philosophical underpinning bemoaned by Palazzo (2002).

Palazzo (2002) believes that America's preoccupation with business ethics is a reaction to the gap between morality and profits. The assumption that economics and ethics do not contradict each other, she asserts, stems from basic religious beliefs in the United States. She contends that this does not just have its origins in the puritan work ethic, but also in the role played by

Jewish entrepreneurs in the development of the American economy. Simply stated, the puritan stance is that divine grace manifests in the worldly success of a person. Hence a rich person cannot be morally bad, as surely he would not be rich. Puritanism may therefore inspire industriousness and frugality. The *doctrine of stewardship* requires that profits made due to this lifestyle are then used for the overall benefit of the community. Hence the rich are seen as the fiduciary of the wealth God gave them, and they should use this wealth to do His work on Earth. Citing the work of Fukuyama (1995), she contends that industrialization and the building of the big American corporates were dominated by Calvinist Protestants. Most managers, CEOs and board members of the major corporates were White Anglo-Saxon Protestant (WASP) males, who knew each other through schools, clubs and churches, and the norms and values that they were able to enforce reflected this background.

She suggests similarly that in Judaism there is no inherent distrust and contempt for business as might have been found in European Catholicism (discussed in more detail in Chapter 6 of the current text). Indeed the positive relationship between morality and business is reinforced through the rabbinic teaching that forbids active deception and any form of tacit misrepresentation in relations with customers. She also suggests, from the German and American literature, that other denominations in America appear to share the same belief in a positive relationship between business and morality. This includes American Catholicism which appears to have a more business-friendly and optimistic view than its European equivalents. Even in the case of Afro-Americans, who may be regarded as the main victims of American capitalism, she quotes Trimiew and Green (1997: 142) in saying: 'The African-American Church essentially accepts the existing political economy, even if that economy was founded and developed upon the degradation and economic exploitation of African Americans.' This may well reflect the inherent conservative nature, and influence, of established churches.

Interestingly, Palazzo (2002) suggests, after Vogel (1993a) that as a result of these influences on American society, particularly the view that there is a positive relationship between economic and spiritual success, the moral expectations of the public towards large corporations are far greater than they would be in continental Europe where the inheritance from a feudal structure of society had led to negative and cynical expectations towards the moral standards of big business. When these expectations of the American public are not fulfilled, they feel let down, far more than their European counterparts who have no such high expectations.

The ease and prominence of the public debate on morality issues in the United States, Palazzo (2002) contends, is due to the small private space that Americans appear to occupy. While, for example, Germans would consider these matters as subject more to private contemplation, American employees would be happy for their companies to prescribe codes of ethics to guide their moral behaviour. She suggests that in the USA the boundaries between public and private life are more permeable. Indeed, from the beginning of building their republic the Americans developed an intermediate level – civil society – between the citizen and the state where moral questions should be discussed openly. This is in marked contrast to many European countries where Catholicism and Lutheranism would not have supported the ideological foundations for such a self-assured civil public arena. Palazzo (2002) in particular points to Germany where business and politics were dominated by the state, and Germans traditionally retreated into their own private spaces and tried to shield themselves from the intruding state. Nazism tried to unite these two spheres. The consequences of this, she suggests, have led to even more resentment against public invasion into private morality, which has persisted up to the present time.

Another aspect that Palazzo (2002) points to in American life is the cross-over between the legal and the moral, where moral behaviour can effectively be legislated for: a reflection of individualistic universalism. Fixed rules are defined for everyone, in order to keep the society of individuals together. She suggests that a corollary of this is that once a certain value is recognized as being important, its general acceptance and legal enforcement are then fought for. This appears to be well reflected in the way American institutions take values and ways of doing things to countries in which they operate. This includes business, financial and military operations. Certainly in very recent years, the American government has, with almost religious zeal, attempted to enforce 'universal' concepts of democracy and liberal attitudes on other nations.

Yet in American society, this has a historical origin in the nature of an immigrant country, where many different cultural groups have come together. Not being able to rely on a shared tradition, a set of rules provides the foundation for social and ethical interaction, while preserving the inherent individualism of the basis of this type of society. European countries have tended to be more homogenous than the United States and possessed more of a common moral foundation, where moral values have been transmitted down the generations, and through common social institutions such as the church. Where societies are more collectivist and communitarian in orientation, what constitutes ethicality may be derived from shared values and bound into a network of social obligations and relationships. They will be held implicitly and communicated informally and tacitly, rather than in a formal, explicit, codified way.

This explains well contradictions in American society pointed out earlier in this chapter. There is indeed much diversity in American society due to its immigrant heritage, and it may be difficult to talk about one American cultural identity. Yet Palazzo (2002) after Vogel (1993a) suggests that it is exactly the cultural immigrant diversity that has necessitated a formalization of ethical values through public debate, and a desire to expound and enforce these values almost in an evangelical way (within the USA and outside) that has forged a commonality among a society of individuals and diverse cultural groups. The individualism and liberalistic attitudes that have been perpetuated by the dominance of white groups may well be opposed to the more communistic views of Hispanic or black groups. Yet it has been this liberal/Puritan/individualistic tradition that has provided the social framework to hold this society together. This appears to be the crux of American society, and the basis of its cultural identity, its concern for and concepts of ethicality, and its proselytizing of such concepts around the world.

It is difficult to understand international management ethics in a globalized world without understanding the basis of American ethical values. This discussion is taken into the next chapters. The contrast between the USA and European countries and US influence in Europe is continued in Chapter 6.

Opening case revisited: the UN Global Compact

In 2000 Kofi Annan, the then secretary-general of the United Nations, presented a new strategic policy initiative for businesses that are committed to aligning their operations and strategies with ten universally accepted principles in the areas of human rights, labour, environment and anti-corruption:

Human rights

Principle 1: businesses should support and respect the protection of internationally proclaimed human rights; and
Principle 2: make sure that they are not complicit in human rights abuses.

Labour

Principle 3: Businesses should uphold the freedom of association and the effective recognition of the right to collective bargaining;

Principle 4: the elimination of all forms of forced and compulsory labour;

Principle 5: the effective abolition of child labour; and

Principle 6: the elimination of discrimination in respect of employment and occupation.

Environment

Principle 7: businesses are asked to support a precautionary approach to environmental challenges;

Principle 8: undertake initiatives to promote greater environmental responsibility; and

Principle 9: encourage the development and diffusion of environmentally friendly technologies.

Anti-corruption

Principle 10: Businesses should work against corruption in all its forms, including extortion and bribery. (UN Global Compact, 2000)

Although this appears to be a continuing development in the same mould as the UN Declaration on Human Rights, discussed at the beginning of this chapter, as Williams (2004) points out, very few American corporations have signed up to this Compact. Certainly, behind the philosophy of this initiative lies the belief discussed in connection with American concepts, that business and ethics are compatible, and that codes can be drawn up to legislate for managers' (universal) ethical behaviour. Hence Annan is quoted by Williams as saying:

Let us choose to unite the power of markets with the authority of universal ideals. Let us chose to reconcile the creative forces of private entrepreneurship with the needs of the disadvantaged and the requirements of future generations. (Annan, 1999)

Williams (2004) argues that although most of the major European companies signed up to the Compact enthusiastically and at an early stage, US companies have been reluctant, mainly on accountability grounds. That is, because there is a lack of an accountability structure, the Compact will not be credible. However, a number of NGOs have criticized the Compact as a 'cover story' and argue for a mandatory legal framework.

Yet it may also be possible that some US corporates are reluctant to sign up, because of the increased levels of accountability they may have to be subjected to. For example, a look on corporate social responsibility watchdog websites such as www.corpwatch.org or www.crocodyl.org will provides interesting reading on such iconic brand representations of American globalization such as McDonald's and Coca-Cola. For example (posted on www.crocodyl.org, 2009 – last accessed 4 October 2009):

In August 2001 a McDonald's operating in Surrey, England was fined 12,000 pounds for overworking school-age employees late into the night on school days, often without rest breaks. One 15-year-old girl served burgers and fries for 16 hours during a Saturday. A McDonald's spokeswoman said the company usually only hired employees above school-leaving age, and deeply regretted the lapse. (BBC News, 31 July 2001)

In July 2001, the International Labor Rights Fund and United Steelworkers filed a lawsuit against two Coca–Cola bottlers in Colombia accusing the plants of hiring paramilitary groups to kill labor union organizers. In 2003, the US District Court for the Southern District of Florida dismissed the case owing to a lack of jurisdiction. The ILRF and USW brought a new complaint against Coca-Cola and its Latin American Bottler, Coca-Cola FEMSA in June 2006. US District Judge Jose E. Martinez dismissed the case stating a lack of evidence linking the murders of union leaders to an alleged conspiracy between paramilitaries and bottling plant officials in September. Sinaltrainal, the major Colombian labor union involved in the allegations, is appealing the ruling to the 11th Circuit Court of Appeals in Atlanta. Legal proceedings against Coca-Cola in Colombian courts have all been shelved; no entity has been held responsible for the killings. (Associated Press, 2 November 2006)

Coca-Cola workers in Turkey and Indonesia have faced mass firings after their efforts to improve labor conditions. Employees of at least two of Coke's bottling facilities in Turkey found themselves jobless after openly working to initiate union activity. Workers protesting the firings faced police violence. Police also attacked Turkish laborers and their family members during talks with the management at one plant. (United Students Against Sweatshops (USAS), 28 July 2005)

According to the All-China Federation of Trade Unions, McDonald's violated China's labor laws by underpaying part-time workers. Minimum wage is $.97/hour for part-time workers, but McDonald's pays only $.52/hour. (China Radio International, 11 April 2007)

In June 2007 a research team from the India Resource Center visiting a Coca-Cola bottling plant in Sinhachawar, found that the facility was pumping wastewater and hazardous waste into nearby farm fields and a local canal that empties into the Ganges River. The Central Pollution Control Board of India had already asked

Coca-Cola to clean up eight of its plant sites in 2003. (India Resource Center, 4 June 2007)

This of course is not to suggest that European companies and those from other parts of the world are not involved in similar practices, and that other large US corporates do not refrain from such violations of the principles contained in the UN Compact.

Implications for international managers

Although this chapter has taken a rather discursive approach to looking at values and ethicality in and from the United States, this critical perspective has been necessary in order to place the USA within its geopolitical position in the world – arguably a very important and strategic position – and to reflect on the nature of the historical, institutional and cultural influences on the American cultural identity, or identities, and implications for American perceptions of ethicality, and what that means for the rest of the world. However, we should not lose sight of the implications this all has for studying and practising international management.

The first aspect is the perceived universality by (American) managers of ethical principles that can be applied anywhere, and perhaps a perceived universality of American management principles by managers elsewhere, that may get confounded with perceptions of ethicality. To state this in a different way, American management principles are taught in many countries around the world and are widely accepted and adopted. Yet these are products of a particular value system stemming from the historical and other influences discussed in this chapter. The sanctity of individual 'liberty', democracy including participation in the workplace, reward for individual achievement, a 'doing' attitude often leading to short-termism and coupled with an internal locus of control, are all products of a particular cultural value system with its roots in white, protestant American society. This has led not only to the formulation of human rights of individuals and its implications for the corporate sphere (UN Compact), and at the same time downplaying the collective responsibilities of individuals as part of a community and nation, and a nation's right to develop following its own trajectory, but a value system that often comes into contradiction with its own tenets (e.g. free trade and unfettered competition), as well as those (managers, staffs, community) in other nations that come into contact with American managers. Coupled with a sometimes missionary zeal to do the right thing by introducing certain principles into foreign subsidiaries, for example, certain things start to happen that may be called into (ethical) question.

- Home country principles are introduced that may be contrary to values in the host country: what is the ethicality of using economic power in a corporate situation to introduce one's own value system?

- Host country principles are adopted which might be contrary to home country values and the values of home country managers: what is the ethicality of adopting host country values (perhaps to gain competitive advantage, in the case of paying bribes – if indeed this is a reflection of host 'values'), which are in contradiction to value systems from one's home country?
- Supposed concepts of universal human rights are infringed because they contradict the interests of the perpetrating corporate: what is the ethicality of not living up to the high moral standards prescribed and accepted by one's home country, and ostensibly the 'international community', which have been propagated by a country's access to international power structures (such as the United Nations), but which can apparently flout those standards when it suits?

Of course, this latter condition may be rather exceptional, yet as we have seen from this chapter, and Chapter 2 in connection with US Federal legislation regarding payment of bribes, there are always allowances for exceptions (the Foreign Corrupt Practices Act excludes payments made under duress or extortion; and 'grease' or 'speed' payments; and, of course, 9/11 has provided an exception that has led the United States to come under criticism of infringement of human rights: see for example Castellino, 2009).

One approach that this book tries to avoid is the comparison between 'cultures': Americans are like this, and (say) Germans are like that. Hence the current chapter has tried to take a processional and explanatory approach rather than a content one. It has tried to explain 'why' and 'how', but not so much 'what'. It has therefore tried to explain the position of the United States in the world, why this is important, and why it propagates certain cultural explanations or accounts of life, business and the management of organizations. Many existing texts have taken the view that it is far more useful for managers to understand that (say) Germans are like this, and this differs from Americans in the following way. The current author disagrees. It is far more useful for managers to try to answer the questions first outlined in Chapter 2 and again discussed in the current chapter in connection with Flyvbjerg's (2001) *phronesis*. This is not to propose a quick fix (answer these questions and you will be managing ethically, in the manner of Blanchard and Peale's, 1988, *The Power of Ethical Management*), but for managers to interrogate and understand certain aspects of the attitudes and actions, as follows.

1. What *choices* are available to individuals and organizations in the decisions they make? In theory managers have got infinite numbers of choices in any decision situation, and this may be an assumption made when one's cultural values are in effect invisible, as discussed above, particularly as informed by whiteness studies. But choices may be limited by one's living in a liberal, individualistic, achievement-oriented society. Yet in an international situation, an American manager's 'culture' may become more visible. There may be a choice between

paying a bribe or not; or employing staff on subsistence wages or not; or polluting a local environment or not. More visible choices would seem to become available owing now to the juxtaposition of two or more 'cultural spaces'. Decision making is about choice. Ethical decision making is about the values that inform choice, and there is always an ethical element in decision making when it involves (as all corporate decision making does) different stakeholders (in the modern language of business ethics and corporate social responsibility). Of course, choices are influenced by the following:

2. What *values* influence or govern these choices? Our values reflect the Third Space (in the language of Bhabha, 1994) we occupy. As the current chapter discussed, this is the result of a process involving interaction among societies, institutions, organizations, communities and individuals, and also involving some of the other questions listed below. One's cultural space within American society, which influences the values employed, was discussed in terms of the history of the United States as an immigrant destination, and the tension between integration and diversity. From a management perspective, it is perhaps important to attempt to understand how one fits into that wider society, and how American society fits into the world community. Carroll and Gannon (1997) point to the public education system perpetuating the idea that American society is the best in the world. It may be necessary to critically examine this assumption and to understand the values that underpin it.

3. What *rules* are followed (or not followed) in order to make such choices? Palazzo (2002) points to the prominence of teleological thinking in American ethical decision making, specifically utilitarian approaches that focus on the assessment of the results of decisions being to the benefit of the greatest number of people. Yet this fails to recognize the importance of deontological approaches in the formulation of corporate codes of ethics: an assumption that a company can legislate for good behaviour. Rules of course can be teleological in nature (e.g. assess the impact of a decision on different stakeholders) or deontological (e.g. do not pay bribes). The former may be more flexible in a cross-cultural situation, but may still transgress rules adhered to in other Third Spaces if not properly examined in relation to different rule systems (e.g. Shar'ia laws on not paying interest). An interesting example is the rule (e.g. from the UN Compact) concerning the employment of child labour: 'Principle 5: the effective abolition of child labour'. Clearly there is a case for abolishing the exploitation of children. Following the introduction of the Child Labor Deterrence Act in the US Senate in 1993, 50,000 children lost their jobs. It had a particularly devastating effect in the garment industry in Bangladesh, where child workers themselves found it difficult to understand that this was motivated by a humanitarian concern for their well-being. Senator Tom

Harkin, who introduced the bill, was sponsored by a key US trade union. Cheap imports from the Third World were seen as undercutting American workers' jobs (Schech and Haggis, 2000).

4. How do these rules *control* the levels and nature of choice in a society or an organization? Values also control, or at least influence, the nature of choice, but are not formally codified. Values comprise tacit information, and also can be at variance to rules. One can think of the variance between (originally) colonially imposed institutions in Africa and local community or societal values that may be at variance to the rules imposed by institutions (Dia, 1996; Jackson, 2004). This may include institutions that we take for granted such as the capitalist mode of production and the Western concept of the firm (Jackson *et al.*, 2008). This may have widespread acceptance in Africa, yet may still be at variance to more communalistic values relating to modes of organizing and production. Formally, or informally, prescribed rules around institutions limit and facilitate choice. From an American liberal perspective, the institution of the firm in a free-market economy may well give the impression of creating choice through freedom of action. Yet this may also limit choice. One can think of underskilled individuals; or perhaps minority groups such as the Ogoni people in the Delta region of Nigeria where the oil company Shell operates, perhaps in the interests of free-market economics, but apparently not without severely curtailing the choices available to the local people.

5. What are the *power* relations among the different stakeholders within the organization or society that control the rules and the values that influence choice? The point about the Ogoni people brings us to the management of the power relations among stakeholder groups. Often, as in the case of Shell and the Ogoni, this relationship may be apparent, but what about the more subtle aspects of American international management? If an American firm is in the position of employer of local people, or bringer of technology to a developing country, or bringer of managerial expertise in an international joint venture with an East European firm, the acceptance of the American manager's position may not just be a matter of an economic dependency relationship, but also may be based on the internalization of ideas of superiority, as partly explained by postcolonial theory. It may not be just the American manager who is blind both to the cultural influence and power relationship; it could also be the 'recipient' in the host country.

6. What different *objectives* do the different *stakeholders* have that influence choice in decision making? This really follows on from the last point. Although different stakeholders may well have different objectives based on varying cultural influences, as a result of power dynamics where one cultural Third Space is dominant over another, perceptions of objectives may be similar, even though it may be against the ultimate

interest of one of the weaker stakeholders. Even within the United States, the dominant 'cultural identity' may well be internalized by less dominant groups. However, postcolonial theory also allows for protest against dominant ideologies. It is perhaps incumbent on the part of (mostly white) American managers to understand such contradictions of influence on different stakeholders, to understand more about their own and others' cultural identities, and how this affects objectives of the different stakeholders and the interaction among them.

Questions for managers
1. How would you describe the cultural influences on your life, your values and your work?
2. What specific values and rules do you need to follow in your job, and how do these limit or facilitate choices that you have in your decision making?
3. How would you handle the choices available to you when your cultural Third Space comes into contact with another's Third Space? Does your organization have any rules, guidelines or advice for this?

An agenda for research

It is also incumbent on management researchers that they render the formerly invisible visible. This applies right to the core of social science: that value-rationality is given priority over analytical rationality (universal, context independent knowledge), and that the 'seat' of rational thought and universal approaches to management ethics is adequately scrutinized (it may be a truism that no where else on Earth other than the United States would assume a universal rationality for ethical thought). The current chapter has been a necessarily long one, as it has been important to fully discuss the constitution of American 'culture' and its position in the world. Any research agenda should attempt to make this transparent, rather than invisible. As Flyvbjerg (2001) points out, it is impossible to take a view from nowhere. In elaborating on a view from somewhere, it is also important to explore the multiplicity of that somewhere: the United States as a tension between diverse social and cultural interests, and a unifying (sometimes codified, sometimes not) set of rules and values (what Schildkraut, 2007, has called 'incorporationism').

As we saw above, any analysis should attempt to incorporate a modern interpretation of *phronesis*; an understanding of geopolitical power relations based on postcolonial and dependency theories; a concept of cultural cross-vergence; an integrating theory of cultural intersections/interfaces; and an understanding of the role of the United States in a modern globalized world. Flyvbjerg's (2001) four *phronetic* questions may be useful for constructing a research agenda in this area.

Questions for researchers

1. Where are we going? In terms of modern America's role in the world, coupled with setting an agenda for a universal ethics (not just the Universal Declaration of Human Rights and UN Compact), and its critics and alternatives (China, Africa, the Arab world) where is this heading? What are likely to be the outcomes? How can we research this, and what implications does it have for the way we do research on management ethics?
2. Who gains, and who loses, by which mechanisms of power? What are the mechanisms of power, how can we research these, and what implications does this have for our research on management ethics?
3. Is it desirable? To what extent can we or should we, as social scientists, make a judgement on whether the project's direction and outcomes are desirable? How can we evaluate this, by using what set of values? How can this be regarded as scientific?
4. What should be done? How can this actually make a difference to policy makers, business leaders and managers?

6 Institutions as culture, and the invisibility of ethics: a New Europe

Europe, as it exists at the beginning of the twenty-first century, is a product of multiple and complex influences that are often encapsulated in the word 'globalization'. The current author's first intention was to write two chapters, one on West European countries, and one on Eastern and Central European or 'post-soviet' ones. Although there would have been some justification for this in terms of very recent history, put in the context of an evolving colonial and intra-European dynamic over the last few centuries this seems rather an artificial division. Even in the last ten years, the term 'post-soviet' has really lost its immediacy and relevance. However, to lump a whole continent together in one chapter, where one chapter per country could be justified, seems an enormous task. Yet the quest of this book is to look more at the international dynamics of cross-cultural management ethics, to eschew simple comparison, but to also consider rich description/data from specific countries, and to consider intra-country dynamics. It is of course only possible to do this through considering a limited number of countries in this way, rather than for example the twenty-seven countries that now form the European Union (EU) as well as the European countries that are not within the EU, including Russia (the largest of Europe's total of fifty sovereign states).

European countries have variously colonized the Americas and Africa, colonized each other, and have been colonized by outsiders, such as the Moors of North Africa. Christianity (Roman Catholicism, Protestantism and Eastern Orthodox) predominates, with significant Muslim and Jewish populations. It is very unlikely that one can speak about a 'European (cultural/social) identity' yet it is also unlikely to be possible to speak in isolation of a German, Russian, Polish, Spanish or British identity without considering the historical and current dynamics, both internally and externally, of this continent. The EU project itself might also be regarded as the 'European dream' although as something quite different to the American dream: as Cortina (2008: 11) suggests, 'achieving much higher levels of equity in the economic sphere than other models', and having something different to offer in the approach taken in Europe towards 'economic ethics'.

The current chapter, taking its lead from Chapter 5, focuses firstly on differences with America and indeed American influences on Europe. It focuses on West Europe and its relationship and influences on Eastern and Central Europe. It looks at the influences on Europe as a whole of the dismantling of the Soviet Union. The wider international interaction and influences are also focused upon, including its previous colonies and implications for immigration and cultural identity, and more recent possible influences such as from Japan and China. The question of whether Britain is different, a part of Europe or a small island off the east coast of America, is also taken up.

Opening case: going West

In April 2007 the German publication *Spiegel Online* carried a story entitled 'Eastern Europe Pricing Itself Out of Cheap Labor Market'. This was an article on the workers of the Czech car maker Skoda going on strike for higher wages. They had asked for a 12 per cent increase. Although this seemed a high demand, they were looking to approach the level of monthly income of their counterparts in Volkswagen's German factories. Skoda has been one of Volkswagen's success stories, selling a record of 549,667 cars the previous year and highly profitable. Already workers earned 10 per cent higher than the Czech average. In recent years the former Soviet bloc countries had seen growth above the rate in the Euro zone, with wages doing correspondingly well. In the previous years, 2002–6, median hourly wages had increased by 45.5% in the Czech Republic. In Slovakia they had increased by 67.7%, in Hungary by 70.1% and in Latvia by 168.3%. Poland had a more modest rise of 29.8%, but even this was well above increases in the Euro zone. There was also evidence that skills shortages were beginning to push up wages further.

The concern, both perhaps from Skoda, and from experts on the region, was that if such demands from the Skoda workers were met (even though Skoda could afford it), and if pressures to increase wages were given into, then Eastern Europe could price itself out of the market. The article suggests that this has already happened in Mexico, Singapore and Thailand, and there is evidence of (Western) companies already looking past Eastern Europe in search of cheaper markets, to such countries as Ukraine. However, it is still likely that the higher standards of education in Eastern Europe will remain an attraction. The article points to the boom in the Romania IT industry with growth in 2006 of 35 per cent to over US$1.6 billion, as a product of such high education standards in the former Soviet bloc countries (Spiegel, 2007a).

In the previous month (March 2007) *Spiegel Online* carried an article entitled 'Going West for the Good Life'. This was a story of the 'hundreds of thousands' of East Europeans who travelled in search of work mainly to the UK, Ireland and Sweden (the first countries to open their doors to new accession members) when Poland, the Czech Republic, the Baltic States, Hungary and Slovakia joined the EU. Neighbouring countries such as Germany and Austria restricted immigration by imposing interim rules valid until 2011. The article reported that the Polish Ministry of Labour estimates that 2 million out of 38 million citizens were currently seeking employment outside their country, and that Ireland alone was home to around 196,000 of these. Most of the immigrants belong to the most economically important stratum of society, being under 35 and a quarter having finished higher education. Even with Poland's 14 per cent unemployment rate, and Slovakia's 13.3 per cent rate, they both suffer a shortage of qualified workers as a consequence of this exodus.

Wage differentials can be substantial. The article claims that even the miserable wages of Western nurses are attractive to trained East European nurses, and doctors can earn ten times more than back home. If the previous article suggests that capital is following cheaper labour markets, this one is suggesting that workers in Europe are going in the opposite direction. In the health sector, it reports, doctors from Germany, France and England are going to the United States, the Czechs and Poles are taking their place, and in turn the Bulgarians and Romanians are taking their place.

The article reports that even though the UK has now closed its borders to Bulgarians and Romanians to prevent another huge wave of cheap labour, after these two countries acceded, much of the 2.7 per cent economic growth of the UK can be attributed to the inflow of immigrants. Although not actually depressing wages they prevented their rapid rise. They increased domestic demand and paid taxes. They also took jobs that the British no longer wanted (Spiegel, 2007b).

America and Europe

Crane and Matten (2004: 27–8) point to differences between America and Europe by focusing on what they regard as six key questions. Firstly, 'Who is responsible for ethical conduct in business?' They suggest that the strong

American culture of individualism puts the responsibility onto individuals for their own success. So if there is a need to solve an ethical question, the individual is expected to be responsible for making the right choice. This very much reflects the large literature on individual ethical decision making. They contrast this with the situation in Europe where traditionally it has been thought that it is not the individual or even a single company's responsibility for solving ethical dilemmas, but the responsibility normally of the state as an overarching and collective institution. From Enderle (1996) they suggest that in Europe business ethics has focused on the choice *of* constraint, whereas in the USA the focus has been on choice *within* constraints.

Their second question is 'Who is the key actor in business ethics?' This follows from the previous one. In Europe this points to the collective institutions of governments, trade unions and corporate associations within a tight governmental institutional framework, which includes a network of regulation around workers' rights, social and medical care and environmental issues, among others. They point to the strong influence of the Scandinavian welfare state, the German codetermination system and the position of the trade unions in France. In the USA the institutional framework would be far looser and the key actor would be the corporation. This points to the much higher preoccupation in the USA with business ethics among the corporate and academic sectors, and the fact that corporate misconduct carries greater enforcement and harsher penalties than in Europe because individual companies are considered responsible.

The third question Crane and Matten (2004) point to is 'What are the key guidelines for ethical behaviour?' They suggest that the substantial differences in legal framework between the USA and Europe necessitate different approaches whereby the key guidelines for ethical conduct in Europe tend to be codified in a negotiated legal framework for business, and in the USA businesses tend to initiate these themselves in the form of corporate codes, although likely motivated by the Federal Sentences Guidelines.

The fourth question they point to is 'What are the key issues in business ethics?' Again, this comes back to the emphasis on the individual and the corporation in the USA, and on collective institutions in Europe. As the state does not fully legislate for the relationship between the individual and business in the USA this is deemed the responsibility of the corporation. Hence American textbooks tend to emphasize privacy, workers' rights, salary issues and whistle-blowing issues among others, whereas the Europeans' texts tend to deal with more overriding, macro issues such as ethics and capitalism and economic rationality.

Finally Crane and Matten (2004) look at the question 'What is the most dominant stakeholder management approach?' They suggest that European corporations tend to be smaller, not so dominated by the drive for shareholder value maximization, and include multiple stakeholders rather than just shareholder interests that may typify US corporations. The governance structure of many European firms also suggests this, with large executive and supervisory boards with interlocking interests with large financial institutions.

Yet Europe, as we have already pointed out, is not homogenous, and has substantial differences among its many countries. However, despite general differences between America and European countries there is no doubt that the USA is having an influence on a number of aspects of management ethics in Europe. For example, as Langlois and Schlegelmilch (1990) pointed out two decades ago, the uptake of corporate codes of ethics in Europe appears to be driven by the activities of American corporates in Europe. Crane and Matten (2004) point out more recently that globalization has increasingly led to a move towards greater deregulation of business activities, putting more emphasis on individual corporations to self-regulate, and putting European corporations into a similar position to their American counterparts. This may be even more so, they suggest, in the case of East European countries where economies in transition are bound to have a weaker state and law enforcement and more likely to be influenced by the type of approaches to managing ethics taken by American corporations. This may be the case particularly as American investment in these countries grows.

It may be, however, that in exploring differences, first between European countries and America, and then looking at influences on European countries from America, the issues may be even more fundamental, starting from the concept of 'culture' itself. In Chapter 2, the differences between European social anthropology and American cultural anthropology were alluded to through the work of the British social anthropologist Goody (1994). He states (1994: 251) that: 'In a widespread European view, culture is seen as the content of social relations, not as some distinct entity ... That is to say, it is the 'customary' part of social action, not one which constitutes their entire field of study and about which one can have a separate body of theory.'

Hence the 'European' view, if it can be posited as such, does not lead to the somewhat artificial split between institutions and culture. One does not lead to the other. They are part of the same socio-cultural phenomenon described by the simple model presented in Chapter 2 in Figure 2.2. The socio-cultural domain can be represented by *context* (social order, rules and institutions), *content* (knowledge, meaning and values) and *conduct* (social interaction). It is difficult to say that one or two drives the third, as there is an interactional effect among the three, including conflicts (which can give rise to ethical dilemmas). Hence social interaction, while creating meaning and ultimately the nature of institutions and rules, is undertaken within a framework of rules (institutions). Generally in theory, values should be in harmony with societal rules and institutions. The nature of institutions in a society should reflect predominant values: values give rise to rules that are generated and governed by institutions, and these rules propagate and evolve values within a society. Nothing can happen without human action (meaningful behaviour in Silverman's, 1970, terms) and human interaction. But human action and interaction are tempered, governed and even enforced by the social order (*context*): firstly rules about how that human interaction should be con-ducted; and secondly in terms of power relations (for example one party to that interaction may be more powerful than another). That may work fine when rules and values, meaning and social order, knowledge and institutions are in harmony and reflect one another. Yet when they do not, human inter-action may for example take the form of resistance or compliance: staff in a company in the Czech Republic taken over by a German manufacturer may resist the imposition of German management methods as they perceive them as being out of line with how they see things ought to be done; or managers, as often is the case in similar situations, may be hungry for Western man-agement tools and know-how, seeing them as superior and welcoming them (the denigration of non-Western ways of doing things, values structures and knowledge, and the internalization of such negative attitudes, may well be another example of the 'Orientalism' described by Said, 1978, and taken up in postcolonial theory: see particularly Chapters 2, 5 and 9).

Rules and values are most likely to come into conflict at the point of a socio-cultural interface such as an international joint venture or foreign company operating in a local community, locals working with expatriate managers, or the imposition of a foreign institution in a local community. In general globalization may be described as a process that brings together different cultural spaces (Third Spaces, as discussed in Chapter 5) at specific socio-cultural interfaces. This may bring into disharmony or conflict rules and values. When institutions and rules are imposed or adopted through unequal power relationships, they may come into conflict with local values. This may be a major reason for ethical questions arising. Although cer-tainly not unique to the current continent under discussion, this may exactly describe the situation in the post-colonial, post-WWII and post-Soviet

Europe of today. But also these issues are not unique to a discussion of globalization, as difference between the more powerful in society (by social class or gender) suggests differences between those who make the rules according to their values and interests, and those whose values or interests come into conflict with institutional rules.

The tripartite dynamic of context, content and conduct is rather a simplistic construct, and must be combined with a theory of socio-cultural interfaces and power dynamics, if we are to understand management ethics in Europe, and indeed other cultural phenomenon in any part of the world. Modern or the New Europe does not represent, as perhaps the United States does, a quest for universalism and by implication an invisibility of culture. It represents an attempt to act and interact within and across cultures (see Jackson, 1993a), that is, to be conscious of 'culture', to make this explicit, and to interact across Europe (and the rest of the world) with this in mind (although its colonial past may come back to haunt it).

However, apart from the conceptual base discussed above, which includes social institutions and structures within a definition of culture, there may be another reason why there is seen to be a tighter fit between symbolic culture (values) and institutions (rules) in the context of many European countries. The explanation may be in the differences between America and European countries as explained by Crane and Matten (2004) and others: that questions of ethicality reside with the individual and the individual corporation in the United States, but with collective institutions in countries such as Germany, France and the Scandinavian countries. This apparent close fit in European countries, and the fact that ethical issues are not dealt with so much by individuals and firms, may at least partially render ethics invisible. Hence the common finding in empirical studies that German managers appear to be less ethical than American managers. Jackson (2000) has suggested that issues which have an ethical content for individual American managers do not have an ethical content for their counterparts in Germany. Ethics is not such a major issue for German managers as it is for American managers. Ethics in (at least) Northern Europe may be so bound up with collective institutions, and not a matter for individuals, that the fit between institutions and culture on this major issue of values is closer than it is in America. Context and content are a tighter fit.

Although rapidly moving towards a tautological explanation, if an awareness of ethical issues can be explained by a disparity between the way things are (context), and the way things ought to be (content) (see Figure 2.3 in Chapter 2), a tighter fit between these two may suggest why ethical issues are not paramount on the agenda of German managers.

However, dynamics in and with Europe may be changing this situation. Whereas the academic study of business ethics was the province of American (and then British) business schools, that has changed over the last two decades (in fact since Langlois and Schlegelmilch suggested they were changing in 1990). Yet this has also been part of the development of university business schools in Germany (in 1997 van Luijk had counted twenty-five university chairs of business ethics in Europe). This may well be due to American influence. Certainly this has been one of the changing dynamics over the last few decades, and even since World War II. The increasing presence of American multinational companies (MNCs) in Europe must be at least one instance of an increasing discrepancy between *what is* and *what should be*. Not only have MNCs brought in different cultural spaces that interface with local cultural spaces and provide discrepancies between *what is* and *what should be* (and this does not just apply to American MNCs of course), but American MNCs have come with an emphasis on the responsibility of the individual and the corporation towards ethical issues, which may have come into conflict with the common European emphasis on the responsibility of collective institutions, that simply does not exist in the United States.

Of course the responsibility for a shift in Europe towards an American model cannot be entirely attributed to the influence of American corporations. Yet the turning more towards neoliberal economic policies of the EU, which have no doubt influenced changes in individual EU countries, may be attributed to growing globalization and the obvious effect of American institutions. However, Iankova and Turner (2004: 77) argue that 'the rise of Thatcher/Reagan/Friedman "free market economics"' is paradoxically driving a resurgence and consolidation of social partnership relations across the new (both West and East) Europe. The social partnership relations they describe, which have been a feature of social market economics of many continental European countries, is the 'regularised bargaining relationships between organised business and labour, often tripartite (with the state playing more or less engaged roles), to set basic wage and employment standards as well as to influence broader economic and social policy' (2004: 77). Behind this is the concept of a social Europe. Iankova and Turner (2004: 78) describe it thus:

'Social Europe' – a theoretically vague term but also a much debated political concept – has at its heart a collective societal effort to limit social inequality through government intervention, with an active role played by organised 'social partners' representing labour and business. Social Europe envisages economic success building on deep social foundations, on a shared belief that the fruits of capitalist enterprise should be distributed across society in policies of social and economic security. First and foremost a concept of comparative capitalism, social Europe contrasts sharply with the US model of capitalism featuring individualism, minimal state involvement in the economy, and adversarial relations between labour and business rather than dialogue and concertation ... Despite the wide variation among European countries in terms of social policies, the gap separating them in particular from the United States is much wider and more significant.

It is partly the result of the strength of the concept of a social Europe, the reaction to a change towards a free market in both the West and East, and in the East a buffer to the quick move from a protected, socialist economy to free-market economics, which have in a way strengthened social partnering. This is so even in the UK with a movement towards greater integration with the EU, and in Poland, that although slow to adopt such policies after its initial 'shock therapy' move towards a free market in the early 1990s, was also keen to conform to EU accession norms.

This maintenance of a social Europe and a stress on a partnership between business organizations, organized labour and, in many cases, government may at the same time have provided a contrast with policies of American MNCs in Europe, and thus raised ethical issues through a distinction between *what is* and what *should be*. Yet this may also have provided a buffer between this disparity. In other words, this cannot be regarded as a case of cultural disparity between American and European ways of doing things. To a large extent, American corporations would have had to conform to European institutional norms in order to operate.

There is another area, however, that might cause ethical issues between *what is* and *what should be*: the difference between the relative short-termism of American firms focused on shareholder value and the longer-termism of German and possibly French corporations (on a par with Japanese corporations perhaps) with their strong ties with banking institutions and government and a lower focus on shareholders' short-term interests. Short-termism may lead to cutting corners and making decisions that raise ethical issues (Jackson, 2002b).

The other dynamic within Europe that may be causing discrepancies between *what is* and *what should be* is the interaction between West and East, between countries of Western Europe and countries of the former soviet bloc, both within the EU, and with countries outside the EU such as Russia. For example, the opening case points to one possible dynamic of West European firms operating in the East and Central European countries. When Volkswagen first took a stake in the ailing Skoda in the Czech

Republic in 1991, a number of issues arose in the relationship between Czech and German managers (discussed in Jackson, 2002b). Certainly one of the complaints from Czech managers was that too many German regulations, attitudes and behaviours had been transferred, with a lack of respect by the expatriates for what had worked well in the past in the Czech company. The other main area of contention was the differential in pay between locals and expatriates, with expatriate managers earning far more than local managers. This appears now to have taken on a macro dimension within the EU: capital seeking out cheaper labour markets. In a way this may reflect dependency theory (discussed in Chapter 5), although arguably this is not necessarily leading to Eastern and Central Europe's underdevelopment. The motive force in warnings such as from the article in *Spiegel* in the opening case, is the search for cheaper labour markets with a good standard of education. The quest for higher wages by workers in Eastern and Central Europe, although having been partially met, appears ultimately to be at odds with the interests of Western capital. Companies from Western Europe may well take their business elsewhere if wages in the accession countries become on a par with those in the West.

The corollary of this is that low wages in countries such as Poland and the Czech Republic have created a movement of workers within the EU towards the West. This has been good for economies such as the UK, but has caused skills shortage problems back home in lower wage areas.

One ethical consideration that exists regarding the international dynamics of the transfer of production and knowledge from normally richer, more developed areas, to poorer less developed areas, is the benefit to the poorer areas (a utilitarian consideration, but also deontological in the intent of the decision to take production East or South). In the case of the EU, this question should perhaps be, has 'Social Europe' been transferred to Eastern and Central Europe? Certainly in Iankova and Turner's (2004) estimation this appears to be the case despite, and perhaps because of, the move to a (free) market economy. The move also to higher wages in Eastern and Central Europe appears to represent a benefit, until one hears that this may be a reason for Western companies to withdraw from these markets in search of cheaper labour elsewhere. Also the free movement of labour within the EU appears to have disrupted the labour markets in individual countries: taking skilled labour away from the poorer countries, and holding down wages in richer countries.

Another ethical question appears to concern the nature of the knowledge relationships between West and East. To what extent is local knowledge disparaged, by both Western managers and locals? Cases, such as that of the Volkswagen–Skoda relationship (discussed in Jackson, 2002b), appear to indicate this disparaging. Yet this in itself raises important issues for both managers and scholars. Is this disparaging justified from an 'objective' point of view? That is, Western ('modern') management know-how is better than the inefficiencies of the Soviet systems, and any leftovers that managed to survive from the pre-Soviet era. Or, is this disparaging a product of the 'Orientalism' described in postcolonial theory: a type of 'false consciousness' in the Marxist sense, which has been propagated by the dominant player in a power dynamic, and internalized by local players? From this arise two further questions: Is this important? And, if so: How do we find it out?

The first of these questions appears to be an ethical one, the type that might permeate any subject of social scientific study. It is a value judgement of what is important and what is not. Within it contains the whole issue of globalization and whether or not this is seen as a benign force, or otherwise. The fact that this may not be asked in the first place may reflect poorly on the nature of the scholarship involved. From the value-rational perspective of the *phronetic* approach outlined by Flyvbjerg (2001) it is an essential question.

The second question is one of operationalizing our concepts. I would suggest that postcolonial theory is difficult to operationalize empirically. Certainly we can point to disparaging attitudes towards countries in a less dominant position from colonizers and whatever modern equivalent we might point to (activities of MNC, expatriates operating in a developing host country, activities of development agencies and the premise their work is based on). However, how do we adjudge that a statement by an interviewed local manager or worker who says that they welcome Western management is either a demonstration of the ideological outcome of a power dynamic (a false consciousness, or an internalization of the dominant partner's disparaging of local culture); or is a statement of objective 'truth'. There may be two ways. Firstly, postcolonial theory allows for the possibility of protest against the dominant ideology. An interviewing of a wide sample across different levels in the organization, and across different socio-economic groups, may reveal disparities. This is of course in addition to interviewing both locals and expatriates. Secondly, we can refer back to a discrepancy between what is, and what ought to be, discussed above. Ask interviewees about home/community culture versus work/organization culture. If there are differences this provides an indication of the outcome of a power dynamic: local cultural and foreign institutions; values being different to rules; *what ought to be* out of kilter with *what is.*

Yet, if we accept that in social science there has to be a view from somewhere, then we need to start from a position of understanding the interfaces at which knowledge exists, including the position of the researcher or manager. This should be an integral part of any 'analysis and interpretation of the status of values and interests in society aimed at social commentary and social action' (Flyvbjerg, 2001: 60). So far this chapter has been concerned with the interaction of European and the United States and between East and West Europe. It is not possible to examine all countries of the EU and of the greater Europe, but we can point to some of these in relation to possible corollaries of management ethics.

Europe: similarities and differences

Van Luijk (1997) examines differences among the European countries in six categories that may influence the nature of ethical discourse: style of philosophical reflection; weight of ideological forces; state of economic development; distribution of social power; academic institutions and business education; and open or closed society.

Firstly he looks at the way countries differ in style of philosophical reflection, where Germany has a tradition of fundamental and metaphysical philosophy that has tended to emphasize all encompassing issues such as the relationship between economic and ethical rationality: treating ethics as a quest to justify norms and values, rather than merely a consideration of specific moral dilemmas. Such justification would normally be sought in discursive or dialogue ethics where validity is achieved through that which well-informed and impartial persons could agree through solid argument. A later definition by Beschorner (2006: 127) asserts that (German) 'Discourse Ethics is a procedural moral theory of interactionism that attempts to develop normative orientations for practical purposes based on the idea of fair dialogs'. In France, van Luijk (1997) suggests that although the philosophical tradition has been to comment on classical texts, moral philosophy as a systematic discipline is only recently making a resurgence. In Britain the tradition has been with empiricism, with a recent emphasis on applied ethics and practical questions.

The second heading under which van Luijk (1997) considers European differences is the weight of ideological forces. Here he contrasts the influences of institutions such as churches, political parties and what he refers to as 'national values'. Hence in the Netherlands, the most secularized country in

Europe, churches have suffered a dramatic loss in public influences, whereas in Italy the Catholic Church still plays a major role, coupled with the ideology of the free market and still strong remnants of Marxism. He also suggests that religious influence is still strong in Belgium and Spain. The political influence of social democracy is strong in Scandinavia, particularly in Sweden, together with secularization. Following World War II, he suggests, Germany had to develop a new national ideology, modelling itself as an economically successful country with a social market economy as the mark of good conduct, and based on conservative political convictions supported by the Christian churches.

His third categorization is the state of economic development, and suggests that economy is important in moral notions of solidarity, using the example of Italy, and the notion of separation of the prosperous north from the poor south of the country. He also points to transformations in Spain and Ireland from predominantly agricultural countries promoting tourism as a source of revenue, to industrialization that has transformed also the approach to social welfare and the distribution of responsibilities between government and private agencies and persons.

The fourth heading of van Luijk (1997) is distribution of power. He suggests that in Britain and France the social order is predominantly based on class relations, contrasted with countries such as Sweden, the Netherlands and Germany, which emphasize egalitarianism. In Italy family values are emphasized with the family having a central role, for example in business. This is also partly the case in France. Yet a cross-cutting theme is the extent to which power is distributed in the work situation in terms of the level of industrial democracy: the extent to which social problems are addressed through consensus or conflict. This has already been referred to through Iankova and Turner's (2004) discussion of social partnerships. Yet this differs considerably country by country, and particularly between the UK and other West European countries. The codetermination laws of Germany and the Dutch systems of workers' councils make for a different approach to that in the UK, where unions have been weakened in industrial negotiations, where their role in decision making tended to be conflictual and confrontational. In countries such as Spain where union membership is low, but trade union influence through national agreements is still high, the situation is different again. In simplistic terms, if Hofstede's (1980a/2003) understanding of *Power Distance* has credibility in comparative studies, this differs considerably among countries such as Belgium, Spain, Italy and France with higher *Power Distance* values and the Netherlands, Denmark and Sweden with lower

Power Distance values. Central and East European countries are unknown territory for Hofstede's original study, but the GLOBE study's measure for *Power Distance* 'as is' correlates with Hofstede's original *Power Distance*, and indicates many East European countries (together with France, Spain and Italy) in the upper quartile of *Power Distance* (House *et al.*, 2004). It is not surprising that the GLOBE's *Power Distance* 'should be' does not correlate with Hofstede's *Power Distance*, as with the GLOBE study itself not only do countries show 'should be' scores much lower than 'as is' scores, most of the East European countries have moved to the third quartile of 'should be' scores. It is unlikely that too much can be read into this in terms of an ethical dilemma between rules/norms (as is) and values (should be) for the East European countries, as all countries show this tendency.

The fifth heading under which van Luijk (1997) considers European differences in approaches to management and business ethics is academic institutions and business education. Germany, for example, has considered that it is not the business of universities to train people directly for business. There has not been a tradition of business school as there has been in the UK. In France the training of future managers has fallen to the *Grandes Ecoles*. Originally these were mainly engineering schools for France's elite, but increasingly business schools have been instigated on this model. Yet these still reflect what Trompenaars (1993) has referred to as Ascriptive, in contrast to Achievement societies, where roles are ascribed in accordance, in this case, to the holding of a diploma from a particular institution: much in the same way as the traditional role of a degree in the UK from the 'Oxbridge' system as a route into the higher echelons of the civil service and business. Van Luijk suggests that under this type of system it takes a strong personality to be committed to ethics in business.

His sixth and final category is open or closed culture. This is the extent to which a country is open to other cultures. He points to the need for Scandinavian business people to speak English and to travel to stay in touch with important markets, coming into contact with common usages and what constitutes moral decency on a transnational scale. In some part he contrasts this with British and Irish business people who do not have to learn foreign languages and simply have to accommodate themselves to odd forms of pronunciation and 'unfamiliar ways of thinking expressed in familiar sounding sentences' (van Luijk, 1997: 1586). He also points to the increasing influence of immigration in European countries that has changed the dynamics of national identities. Although this aspect was well discussed in the context of the United States in the previous chapter,

Europe, and different European countries, may well present a different dynamic. In the current decade, Britain for example has different policies to France, where the latter has banned the wearing of any dress or signification in schools that can be considered religious, such as Islamic traditional dress, favouring assimilation, and Britain has a more accommodating and multicultural policy.

Germany and the development of discourse ethics

There may be other ways to conceptualize the wider context of differences to approaches to management ethics in Europe, yet van Luijk's provides a beginning. It is perhaps more important now, in exploring those differences and similarities, to look at some of the many and diverse countries in Europe, using van Luijk's categorization as a basis, but also exploring in more depth a country's interaction with other countries. A fairly central country in Europe (politically and economically) is Germany. Yet the national boundaries of Germany have changed considerably during the course of the twentieth century. In the current author's earlier career in teaching cross-cultural management he made use of an interesting suggestion by Guy and Mattock (1991) that we should focus on three aspects in order to try to understand the 'culture' of a country: topography, religion and history. The concern for trying to understand culture, from the current author's perspective, was the image of a manager landing in a country as though in a space ship from an alien planet (Jackson, 1993a). How could they start to make sense of this? Certainly tools such as that provided by Hofstede's value dimensions may be useful, but may be too superficial when considering just one country: although it is useful to know how that country may differ and is similar to its neighbouring countries (or the 'alien planet' from which the manager comes: bearing in mind the difficulty of taking a view from nowhere). Social anthropological methods of prolonged participant observation may be useful if one has a year or so to spare, although even this more detailed ethnography often lacks a historical perspective.

To demonstrate the possible influence of topography on culture Guy and Mattock (1991) suggested an exercise for students. First draw a simple sketch map of Spain, with its boundaries and show its capital. Now, do the same for Germany. Almost all European students can easily do the first, yet sometimes even German students find it difficult to do the latter. The authors show that since 1640, Spain has remained the same, with its border with Portugal, and the capital Madrid in the centre. They also show how, in 1648 the Electorate of Brandenburg was a collection of around 300 Germanic states comprising mostly fragments of a shattered Holy Roman Empire. In 1866 the Second German Reich, although unified, occupied a different land-mass and shape. The German Republic of 1919 was far smaller after World War I, and again in 1942 the Third German Reich occupied a larger land-mass and a much altered shape. In 1948 this became different again, if one only includes the Federal Republic of Germany, and in 1990 after unification Germany has a much altered shape and occupies a smaller land mass than in previous times. The authors' point is that Germany has an ill-defined out-line, unmemorable but also changing even in the twentieth century. It has hardly any physical boundaries. This contrasts with Spain which has well-defined borders. They contend that to be Spanish is well defined, despite strong regional identities (Catalan and Basque for example with different languages). There is much less security in what it means to be German, they contend. The proffered German love of order (*Ordnung muss sein*), which in recent years has been supported by cross-cultural management scholars by reference to Hofstede's Uncertainly Avoidance dimension, Guy and Mattock (1991: 24) propose is 'in part a response to the vagueness of their national border', and perhaps to an emotional insecurity about 'Germanness'. Of course, the authors would also connect this with the importance of history, which interacts with the topography of a country, and perhaps also with religion (of which more later).

These three aspects together may well indicate the possible nature of cul-tural identity, but also in the case of countries in Europe such as Germany which have had transient borders over the years, the nation state may not necessarily be a static thing. Whether or not it is the most useful unit of ana-lysis is contestable. Often the answer to that question is: what are you to other people? Or, what are you in relation to other people? Possibly a Bavarian to other Germans, or a Catalan to other Spaniards; but German to non-Germans, and Spanish to non-Spanish. Certainly in terms of the increasing interborder interactions within Europe the nation state has become a defin-ing entity as far as 'culture' is concerned. However, because of this interaction across Europe and globally, what constitutes Germanness, or Spanishness, is changing.

In Chapter 5 we looked at some of the differences between America and Europe, using Germany as a reference point and focusing on the analysis of Palazzo (2002). She suggests that, at the time of writing, there was still resist-ance to a specific consideration of ethics in German corporations, despite a number of corporate scandals at the end of the 1990s and into the next decade, and globalization with (international) pressures to address issues more directly. She summarizes the traditional German view as:

1. A basic antagonism between business and morality arising historically from feudalism, and both Catholic and Lutheran traditions;
2. A stricter separation between public and private spheres such that moral issues are for individual deliberation outside the work place;
3. The relational understanding of norms and values such that more discursive, interactional methods of addressing issues should be used;
4. A more pessimistic evaluation of human potential for moral improvement; and an idealistic intellectual style, starting with theoretical and principled assumptions rather than pragmatic considerations.

As a result of this basic antipathy between business and morality, German companies often prefer to talk about corporate culture rather than ethics. Guidance may be seen to be provided by mission statements rather than directly through codes of ethics. However, increasingly codes are being drawn up by the large international corporations such as Volkswagen which itself went through a scandal in its relationship with the trade union in 2005. Palazzo (2002) also believes that the relational value basis of business culture is changing in Germany: a move away from the more traditional informal discursive control mechanisms to more formal mechanisms. Even so, she reports that companies are still reluctant to go too far in the direction of American-style ethics programmes as a means of preventing corporate crime. The concern is that this could be seen as a form of self-accusation.

The other dynamic that she points to is the increasingly diverse and heterogeneous workforce, together with a loosening of agreement on traditional values and norms. Perhaps also the process that was explored in Chapter 5 is also active here: the loosening of community and communalistic sharing and understanding because of the increased diversity from immigration means that society is becoming more individualistic. Shared and internalized norms and values are no longer as strong across society. This may also mean a greater distinction between institutions (context/rules) and symbolic culture (content/values), where a society becomes more heterogeneous in terms of its values, and institutions become more explicit in terms of the imposition of rules to moderate among and bring closer together disparate value systems. The process in Germany at corporate level may also be becoming more directive rather than agreement seeking, if Palazzo's observations are taken to their logical conclusions. Certainly a commentary in the US publication *Business Week* on the Volkswagen scandal pointed a finger at the German codetermination laws as an 'underlying cause of the country's economic stagnation' (*Business Week*, 2005). However, Iankova and Turner's (2004) thesis regarding the spread of social partnering in Europe somewhat contradicts this trend. Yet clearly there are contradictory trends and motive forces in Germany and other European countries.

Undertaking a reanalysis of GLOBE data to focus on ethical leadership, Martin *et al.* (2009: 139) show that the more traditional focus in Germany explored above is still pervasive:

In general, the quantitative and qualitative results suggest that within Germany, ethical leadership continues to be largely embedded within the organizational system, i.e. within a shared set of implicitly held expectations 'of the nature and scope of the company's responsibilities' (Vogel 1993b: 169). This shared understanding of the nature of the company's responsibilities is, in turn, 'shaped by the norms of the community' (Vogel 1993b: 169). At the same time, there is evidence that ethical behaviour and the ability to lead ethically are embedded within the individual, who self-regulates and is trusted to do so as a member of the moral community. As such, leaders are expected to demonstrate trustworthiness, and to encourage, empower and build confidence in staff to work within the parameters of the system.

They add that German managers are still reluctant to use the more prescriptive approach of American managers, preferring self-regulation. Indeed employees might see this prescriptive approach as a lack of trust by the manager. This has implications for the type of characteristics a German leader is expected to have. They are expected to have integrity, but also the expectation is on how the leader behaves towards others. This involves gaining support and trust from employees. However, these findings are deduced from GLOBE research undertaken at the beginning of the 2000s, and still involve a time lag of around a decade. There is clearly room for current and ongoing research into changes as a result of more recent dynamics, not only involving influences of American MNCs, but also the increasing influx of guest workers and immigrants as a result of the enlargement of the EU.

The role of social partnerships in Germany and in other European countries is reflected in the nature of *economic ethics* (rather than *business ethics*) in the German literature. Certainly one of the major streams, discourse ethics, reflects the emphasis of social partnerships and a wider stakeholder base found in Germany. While a utilitarian emphasis, together with a deontological approach such as the reliance on codes of ethics, and universally applicable principles such as the Declaration of Human Rights, may predominate in the United States, the emphasis here is on gaining agreement on ethical issues, even pre-empting them by creating dialogue.

This has already been alluded to above by referring to Beschorner's (2006: 127) work which suggests that 'Discourse Ethics is a procedural moral theory of interactionism that attempts to develop normative orientations for practical purposes based on the idea of fair dialogs'. Although appearing to develop out of Germany and Northern Europe, the concept of discourse ethics can be allied to the idea of a social Europe, and has been taken up in other countries. Perhaps an unexpected place, with its Catholic base, is Spain.

Spain: ethics and the role of Catholicism

The reader may forgive the current author for beginning this section with an anecdote used in his previous teaching. The story involves his driving in his car in his native England, with a passenger, a colleague from Germany. The colleague points to a road sign that indicates that there is a speed camera further along the road. He asks what this is. The current author begins to explain to him the concept of a speed camera, when he stops him by saying that of course he knows what a speed camera is. He is referring to the sign that warns the motorist of a speed camera. In Germany, he states, of course there are speed cameras, but no warning. If you are exceeding the speed limit and there is a speed camera you get caught. Later the author was relating this incident to a Spanish colleague. She said that in Spain the police quite often hide behind bushes with mobile speed cameras. It is not unusual the next day to find the bush burned down.

Perhaps this provides an example of the pragmatic approach of the British where the police authorities simply do not have the money to install cameras in each of the metal boxes constructed along the highways for this purpose. The signs act as a deterrent. There may or may not be a camera in the box, but the sign has the effect of making the motorist slow down nonetheless. In Germany it may be the principle that is important. It is against the law to speed, so if we catch you out you are in trouble. Cortina (1998), in looking at business ethics in Spain, refers to certain moral representative characters of each culture that provide a moral reference mark, such as the public school headmaster, explorer and engineer in Victorian England; and the Prussian officer, the professor and the social democrat in Wilhelm's Germany. She suggests that even for modern Spain the best representative characters of the moral system of values would be the warrior, the saint and the rogue. She suggests that none of these is concerned with wealth creation. The warrior is after glory, the saint renounces wealth, seeking unity with God from a position of disinterestedness and detachment. The rogue is an antihero, living without working, bucking the system and surviving. It is this attempt to survive at the expense of other people's stupidity that leads the rogue to discover that the great ideals are only facades rather than reflecting the reality of the situation. As a result, she suggests, he comes away from all his endeavours thoroughly fleeced.

Cortina (1998) further asserts than none of these characters place value on productive work and wealth creations. This may be the reason why despite its strategic position for trade and its being part of Europe, Spain has not obtained the levels of industrialization of its other European neighbours. This, she suggests, may be a cultural attribute, a lifestyle question, and linked to Catholicism, with traditional Catholic culture in Spain curtailing wealth creation. However, this assertion is contested, as she points out, not least because one of the more influential Spanish streams of philosophical thought, the Salamanca School (sixteenth century), not only did not condemn trade and wealth creation, but appeared to have made contributions to classic liberal thought: pointing to the importance of trade for carrying out work as a community, and in peace, and seeking the common good in the different parts of the world. However, another factor was the dominance of the nobility in support of the king and church over the nascent bourgeoisie. This was the case right through the nineteenth century, explaining Spain's backwardness in trade and industry up to and beyond this period. Yet there were also considerable differences between the different Christian kingdoms of Spain, particularly between Castile and Aragon (comprising Aragon, Valencia, Majorca and Barcelona). The latter developed an active commercial system throughout the Mediterranean and contributed significantly to the financial resources for the conquest of America. However, Cortina (1998) remarks on the fact that the most highly industrial regions of modern Spain, the Basque country and Catalonia, are where the Catholic Church is most dominant. Having said this, she believes that the Basque country's connection with England, and Catalonia's with the rest of Europe, was more of a factor in industrialization than the Catholic Church.

The nineteenth century also heralded a disjuncture between liberalism and the Catholic Church. This was a censure of modernism, as well as of economic liberalism, which was now being seen by the church as the desire for individual gain albeit the driving force of the economy. It was seen as endangering the common good. Cortina (1998) provides the view that it was the church's social doctrine that provided the halfway house between selfish individualism as the economy's driving force, and collectivism (such as in Marxist doctrine) that cancels out personal conscience. She traces this as the root of the social market economy in Spain. Business and entrepreneurs that abided by this social doctrine under Franco developed such a social model that gave rise to a strong cooperative movement. Under Franco Catholicism became the official doctrine of the state, later to be overturned after his death in 1975 in the new constitution of 1978. This heralded a period of some confusion over ethical matters, where three influential groups rejected ethics: the traditional Catholics asserting that there could be no lay ethics outside the moral foundation of the church; the Positivists who believed the economy and business should follow the dictates of economic rationality; and the Marxists who rejected capitalism and assumed that there could be no ethical business, that it is part of the bourgeois ideology and that the firm is a place of class confrontation and not of cooperation.

Yet in the meantime Spain was busy building its welfare state: schooling, health care and social benefits were granted for all through state interventions and tax policies. This was a new departure for Spain, but nonetheless represented a convergence of social democracy and the church's social doctrine (Cortina, 1998). However, this takes us into the 1980s (Thatcherism/ Reaganomics) where Cortina believes the character of the 'rogue' could often be seen through financial speculation (*cultura del pelotazo*). There were a number of corruption scandals at this time. This led to an upsurge in interest in business ethics in the 1990s. In business itself, this appears to be a reaction to scandals and an attempt to make legitimate the company's *raison d'être*, as well as regaining trust, but Cortina says little about what is actually happening as a whole in Spanish business and organization. She does allude to the moral theory that is emerging from the business schools and universities. This has led to separate schools of thought: based on the church's social doctrine; on the tenets of economic liberalism and personal ethics; on the social market economy focusing on the common good (also in line with the social doctrine); on ethics as an important part of organizational culture and organizational learning; and (the group to which Cortina herself belongs), dialogue-oriented business ethics, the discourse ethics of the German and Social Europe tradition.

Cortina (1998) concludes that this background of globalization, the building of a social Europe and protecting people's rights in both Spain and Europe and the world as a whole, entails the need for a dialogue among those different groups affected by business activity, among those different theoreticians from the schools of thought described above, and across different cultures, allowing different contributions through this intercultural dialogue.

By exploring two diverse countries, among the many that constitute the European Union, it is possible to discern the quest to build a social Europe, and the apparent corollary of this in discourse ethics. Catholicism has been a major influence in continental Europe, as has feudalism. Both these influences have been seen as inhibiting business activity, whereas the lack of these strong influences in the United States has been seen to fuel the development of a free-market economy, and associated approaches to management ethics in pragmatism, utilitarianism and a form of deontology in the quest to develop codes of ethics which set down principles that managers and staff are expected to adhere to.

Despite the strong influence of Kantian deontological ethics, particularly in Germany, it would seem that more modern influence from Hegel and more recently Habermas is more in evidence through discourse ethics. Yet what are the influences on the new EU members from the former Soviet bloc? In the next few pages it is possible to allude to this, yet the focus will be on Russia, as it stands outside the EU. Is it rushing headlong towards a free-market economy? Is it retaining some of the vestiges of the Soviet system? Is it linking in with Europe's social democratic approach, and is discourse ethics relevant here? Also, what has Russia left over in the countries of Eastern and Central Europe?

From the beginning of this chapter, Europe has been seen as a dynamic. The quest of this chapter is to present the contributors, processes and consequences of that dynamic, particularly its impact on the values of management, and what managers do. There is still some way to go. Britain, perhaps regarded as a cuckoo in the European nest, provides its own inputs into this dynamic. Islam also is increasingly important in trying to understand this dynamic. Turkey, a long-time applicant to the EU, provides a link to a more thorough discussion of Islam in the world in Chapter 7. Finally, what holds the current chapter together is a need to find out the implications for managers: their values and their actions.

Russia: towards a social Europe, or free-market economy?

Russia appears not to have a long tradition of evolving ethical theory, with some commentators asserting that the more recent transition to a market economy has caused much moral confusion, and certainly legal confusion in conflicts between communist ideology and the move towards private property and market dynamics (Apressyan, 1997; Puffer and McCarthy, 1998; Avtonomov, 2006). However, Apressyan (1997) states that there were 'certain traditions of ethicality and socially responsible business in Russia' prior to the Soviet period, increasing in importance after 1861 and the abolition of serfdom, but then destroyed after the 1917 October revolution. Puffer and McCarthy (1998), for example, see the main influences on current management ethics in Russia as: (1) the culture, history and religion of Russia over the centuries; (2) communist ideology and the central planning; and (3) the current transitional context including the legal system, government policy and social values. They see as a main contributing factor Russia's turbulent history of oppressive regimes that have created confusion about the role of business in society. A high value placed on strong authority and collective behaviour, including the communist era, has had a major influence, they assert. Through the Russian Orthodox Church, tsars, landowners and communist elite, the population has been mainly subjugated to the values and behaviours of leaders. They believe that this has stifled individual freedoms, and together with social and economic controls, has repressed business. The Orthodox Church appears to have not valued work or business as a religious virtue in the way that Protestantism had. They argue that people who engaged in business were morally suspect. Rather, the Church emphasized obedience and deference, as well as collective values. Puffer and McCarthy (1998) conclude that the environment for centuries has been one of central control, oppression and lack of individual freedoms. This carried on under communist rule, with the exception that the Communists tried to instil a work ethic. This was more designed to serve Communist goals. Reward systems were designed to recognize collective achievements rather than those of the individual. Now, Puffer and McCarthy (1998) conclude that this was not very efficient, saying that people had little incentive to work hard, and to take responsibility for their own actions. They state that people were mainly disillusioned with this. They also relate the role of unrealistic state production targets, which were mainly subverted by factory managers inflating production figures in order to meet these targets.

Communism as a socio-economic system is widely denigrated, particularly with the excesses of the Stalin era, and then the ultimate collapse of the Soviet system at the end of the 1980s. However, the achievements of Russia from a largely agrarian and semi-feudal society in 1917, to it becoming a global superpower, with advance technology sufficient to put a man on the moon, and blow up the planet by the 1960s, as well as the ability to largely abolish poverty, belies a view of gross inefficiencies and a socio-economic system that demotivated people and discouraged work. This perhaps goes back to the discussion in Chapter 5 on human rights versus development, for example in the context of China. There is no doubt that the Soviet system's final collapse was due to both internal and external contradictions. Perhaps the repression of individual freedoms just became too much, or the pressures from international capital proved too much to sustain a protected system based on internal markets within the USSR. Perhaps the prospects of gains from rent-seeking activity by the elite became too attractive.

This has no doubt come at a cost to social aspects such as full employment throughout the former Soviet bloc. The advent of private property and private enterprise at the end of the 1980s has no doubt caused problems and confusion, as Puffer and McCarthy (1998) relate. Communist philosophy, which must have been so heavily imbued within the population for it to have survived for so many years, did not recognize private property or profits. Yet both became legalized and mandated. Many laws were passed, but often contradicted one another, and amended or rescinded. Often they were inconsistently enforced. Little direction was provided for the conduct of business or the management of commercial enterprises. People entering such management responsibility included former party officials, managers of state enterprises, and also criminal elements, often with quite different values: those of the former communist system, those with more 'universal' or religious values, and those with criminal or unscrupulous motives. Puffer and McCarthy (1998) also assert that others would simply have been ignorant of a market economy and what constituted ethical behaviour in these circumstances.

Russia appears to be quite different to many of its former satellites such as the Czech Republic and Poland which have continued with the separation of the state from business. Avtonomov (2006) maintains that under Putin, the state and its interests were strengthened. This includes state control of the mass media and large profitable enterprises such as energy and railways. In fact Avtonomov likened Putin's ambitions to those of Pinochet in Chile: to enforce neoliberal economy policy through authoritarian rule. He believes that this return to state control has been influenced by Russia's history of absolutism, with a weak or non-existent civil society as a counter to the 'simple hierarchical societal structure with relatively homogeneous agents subordinate to absolutist power' (2006: 7). One of the side effects of state influence is the continuous state pressure on business: continual visits 'from local police, fire and sanitation inspectors which in principle should promote consumers' interests but in practice want nothing but bribes' (2006: 7). This means that often the huge burden of certification and licensing can be flouted with fake products as well as potentially harmful ones being on sale. Eighty per cent of consumer goods need certification, with 4,000 agencies involved (compared with ten in the EU). Avtonomov (2006) asserts that local civil servants have largely taken over the rackets that were previously the preserve of criminal gangs. Policemen receive the major part of their income from such activities according to a survey carried out in 2000–2. Prices for such services include US$1000 for the suspension of investigation into your business, US$10,000–20,000 to be released from custody and US$10,000–30,000 to get your competitor arrested.

For Avtonomov (2006: 8) the main issue in considering business ethics is the balance between state, market and social justice. He concludes that the 'Russian experience in balancing state and market can be called predominantly negative. We started with having too much state (in the Soviet times), then we had too much market (under Yeltsin), and now it looks that we have too much state and too much market simultaneously: the business is over-controlled and some state functions are commercialized.'

In addition to this balance between state and business, which Avtonmov concludes is not in a situation of mutual mistrust, Russians do not regard their country as socially just. There is a mistrust of businessmen, although he adds that at the same time a large part of the population wants their children to go into business. The state still has a high level of legitimacy owing to the tradition of paternalism, yet he states that (at the time of writing) Putin's state does not want to be paternalistic, pursuing a neoliberal 'minimal' social policy. It would appear from Avtonomov's analysis it is exactly the components that make up Europe's social partnering (namely business, civil society and state) that exist in Russia in a state of mutual distrust. Where relationships exist between business and the state, this partially exists in a relationship of corruption. Civil society remains very weak. However, the change to a market economy and the new labour laws of 1990 changed the status of Russian trade unions from being of the state and party apparatus to effectively becoming, as non-governmental organizations, the largest civil society organizations.

Their previous role was in the enforcement of labour law, and maintaining industrial harmony in line with managers' responsibilities. As the party and the state represented workers' interests, and organizational managers were the custodians of the interests of the state and workers, there was no contradiction for the trade unions in aligning with management. In a market economy this has somewhat changed, with trade unions facing a new role in protecting the interests of the workers. This new role also was pushed along by the radical workers' protests in 1989 being undertaken outside and against the official trade unions. In fact, these 'unofficial' protests and industrial actions, which contributed significantly to the downfall of the Soviet system, gave birth to a whole number of trade unions independent of the traditional ones. Yet these have been difficult to sustain over the years. They have however made an impact on the traditional unions that take more seriously their role of protecting the interest of workers. With vested interests in the continuation of state support at higher levels in the trade union structure, local initiatives have often not been supported by regional headquarters. Clarke and Pringle (2008: 24) state that:

In Russia, there has been a steady decline in worker militancy since the containment of the protest of the 1990s and economic recovery since 1998, but relative social peace and the collapse of political opposition has deprived the traditional trade unions of their political leverage and enabled the Putin regime to try to marginalise them. In this context the traditional unions had no alternative but to move to revitalise their base in order to defend their political position by demonstrating the value to the government of the institutions of social partnership.

This may well be an indication of the move towards European social partnering. Yet as Jackson (2002a, 2002b) noted, there appears to be a movement towards some of the hard aspects of managing human resource management in the early 1990s, almost as part of an eagerness to adopt Western, and perhaps American, management know-how, rather than, for example, German approaches to social democracy. This may well be changing in the light of more recent events, although Putin's government appeared to be forcing through neoliberal economic solutions. Iankova and Turner's (2004) thesis that the transition to a free-market economy is ironically driving initiatives in social partnering may well apply to Russia, despite it still remaining distinct from Europe. Russia is the EU's third biggest trading partner and has signed a number of agreements with the EU including economic cooperation.

The transition to a market economy has raised particular ethical issues that organizational managers are having to deal with. Puffer and McCarthy (1998) list:

- extortion, by the Russian mafia and, as discussed above, often government officials;
- managerial buy-outs of enterprises where former state enterprise managers have subverted the intention of creating citizen shareholders, by accumulating large percentages of shares in their own enterprises, allowing them to exercise power, often detrimentally to the enterprise, gaining rights and benefits cheaply with little responsibility and risk of failure, and going against well-established norms in Russian society of fair and just behaviour in transactions with others;

- breaking contracts including non-payment of debts to companies by the government and delaying wage payments to state employees, of pensions and student grants;
- ignoring arbitrary laws which appear not to make sense to business people, like manipulating production figures in the Soviet era, but in the transition period ignoring contradictory laws where the authors believe managers are applying situational ethics, yet this might be detrimental to the principle of deferring to authority and to the transition to a market economy;
- personal favouritism (*Blat*), which has been a common practice in Russia for centuries, and involves currying favour with influential people to get favourable treatment, sometimes with money changing hands, may be considered against principles of fair dealing yet may have been necessary in order to survive;
- employee layoffs, which have historically been considered unethical in Russia, and have often been resisted in the transitional economy which by and large have ultimately made large-scale redundancies inevitable.

Although Puffer and McCarthy (1998) apply Donaldson and Dunfee's (1994) integrative social contracts theory to these issues, by way of assessing whether or not management actions could be considered ethical or not within the Russian transitional context, this may well be missing the point. Donaldson has devised this and other methods or principles to decide (perhaps 'objectively') whether or not an action can be considered ethical or not. Laying down such principles for ethical behaviour appears important in the American context. What appears to be important in the context of a social Europe is the ability to discuss and gain agreement on what is ethical by the actors themselves (discourse ethics). It is not clear the extent to which social partnering in Russia provides an opportunity and a context in which to do this.

Closing case: Turkey and the EU

Turkey is only partly in Europe, has mainly a Muslim population and has been a candidate to join the EU since 1999, although as far back as 1963 it had signed an association agreement with the then Common Market that promised eventual membership of the trading bloc. In order to join the EU a country must show that politically it has a stable democracy with institutions that guarantee the rule of law and respect and protect human rights. Economically it must be a functioning market economy and able to cope with membership of the single market. In legal terms it must be able to comply with the obligations of membership and adopt the body of EU law. Turkey has done much to address issues surrounding its record on human rights. It has lifted bans on Kurdish broadcasting and has released Kurdish activists from detention. It has also introduced a package of reforms which have abolished the death penalty, outlawed torture in prisons and curbed military influence. Yet there have been some hiccups along the way such as the desire to keep a clause in the penal code banning adultery, which was later dropped.

Those in favour of Turkey's membership point to the prospect of the country's potential economic growth as a result of membership, the vitality of a young workforce, as well as a huge army and a bulwark against Islamic fundamentalism. Its strategic position straddling Europe and Asia is seen by some as a plus. Yet there is also opposition. This has involved objection to including a predominantly Muslim nation which is largely in Asia within the EU. This would increase the proportion of Muslims in the EU from 3 per cent to 20 per cent. Similarly, objections appear to be around the extension of EU borders to Iraq, Iran and Syria, which may threaten stability. Critics also argue that its sheer size and levels of poverty could drain the resources of the EU, and there could also be a wave of Turkish migrants across Europe (from BBC News, 2004).

We have seen that there appears to be both contradictions and synergies between the EU's apparent drive towards neoliberal economic policies and social partnering. In order to meet the criteria for EU membership, Turkey has undertaken a whole series of reforms driven by such economic policies. Acar (2009: 19) tells us that:

Based on the Turkish government's serious efforts between 2002 and 2004, which included a series of economic and political reforms, EU authorities were satisfied that the Copenhagen criteria have been observed. Accordingly, Turkey and the EU started accession negotiations on 3 October 2005. Despite strong objections and resistance by the state bureaucracy, judiciary, political opposition and the labour unions, the JDP government carried out a large privatisation programme between 2003 and 2008, producing revenue of nearly $40 billion.

This has had the effect of significantly increasing FDI and making Turkey the sixth largest economy in Europe. Acar (2009) posits that there is no inherent contradiction between Islam and democracy and a free-market economy, and the fact other Muslim countries are not democratic and do not have free-market economies is more to do with historical circumstance than with Islam. He points to the fact (2009: 17) that 'Muslim scholars agree that the principle of *shura* (consultative decision-making) is the source of democratic ethics in Islam. The first Islamic state was based on a social contract, was constitutional in character and had a ruler who ruled with the explicit written consent of all the citizens of the state.'

Yet to what extent is Turkey building a system of social partnering? It would seem that ignoring the opposition of labour unions in economic reforms does not indicate a move towards dialogue and discourse ethical approaches to management decision making. Certainly Cam (2002) has presented evidence to suggest that Turkey's move towards a free-market economy, among much internal advice from neoliberal economic experts and agency, has led to a rise in temporary employment, a decline in unionization, workers' employment prospects declining and earnings falling in real terms. He argues that these reforms have led to Turkey being a better place for capital yet a growing inequality in income distribution and political unrest.

More recently Koçer (2007) has described the partnership between employers and trade unions in Turkey, using the metal industry as an example as 'partnership in coercion'. He sees this as a partnership that is joined in willingly by the trade unions, which supports the interests of employers to the detriment of the union's own membership. He distinguishes this from what has been called in former Soviet countries a 'coercive partnership' where unions are involved reluctantly in a partnership which supports the interests of the employers to the detriment of the union's members. Both types of partnership appear to result from the union being in a weak situation, and posing no apparent threat to employers due to job insecurity. Yet with institutional support, such as in Germany, this may not place the union in a weak partnership position sufficient to represent the interest of employers rather than employees. Other institutional arrangements, such as in Russia where unions have inherited a welfare function from the Soviet era, render unions vulnerable to employer support for their continual survival. So, such coercive partnerships are likely to arise in contexts with low job security, and the institutional/legal structure allowing no protection for unions, and therefore pose no threat to employees. Even in post-1997 Britain institutional arrangements protect trade unions and provide positive incentives for social partnerships. Koçer (2007) posits that in Turkey the anti-union legislation plus low job security provides the conditions for both coercive partnerships where unions unwillingly participate in cooperation that is at odds with their members' interests, and conditions where they willingly cooperate. The latter appears to evolve where the employer has a strong market position and is able to make demands on union leadership, where the union has weak internal democracy, and where there is competition among trade unions.

If these conditions can be generalized to other industries in Turkey, it seems unlikely that social partnering can lead to, or be a part of, solving ethically important issues by discursive methods in organizational and societal decision making.

Implications for international managers

The concept of Social Europe appears to be a strong tradition within the tenets of the European Union, with discourse ethics as its corollary in the field of management ethics. Within this tradition Cortina (1998: 415) suggests that for a company to carry out its work legitimately it should take account of at least five points of reference:

1. An *Aristotelian moment* consisting of analysing business activity (praxis) to elucidate the aims through which it assumes meaning and social legitimacy.
2. The proper *mechanisms* to achieve the aims, which in a modern society are market, competition and search for profit.
3. The legal-political framework of that society, expressed in democratic countries in the constitution and legislation in force. Nevertheless, since constitutions are dynamic, the driving force behind reforms must be a modern ethical principle of legitimacy.
4. A *Kantian moment* as this principle is procedural and responds to the requirements of *critical moral conscience of that society*. In societies with a liberal democracy such requirements are the ones made by the principle of the ethics of discourse, which orders that the interests of all those affected should be taken into account through a dialogue.
5. A *consequentialist moment* in the concrete making of decisions, as is proper to an ethics of *convinced responsibility*.

In practice, how can managers stimulate what Frederik Bird (discussed in Beschorner, 2006: 135) has termed 'good conversation'? He proposes cultivating this through individual and organizational learning processes. The features of 'good conversation', a variant of discourse ethics, include the following features: 'Good conversations are recognizable'; 'Speakers are attentive'; 'Conversations move forward reciprocally'; 'Communications are rational'; 'Communications are honest'; 'Speakers keep the promises they make'; 'The exchanges remain civil'. He notes that ways of cultivating 'good conversation' include the following:

Generally:

1. Encourage people to speak up because it matters and makes a difference.
2. De-professionalize moral discussions and decision making.

3. Allow and encourage organizational dissent.
4. Help people to develop their abilities to hear and be attentive.
5. Allow conversations to develop: avoid premature closure.

Organizationally:
1. Define speaking up as part of every manager's job description, not just as trouble shooters but as quality managers.
2. Transform auditing function from one-way policing to two-way interactive activitites.
3. Institute regular discussions of ethics in each organizational unit.
4. Establish multiple media for employee voicing.
5. Establish training programmes in conflict resolution. (Bird, 1996)

Questions for managers
1. To what extent does your organization follow a discourse ethics process or philosophy, and how useful is this?
2. How can such an approach be developed in your organization?
3. How can this be used or adapted to include 'good conversation' across different 'Third Spaces', and how could it contribute to mutual understanding and synergy?

An agenda for research

Although the comparison of 'business ethics' across different countries may have some use in trying to understand different value structures, and the relative importance of 'ethics' and different approaches, it is very limited in providing a way forward. It may provide limited description, and be initially useful for managers operating across countries and in trying to make sense of differences in regard to ethicality. This usefulness could be significantly enhanced by employing Crane and Matten's (2004) questions discussed at the beginning of this chapter. These are:
1. Who is responsible for ethical conduct in business?
2. Who is the key actor in business ethics?
3. What are the key guidelines for ethical behaviour?
4. What are the key issues in business ethics?
5. What is the most dominant stakeholder management approach?
It may also be useful to focus on the three facets of the socio-cultural domain outlined in Chapter 2, and discussed at the beginning of the current chapter, namely:
- *context* (social order, rules and institutions)
- *content* (knowledge, meaning and values) and
- *conduct* (social interaction).

It is perhaps through these three aspects that we can begin to understand in more depth the individual countries within Europe. However, the
focus in this chapter and the preceding one is on the cultural interfaces
involved: those between the USA and Europe, those between East and
West Europe, those between non-member states such as Russia and EU,
those between Turkey and the EU, and probably the interfaces between
European colonizers and their former colonized (and for example the impact
of national and cultural identities in European countries through immigration). Also to go beyond description involves what Robertson (2002: 364) has
described as 'normative' ('what ought to be', and the province of philosophers) which she appears to pitch against 'descriptive' ('what is', and the
province of social scientists) research, and which the current text suggests
should come together.

Hence, in a way, Flyvbjerg (2001) provides a way forward for social science
to integrate the normative with the descriptive, and discourse ethics may
provide the way forward in practice to make this approach work. Yet Jurgen
Habermas's well-known dictum that 'in discourse the unforced force of the
better argument prevails' may be challenged by postcolonial theory which
indicates that despite one's attempt to neutralize power relations within dialogue, 'mimicry' in Bhabha's (1994) terms (discussed in Chapter 5) may still
reflect the dominant ideology in geopolitical relations. It may be possible to
rationale the neutralization of power in an immediate dialogue, but the overarching geopolitical and historical relations at the macro level may neutralize
this neutralization.

It may therefore be possible to operationalize Flyvbjerg's interpretation
of *phronetics*, by posing and gaining answers to his four questions in a dialogue situation, yet still remaining is the difficulty of operationalizing post-
colonial theory, by identifying the consequences of mimicry in practice.

Questions for researchers
1. How can discourse ethics be used as the basis for exploring and
   agreeing on answers to Flyvbjerg's four *phronetic* questions?
2. How can power be neutralized, or controlled for, in a dialogue
   situation?
3. How can mimicry be investigated and identified?

7 The visibility of religion in ethical management: Islam and the Middle East

It is not possible to explore management ethics in the modern Arab world without focusing on Islam. This is the first chapter in the current book that overtly looks at ethics through a religious lens. As Nanji (1993: 117) says:

Since the modern conception of religion familiar to most people in the West assumes a theoretical separation between specifically religious and perceived secular activity, some aspects of contemporary Muslim discourse, which does not accept such a separation, appear strange and often retrogressive. Where such discourse, expressed in what appears to be traditional religious language, has become linked to radical change or violence, it has unfortunately deepened stereotypical perceptions about Muslim fanaticism, violence, and cultural and moral difference.

These words were penned almost a decade before 9/11 after which so much, but also so little, changed. Issues, such as 'veiling' have for many years provoked ethical reactions in the West. Yet antagonisms between the West's perception of Islam and Muslims' reactions to Western-led globalization have been exacerbated by the attacks on the Twin Towers in New York, and subsequent US-led military action in Afghanistan and Iraq.

The Arab world and Islamic philosophers and scientists have achieved much alongside the growth of civilization in the Middle East together with trade and economic development at a time when Europe was still groping around in the Dark Ages. Islam developed initially in the Arabian peninsular doing much to unify diverse Arab communities, and as a progressive religion did much to overthrow the old tribal ways. Like other religions it also borrowed heavily from these 'pagan' ways and adopted (and adapted) features such as a strong paternalism, communalism and family-oriented society. With the spread of Islam along trade routes, the products of this internationalization came back to Arab society, enriching or perhaps corrupting Islam, but nonetheless developing it. This development has taken various paths. Yet the West's perception of Islam is often coloured by news reports of, for example, the Taliban in Afghanistan. Yet, Nanji (1993: 117) warns that 'no one response among the many Muslim societies in the world, can be regarded as normative for all Muslims'. This is an issue that will be returned to towards the end of this chapter.

Islam might be considered far more pervasive as a religion in society as a whole than Christianity, and often difficult to split from the secular. In the Arab countries, many states are based on Islam, and abide by Shar'ia law, or a particular interpretation of it. As such, Islam provides the basis for an ethical system, with specific principles, many of which can and are applied in a business/management situation. In this chapter, social partnering, which was explored in relation to Europe in the last chapter, is again taken up in relation to the principles laid down by the main sources of Islam. In this context, it is argued that paternalism is seen as a major influence, and is discussed in the positive, non-Western mode that Aycan (2006) suggests. This also raises an important issue for both international managers and researchers: gender relations and the role of women.

Opening case: women and Islamic dress

The following was penned by a young Muslim woman[1] living in London who has chosen to wear the *jilbab*. As a student, she explores the relationship between identity and Islamic clothing, particularly with regard to fashion.

The main focus of Islamic clothing is the *Jilbab*, a long, loose dress that reaches below the ankles, long sleeves together with a headscarf which covers the hair and neck, leaving visible only the hands and face. It is worn by Muslim woman as an identity and is not projected as fashionable attire but rather as a recommendation of their religious belief, Islam. Muslim women in the West are increasingly sporting Islamic attire. The editor of a leading Muslim magazine recently said, 'Modesty is only one of many reasons why a woman wears a scarf. It can be a very political choice too.'

Islamic attire has suffered much controversy in the West. A young student in France said, 'I get strange looks when I wear my headscarf around town. Some have a look of pity, that says "poor girl, she is oppressed"' (quoted from BBC News website article: In Quotes: French Muslim Voices, http://news.bbc.co.uk/1/hi/world/europe/4376500.stm).

The priority for Shariah law is the wearing of the headscarf, which has been opposed by many women activists, who argue that the regulation requiring wearing of the *Jilbab* is in practice discriminatory towards non-Muslims as well as an

---

[1] This is taken from the dissertation work of Hayat Charkaoui, at the time (2009) a third-year undergraduate student at Middlesex University.

invasion of a woman's private life (Parker 2005). Western feminist theory assumes that veiling is proof of the gender oppression of women in Islam and the assurance that Islamic society is not as progressive as Western society. Such expressions support the Islam/West dichotomy, being indicative of post 9/11 chauvinism in the West and an increased defensiveness in Islamic cultures. In Australia the issue has become sensitive particularly since the Cronulla riots and episodes where scarves have been snatched from the heads of Muslim women.

The increased media attention to countries like Afghanistan and Iran in the past several years has caused a renewed fascination in the West with the *Hijab*. Also what is frequently questioned is the status of Muslim women. Even though *Hijab* is more properly interpreted as 'modest dress', it is characteristically used to refer to the headscarf some Muslim women wear, covering their hair and neck, but not their face.

In December 2001, *Time* magazine published a feature entitled 'Lifting the Veil' proclaiming, 'Nowhere in the Muslim world are women treated as equals'. The article made an attempt to comment on modest dress reporting, 'Coverings are technically optional' but added, 'Some women, including some feminists, wear them because they like them. They find that the veil liberates them from unwanted gazes and hassles from men.'

Western feminists like Kate Millet, a prominent American feminist and the author of *Sexual Politics*, has also been condemned heavily for her book *Going to Iran*, where she documents her experiences in Iran after the Iranian Revolution. Homa Hoodfar, a Canadian Muslim feminist suggested that Millet's own story seems to propose that she went in order 'to lecture her Iranian sisters on feminism and women's rights, as though her political ideas, life expectations, and experiences were universally applicable'. From a Western perspective, it seems simple to view oneself as the liberator of 'oppressed' Muslim women everywhere and support them to throw aside the veils that purportedly enslave them.

The Muslim community is not completely homogenous, and attitudes towards modesty vary not only from country to country, but also from community to community. Within the largely Arab/Muslim populated countries of the Middle East there is also some disagreement among people as to whether the Qur'an necessitates Muslim women to wear the *Hijab* (head scarf) or the *Jilbab* (long black dress covering all but the feet and hands). For Arab immigrants into Western countries like the UK, the decision whether to cover or not by the women becomes even weightier in a country where women pride themselves on independence and feminism, often perceiving the Islamic way of covering as repressive. Therefore Muslim women who do choose to cover or veil in a predominantly Western society, are aware that they will stand out in a way they will not in the Middle East.

Although some argue that the *Hijab*, which is a recommendation of Islam, is oppressive to women, it should be noted that Mohammad, the founder of Islam, was amongst the world's greatest reformers on behalf of women. Islam, in fact, may be the only religion that officially specified women's rights and sought ways to defend them.

Iranian women, like Zahra Rahnavard, a playwright and president of Al-Zahra University, insist women in the West have been enslaved by fashion and makeup, turned into objects of sexual attention. 'The veil frees women from the shackles of fashion, and enables them to become human beings in their own right,' says Rahnavard. 'Once people cease to be distracted by women's physical appearance, they can begin to hear their views and recognize the inner person.'

So, whereas some Western women believe that the Islamic *Hijab* is oppressive and therefore hold a dislike to it, some Muslim women feel that Western fashion is oppressive to women as they have been 'enslaved' by fashion and makeup and portrayed as sexual objects.

At question is whether it is possible for Muslim women to integrate in a predominantly Western society without the need to assimilate. The interpretation of 'integration' by Western society is what Muslim women struggle with. It means that they have to decide how to blend with or into the fabric of the society while still retaining their religion, culture and values in a manner that is comfortable and satisfactory to them.

Organizational stakeholders and Islam

In the previous chapter on Europe we have seen that social partnering and the concept of a social Europe is an important one, and may well be, with discourse ethics, a major contribution of the region to international management ethics. We have also seen that a long-standing applicant to the EU, Turkey, a predominantly Muslim country, although a secular state, may not share the same principles of social partnering. This is not to say that all existing EU members share this in practice to the extent of the Northern European countries.

However, Beekun and Badawi (2005) argue that Islam actually lays down the main principles for a multiple organizational stakeholder model. Although this is more a manifesto than a work that draws on empirical evidence or gives examples of countries or organizations that are practicing such a stakeholder approach based on Islamic principles, it is worth looking at these principles through the eyes of these authors (and as they reflect the views of other authors such as Wilson, 2006, and Abuznaid, 2006), in order to better understand the potential contribution of Islam to the discourse on management ethics, particularly in the area of stakeholder management.

Beekun and Badawi (2005) assert that Islam adopts a stakeholder perspective that recognizes the rights of the owner and financiers of the business to make a profit, but not at the expense of the claims by other stakeholders. However, they state that Islam does not see that all stakeholders have equal claims. Owners, financiers and employees, including managers, have claims as a first priority group. The second priority group is that of suppliers and customers, and the final priority group includes all external parties. Unlike other stakeholder models, the authors propose that Islam sees these as moral claims, and that this emphasis on the moral core of business may help to protect rather than militate against a free-market system. Hence, although the moral business can pursue its economic goals, it should not do this at the expense of its moral obligations to society and others who may be affected by the business's actions.

They suggest that it is Islamic normative business ethics that unites Muslim countries and business in terms of the business dealings they aspire to, and that the sources of these ethics are contained in the business teaching of the Qur'an, as the verbatim word of God revealed through the Prophet Muhammad, the *Sunnah* or *Hadith*, which are the 'words, actions and approvals' of the Prophet Muhammad, and the *Ijmaa'* or consensus of scholars and *Qiyaas* or analogy. Both these are derived from the Qur'an and *Hadith*, with analogy being a ruling based on a new situation by using a similar situation dealt with in the Qur'an or *Hadith*.

A fundamental principle in Islam is that of trusteeship, where the human race is considered to be the trustee of God on Earth. As part of this trust, a person must emulate the behaviour of the Prophet. The word *khuluq* used in the Qur'an for this pattern of behaviour is derived from the word *akhlaq*, which they state is the comparable word for 'ethics' in Islam. When a person is acting out the role of trustee, a Muslim is performing an act of worship. Any act done with pure intentions, including work and business, can be considered an act of worship. The authors conclude that the desire to please God through productive work at any level can be a strong motivator for the Muslim worker.

Another principle that the authors contend contributes towards a stakeholder approach in Islam is the concept of justice ('*adl* – 'equity, balance'; and *qist* – 'share, portion, measure'). Muslims are asked to behave justly to all, by doing things in a balanced manner and avoiding extremes. A balanced transaction is also just. At the same time justice involves giving everyone their proper due.

A third principle in Islamic ethics is that of benevolence or kindness to others. The same word, *Ihsaan*, also means excellence, relating to striving for excellence in work, again focusing on behaviour as an act of worship.

These principles, according to the authors, can be seen in the approaches to stakeholder management favoured by Islam. Trust, for example, is important in the relationship of managers to the shareholders in safeguarding investments and ensuring the firm only engages in permitted (*halal*) activities, and that business is conducted in a balanced way according to the concepts of justice (*'adl, qist*) and excellence (*Ihsaan*).

Shareholders as stakeholders

Beekun and Badawi (2005) also state that the need to balance maximizing value with fairness to other stakeholders is seen in the prohibition of charging or paying interest (*riba*). Shareholders' capital is not seen as a factor of production and cannot earn a return. It has to be turned into a physical asset. Islam does not forbid a return on capital. It forbids a predetermined return on money capital which is inconsequential to the outcome of an enterprise. This reflects the concept of justice (*'adl, qist*) in that a shareholder, or banker, should not receive a predetermined income from his capital when other stakeholders are bearing all the risk. Islamic banks provide capital on the basis of a business partnership, where often the businessperson provides the balance. The parties will then share profit or loss in accordance with the proportion of their investment. In any such partnership trust is an important principle, in accordance with Islamic principles.

The authors provide an example of a slightly different type of partnership (*musharakah*) that also avoids interest-bearing relationships, used by the Sudanese Islamic Bank involved in rural development. This is a joint enterprise where all partners share in the profits and losses. Typically the small farmer is unable to offer collateral prior to financing. Instead the Bank will own the equipment such as tractors and water pumps, and will maintain these. The small farmers will contribute their land, management and labour. The Bank also will provide professional services of veterinarians and agriculturalists where these are required. The Bank will receive 25 per cent of any profits, but will bear the losses if for example the crop fails through adverse weather conditions. This partnership arrangement has, the authors add, had a very positive influence on the area.

Employees as stakeholders

Justice and fairness (*qist*, or giving the employee their due, and *'adl*, or behaving in a balanced manner) and the associated concept of paying special attention to employee competence, the authors assert, is key in the firm's relationship with its employees. However, they decry what appears to be contravening this principle in more conservative Islamic nations such as Saudi Arabia where only 3 per cent of the work force comprises women. Hence the basing of a meritocracy on competence rather than other considerations such as gender, appears to have been set aside by a more 'conservative interpretation of Islamic precepts' (Beekun and Badawi 2005: 137). The authors assert that the central concepts of trusteeship, human dignity and responsibility are presented in a gender-neutral way in the Qur'an. They state that the only basis for superiority is piety and righteousness. As part of this concept of fairness, it is also the employer's responsibility to ensure the worker is not exploited, and in fact that he is looked after as a shepherd would look after his flock. Not only does this imply the principle of benevolence as the authors suggest, but also indicates what Aycan (2006) has described as paternalism with her positive inflection on this term. It may well be that paternalism is inherent within an Islamic approach. This point will be returned to later.

Also in dealings with employees, Beekun and Badawi (2005) contend that wage equity has been a key feature in Islamic business for centuries. However, despite the principles of fairness in the concept that fair wages are paid and workers are not exploited, conditions of child labour still exist in Muslim countries (such as Nike's now well-publicized employment of children in Indonesia with the apparent connivance of the government).

Certainly hard work and productivity is encouraged, but this should not be at the expense of the young and weak. So, the authors conclude that, though the welfare mentality might be discouraged, welfare is seen as appropriate.

There also appears to be a discouragement of religious intolerance towards employees where the Qur'an says 'Unto you your religion, and unto me my religion' (106:8). The authors suggest that this is consistent with the practice of providing employees time for prayer no matter what their religion. They give the example of the early days of Islam when Jews in the city of Medina were given such freedoms to live according to their faith, and more latterly in the Saudi food company of Savola following the principles of *'adl*, and *ihsaan* in its relations with Muslim and non-Muslim staff.

Similarly, if the firm has responsibilities towards employees under Islamic principles, so have employees towards the firm, in terms of trust and loyalty. This involves their dealings with the organization itself, in being honest and truthful, but also with regard to external relationships where also the employee is in a position of trust in terms of secrecy and conflicts of interests.

Derivative stakeholders

These include the company's customers, suppliers, debtors, competitors and the environment. Relations with these stakeholders involve putting all contractual obligations in writing and fulfilling these contracts. It also involves not interfering with a free market by such devices as price manipulation such as hoarding (aspects that are likely to affect both customers and competitors). In Islam the principle is that the market is free to respond to supply and demand. Monopolies are not condemned *per se*, for example when utilities operate to facilitate business and for the benefit of society, only when they interfere with prices and the free supply of goods. There are also stipulations in Islam to be honest in business dealings, not to cover up defects in products for example or commit fraud, as there is no *caveat emptor* (let the buyer beware) in Islam. It is assumed that both parties deal honestly with each other and disclose all information about the product. In dealing with debtors Islam extols benevolence and kindness, but not to the extent of being taken advantage of by debtors, as a debt is a trust.

Although Beekun and Badawi (2005) assert that bribery is expressly forbidden in Islam's primary sources, it is prevalent in some majority Muslim countries such as Pakistan and Bangladesh, but mainly absent from others such as Oman, Bahrain and Qatar. Yet they also state that it may be legitimate to pay a fee to quickly expedite a transaction that if not concluded might lead to a major loss or bankruptcy. That is being able to deal pragmatically in order to ensure the lesser of two evils.

Environmental protection also appears to be a key element of Islam with the concept of man as God's vice-regent on Earth, and entrusted with the natural environment. Private ownership rights are honoured in Islam, but not to the extent of causing threat to the public or environment. From early times Muslims were forbidden to slaughter animals in the street or their homes for the sake of public hygiene, nor to install a forge or mill in residential areas. Other similar public health and hygiene issues, and environmental protection are recognized in Islam.

Managing relationships

When looking back to Chapter 4, and the schematic of Table 4.1, it can be noticed that Islamic principles provide almost a complete guide to relationships with the different organizational stakeholders in decision making. As discussed then, management ethics involves anything concerning decisions that affect people. It involves relationships, and the values we attach to making decisions about those relationships. Religions, certainly the monotheistic ones such as Islam, provide guidelines for those relationships.

Responsibility for ethical conduct

In Chapter 6, of the six key questions that Crane and Matten (2004) ask about business ethics in America and Europe, it is worth here attending to the first: Who is responsible for ethical conduct in business? As we saw in Chapter 5, the American emphasis on ethical responsibility is with the individual where private and public domains appear to intertwine, and that enforcement is with the legal system if the excesses of a free-market economy are taken too far. In Europe (Chapter 6) responsibility is with the corporation and other institutions, with the individual conscience and values being left in the private domain. In the Islamic perspective the enforcement mechanism appears to be with the individual in relationship to his or her God. Actions are undertaken as a form of worship, and adherence to the principles of Islam and the word of God. The individual will be held accountable for their action by God. Beekun and Badawi (2005) contend that this is a far more powerful enforcement mechanism than government control.

Islam is, by these authors, deemed not simply a religion, but also a way of life. Saeed and Ahmed (1998) have previously asserted that ethics is deeply engrained in all Islamic concepts, and internationally does not provide a relativist approach but is absolute and deep-rooted with sound foundations. It could be claimed that many of the religious principles seen in Islam can also be found in Judaism and Christianity. For example Werner (2008) points to the Christian concept of 'stewardship' (also explored in Chapter 5 in relation to the United States) whereby God has entrusted the businessperson with the responsibility of their business and employees, and that they will be ultimately answerable to God for their actions.

Islam appears to be a large influence in many countries in the Middle East, the main focus in the current chapter. Yet although Beekun and Badawi (2005) have managed to demonstrate the connection of Islam to a morally oriented stakeholder approach, this is by no means the social partnering approach described in Chapter 6. The nature of the relationship among different stakeholders could be referred to as a benevolent paternalism. This may not simply be confined to Islam but may mix with the Arab culture prevalent in the region.

Arab culture, management and ethics

By first focusing on Islamic perspectives of management ethics, in providing principles for a company's dealings with the varied stakeholders that affect or are affected by managerial actions, and then now turning to Arab culture and management values, it is possible to understand some of the complexities of value structures within the Middle East. Ali (1995: 9) has stated, for example, that

the Arab societies suffer from cultural discontinuities, perhaps the most important factor that impedes the development of [a separate and distinct] Arab management thought. The Arab world, for over 500 years, has been under the direct and/or indirect influence of numerous foreign powers. Arabs, generation after generation, have lost attachments to their cultural heritages and principles. In fact, formal education ceased to exist until the early years of this century and cultural contact with mainstream Arab thought was lost.

Islam and Arab culture

Islam acted as a uniting force among competing Arab states and tribes, although failed to unite them into a single nation. Ali (1995) adds that in the early days of Islam (622–1258 CE) the Arabs made many contributions to enriching civilization and to establishing a state. Islam strengthened values of equity among people and of hard work, while providing the Arabs with a simple and practical ideology: a belief in one god and qualities of 'honesty, trust, solidarity, loyalty and flexibility' (1995: 9). At the same time the internationalization of Islam reflected back on the Arabs who were receptive to foreign ideas. While at this time the Europeans were largely disparaging business and trade as degrading, the Arabs embraced trade and acknowledged the status of merchants. It should be noted that this is also the time that Arab traders were active in North and East Africa, in the colonization of Spain (eighth and ninth centuries), and in Arab army conquests as far east as the Indus river, and as far west as current day Ghana. This also included the slave trade in North Africa, Mediterranean areas and as far away as eastern Europe from 650 CE until 1900 CE.

Ali (1995) notes that Islam emerged in Arabia when Arab communities were thriving commercially and intellectually, rather than giving rise to it. The centralized Ommayyad Empire (661–750 CE) led the opposition to Islam.

But certainly Islam in the Arab world led to the greater integration and consolidation of trade and enterprise, with a 'merchant warrior' class transforming the Arab world into the centre for international trade between Africa, Asia and Europe. Ali (1995) remarks that the capitalist system, developed in Arabia in the first six centuries of the Arab–Islamic state, was the most extensive and highly developed in history before the creation of the world market by West Europeans. In addition, the intellectual life of the state flourished with various schools of thought developing with tremendous influence on governance structures and business practices.

Industry and agriculture did not exist as such, and investments mainly went into expanding commercial interests in Africa, Spain and South Asia. This was initially under the Ommayyad dynasty which was highly influenced by the *Jabria* school stressing adherence to strict rules and centralization. Other schools which stressed rationalism, the power of the mind, concept of liberty and role of knowledge (*Ikhtiar* and *Mutazilas* schools) had more influence on subsequent regimes. Yet Ali (1995) contends that influences of non-Arab Islam contributed to a decline of these more participative approaches and to more authoritarian forms of government. This was very much consolidated with the ascendancy of the Islamic non-Arab Turkish Ottoman Empire from 1412 CE to the early twentieth century, which adhered to the *Jabria* school, saw their chiefs as direct descendants of God (even after Islam) and favoured an authoritarian and centralized state. This led to the demise of the Arab trade associations and business activities in Arabia. This also heralded the influence of a number of foreign invaders into Arab lands, the further demise of trade and business and decline and disjuncture of Arab national life. The economic prosperity going back to the seventh century deteriorated.

Western powers and the Arab world

After the demise of the Ottoman Empire, Great Britain and France as imperial powers divided the Arab world up into small states with authoritarian regimes. Arab traditions of independent thinking, liberty and power of the mind were condemned and subjugated to *Jabira* principles.

Yet even before this, the clash of empires, and schisms in Islam and within the Arab World were having an effect. This included the birth of Wahhabism and its alliance with and allegiance to the Saud family, and then in the service of the British Empire with lasting implications today in the Arabian peninsular (Ali, 2002), of which more later.

Tribal values

Although the Middle East in its relationship with global dynamics will be returned to later, the Arab cultural space that we see today is described by Rees and Althakhri (2008) as still exhibiting a degree of tribalism, which is often incorporated into modern-day political, economic and management systems. It is traditional, family oriented and male dominated, while also being rather conservative in its risk taking. They add that tribalism was instrumental in developing the authoritarian structures in public and private sectors in the Middle East. Yet there appears some ambivalence in the concept of authoritarianism, as while including both hierarchical structures and centralization in decision making, as well as a rigidity, it also is dependent on the person who holds a position of power, and on an open-door policy where certainly consultation, and sometimes participating decision making, is a feature. They back this up by studies undertaken by Ali *et al.* (1997) of managers in Kuwait who appeared to prefer consultative and participative decision-making styles, and a study in the United Arab Emirates by Darwish (2000) that had similar results. Yet participation (if not consultation) appears to be at the same organizational level rather than down the hierarchy. Certainly, as Neal *et al.* (2007) assert, the role of the *sheik* in traditional Arab communities can be seen as indicative of modern-day leadership styles:

the sheik is not a mere autocrat – though he often has near absolute power over subordinates. Instead, the relationship with subordinates is best viewed as 'paternalistic', in that the sheik looks after the needs of tribe members, without passing over rights and responsibilities to them. This relationship is not merely 'top-down', however, but is characterized by high degrees of embedded interaction and consultation. For instance, all members of the tribe, no matter how humble, are entitled to secure a personal audience, and can expect their petitions to be treated seriously, and acted on.

Rees and Althakhri (2008) also argue that because tribal values place great importance on commitment and obedience, this leads to nepotism that appears to be openly allowed in the Arab world. This fulfils the commitment towards relatives and tribal members inherent within this value system. Such is evident in the recruitment of upper-level management, despite qualifications being stressed in recruiting middle- and lower-level managers. They point to one such finding in Kuwait by Al-Kazemi and Ali (2002) which pointed to favouritism and personal loyalty, unwillingness to take responsibility among a rigidity of administrative systems, and the dominance of personal relationships over work relations. This involved subjectivity in appraisal and promotions and reliance on hereditary relationships.

This seems to be at variance to the Islamic values discussed by Beekun and Badawi (2005) which appear to focus on employee competence. Rees and Althakhri (2008) may partially be right in pointing to Hofstede's (1980a/2003) value dimension relating to Arab countries that they are high in *Power Distance*, *Uncertainty Avoidance* and *Collectivism* (see also the discussion in Chapter 3 of the current text). That more recent studies indicate the adoption of Western management theories and practice such as GLOBE's finding that Arab countries exhibit *Future* and *Performance Orientation* and low *Power Distance* may also not fully capture the complete nature of Arab cultural space within the management domain.

Paternalism as a key factor in management ethics in the Middle East

Countries of the Arabian peninsular do not appear replete with strong trade unions. Mellahi (2006) for example has described Saudi Arabia as a 'high-context culture and more collectivist than the rest of the Arab world' (2006: 104) and, as such in the absence of labour unions, Saudis are well protected in employment with much better salaries than expatriate workers. So, according to Mellahi (2006) employees, whether local or expatriate, are not permitted to form any formal association such as a trade union in order to defend their rights (arguably if they have no rights there are no rights to defend). He poses this as an ethical question of the right to representation.

However, as we have seen above, rights and responsibilities are encompassed within the rules and values laid down by Islam. These appear to be comprehensive and all embracing of relationships such as the one between employer and employee. It is absolute, and not simply an ethic, but a way of life for believers. The enforcement of these principles is fundamentally the province of a person's relationship with God. Yet it also seems likely in an Islamic state that the government has a duty to ensure these principles are upheld. This brings us to Mellahi's (2006) assumption of an ethical question of a right to representation. Yet if the state has a duty to ensure adherence to Islamic principles, and assuming those principles are benign, why should we assume that a person has a right to be represented? In the same way we saw above that *caveat emptor* does not exist in Islamic law, because it does not need to exist, so (Western) rights of representation perhaps do not need to exist if rules governing social relations in business are specific, adhered to, internalized to the extent that they are a way of life and enforced through an implicit relationship between a person and God, and further monitored by the state. Why does an employee need to be represented? This is a logical conclusion rather than one based on empirical evidence, which will be examined later.

It is therefore difficult to talk about social partnering in the same sense as in European countries. We have already discussed the nature of industrial relations in Turkey, where Koçer (2007) has described industrial relations as a 'partnership in coercion' (Chapter 6). Yet this also may belie what Aycan (2006) has more positively described as paternalism. That employers, and governments, for example in Saudi Arabia protect their own may be a positive aspect of paternalism within a collectivist society. However, that women comprise 55 per cent of graduates, and only 4.8 per cent of the workforce (Mellahi, 2006), may represent in Saudi Arabia one of the more negative (from a Western perspective) effects of paternalism (a paternalistic state protecting its women, perhaps).

Although paternalism does not just exist in Middle Eastern countries (Aycan, 2006, points also to Pacific Asian countries, such as China, Japan, Korea and India, and to Latin America), Crane and Mattens' (2004) third key question about ethics 'What are the key guidelines for ethical behaviour?' can be answered by reference to Islamic principles. In Europe this was noted to be a negotiated legal framework for business, and in the USA a corporate-initiated code of ethics (Chapter 6). For their second question, however, 'Who is the key actor in business ethics?' this must surely be the paternalistic employer, and perhaps the state, among a lack of formal government regulations and control and laws pertaining to individual 'rights'. If in Europe, this is the collective institutions of government, trade unions and corporate associates, and in the USA the corporation; in Middle Eastern countries the social partnership relationship would be a paternalistic one.

It is therefore important to explore paternalism a little more, as it will feature in other regions and countries as these are explored in later chapters.

Negative and positive connotations of paternalism

Aycan (2006) has pointed out that the term 'paternalism' has negative connotations in the West. For example Demenchono (2009: 283) invokes Kant in believing that 'a *paternalistic* government, treating its citizens like immature children and thus infringing upon their freedom, is "the most despotic of all"'. This is mainly because the welfare of the state is not the same thing as

the well-being and happiness of the population. He applies the term paternalism to denote the enforced spread of democracy by military means to Iraq
among others. Yet surely this is a misappropriation of the term. However, as
Aycan (2006) quotes from Jackman (1994: 10): 'paternalism is a time-worn
term that has indefinite meaning in common use'. In fact Aycan (2006)
defines the term from the Webster's dictionary as 'the principle or system
of governing or controlling a country, group of employees, etc, in a manner
suggesting a father's relationship with his children'. Pellegrini and Scandura
(2008: 567), writing on paternalistic leadership, state that:

> Despite diverse descriptions offered by different authors across time and cultures,
> more recent research typically defines paternalistic leadership as 'a style that com-
> bines strong discipline and authority with fatherly benevolence' (Farh and Cheng,
> 2000: 91). *Authoritarianism* refers to leader behaviors that assert authority and
> control, whereas *benevolence* refers to an individualized concern for subordinates'
> personal well-being. This type of leadership is still prevalent and effective in many
> business cultures, such as in the Middle East, Pacific Asia, and Latin America (Farh,
> Cheng, Chou, and Chu, 2006; Martinez, 2003; Pellegrini and Scandura, 2006;
> Uhl-Bien, Tierney, Graen, and Wakabayashi, 1990). However, it has increasingly
> been perceived negatively in Western management literature, which is reflected in
> descriptions of paternalism such as 'benevolent dictatorship' (Northouse, 1997: 39)
> and 'a hidden and insidious form of discrimination' (Colella, Garcia, Reidel, and
> Triana, 2005: 26).

They further state that in paternalistic cultures, those in authority consider
it their obligation to provide protection to those under their care. In return
they expect loyalty and deference. Yet the extent to which this relationship
is benevolent is often questioned. Some assert that benevolence is there only
because the power holder wants something in return. Hence paternal relationships create obligations. Another way of looking at this is that paternalism is conducive to societal cultures where mutual obligations are a feature
of what Hofstede (1980a/2003) and others have referred to as collectivism.
Aycan (2006) notes that many of the negative attitudes towards paternalism
stem from the West.

It is likely in an individualistic societal culture, where a clear distinc-
tion is made between authoritarian and democratic forms of management
(McGregor's Theory X and Theory Y, or Likert's Authoritarian, Consultative,
Participative management), that paternalistic management does not fit neatly
into one of these slots, and if it does, fits into the authoritarian one. However,
Aycan (2006) sees authoritarianism as quite distinct from paternalism.
Authoritarian relationships are based on control and exploitation where

subordinates show conformity simply to avoid punishment. In a paternalistic relationship the figure of authority, say, the boss, may be involved in the lives of subordinates as would be expected in a collectivist society. This would be seen as part of the leader's care and protection role. This would be seen as a violation of privacy in an individualistic society. Also with an acceptance of the authority of the leader, and an unequal power relationship that would be accepted in a high Power Distance culture, this may again be viewed negatively in a Western society with lower Power Distance. It is for these reasons that Aycan (2006) has suggested that the benevolent aspects of paternalism have been difficult for Western scholars to digest. It is particularly the 'duality between control and care' (2006: 453) inherent in paternalism that is difficult for Western scholars to comprehend. It might be added further that this perception may well colour both the investigation and analysis of such leadership behaviour and organizational relations in non-Western societies, from a Western perspective; and at the same time create issues of ethicality (in Mellahi's, 2006, terms, a right to representation).

Paternalistic leadership and *wasta*

Pellegrini and Scandura (2008) have suggested that problems may also arise because different authors are writing about different things. Aycan (2006) sought to clarify concepts, and in particular distinguished *benevolent paternalism* and *exploitative paternalism*. In the former a leader has a genuine concern for the subordinates' welfare, with employees showing loyalty and deference towards the leader out of respect and appreciation of his protection. In the latter, while the leader's overt behaviour is a nurturing one, care towards the employee exists solely to get the employee's compliance to achieve the executive ends of the organization. Employees will indeed show loyalty and deference, but only insofar as the leader is capable of fulfilling the needs of the employee, and conversely can take away critical resources if the employee fails to provide such loyalty and deference. In contrast with paternalism Aycan (2006) also distinguishes *authoritarian management* which relies on control and exploitation of the employee who in turn shows conformity and dependence in order to receive rewards and/or avoid punishment; and *authoritative management*, which again exercises control, but this time has the underlying motivation to promote the employees' welfare, while the employee respects the leader's decisions and rules as they know that they will benefit.

A relevant aspect of paternalism in the current discussion of management ethics is that it is situational, or perhaps more accurately because it is a relational factor, the extent to which a leader exhibits (benevolent) paternalistic attitudes and behaviour towards subordinates is a function of the relationship between them. Within a collectivist society a benevolent paternalistic relationship may only exist between in-group members, whereas out-group members may be treated in a completely different way (perhaps in an authoritarian way: although Jackson *et al.*, 2008, found evidence in Kenyan SMEs that a form of paternalism was also applied to out-group members). Pellegrini and Scandura (2008) also point to the relationship between paternalism and leader-member exchange (LMX) in the literature. Because paternal leadership is so personal, it is also dependent on the quality of individual relationships with subordinates. Certainly in-group/out-group relationships are important in this, but are not the only factor. This being the case, there appears to be much scope with paternalistic relationships to show favouritism and special treatment to particular individuals or groups. 'Nepotism' (*wasta*) certainly appears to be a factor in relationships in Arab countries (although as Ali, 2005: 190, points out this may be against Islamic principles) as it is in many collectivist societies. Whether or not there is a direct relationship between paternalistic leadership and nepotism is not clear. The fact that the word 'nepotism' carries negative connotations in itself does not mean that personal favours are unethical in themselves. Certainly the Arabic *wasta* appears not to reflect such negative ideas, and in fact reflects the taking care of one's own in a tribal, paternalistic society, as discussed later in the current chapter.

Paternalism and Islam

While Islamic principles appear to favour competence over personal favour, it also looks towards the boss as a shepherd to his flock. Looking after his own flock, as opposed to taking care of someone else's to the detriment of his own, also raises interesting ethical issues.

It is unfortunate that so few studies exist of paternalism in Middle Eastern countries, other than in Turkey (e.g. Aycan *et al.*, 2000; Pellegrini and Scandura, 2006). Evidence from other Islamic countries such as Pakistan (Aycan *et al.*, 2000) and Malaysia (Ansari *et al.*, 2004), does not however establish a relationship between paternalism and Islam. Yet certainly the account given by Beekun and Badawi (2005) of Islam and the stakeholder model suggests the boss looking after his people as a shepherd would his flock. There is also an indication from Ali (2005) in his account of power and authority in Islam that if the leader did not behave in this way, that is in a fair and benevolent way, then those governed had the right to depose the ruler.

It may be difficult to generalize from Turkey as a secure state, to the Islamic states of the Arabian peninsular, for example. However, although a study in Turkey by Erben and Güneşer (2007) has limitations, it does appear to support a relationship between a benevolent paternalism and positive ethical climate, and employee commitment to the organization. It is particularly interesting that within this context employees see paternal leadership as a positive ethical influence.

However, following on from the discussion in Chapter 6 regarding the role of discourse ethics and social partnering within a social Europe, the logic of both the content of management ethics (its principle: based on Islam in Arab countries), and the process of developing understanding of what is ethical and what is not (based on paternalistic relationships and their outcomes in the Arab world as opposed to social partnering in Europe), may have completely different dynamics in the Middle East.

Women in Islam

From a Western perspective, it could be proffered that a common perspective is that we have nothing to learn from the management of gender-related issues from the Arab world. The view from the West, and from many (presumably Westernized) Muslims is quite the reverse – as we have seen from the introductory case study, the role of women in Islamic cultures is seen from the West as subservient and of women being repressed, even to the extent of being seen as a human rights issue.

It seems that it is possible to approach the perception of the role of women in Islamic countries at least in three different ways:

1. Women have few rights in Islamic countries. These countries therefore are backward and have everything to learn from the West.
2. Islam, as a religion, was very progressive towards the role of women, but became corrupted as a result of influences originally from tribal Arab cultures, in colonial times as a result of collaboration between colonists and conservatives, and now as a defence mechanism against the West.
3. Modern Islamic states protect women from unwanted sexual attention and focus on women not as objects of men's desires, but on the inner person and what they have to offer as human beings. As such this is simply a different way of looking at the role of women, and the West could learn something from this.

Coleman (2006: 26), who appears to provide support for the second view, tells us that:

Contrary to the claims of secularists who deny the compatibility of Islam and modern notions of women's rights, Islamic attitudes on the question actually vary quite widely. According to "Islamic feminists," Islam is actually a very progressive religion for women, was radically egalitarian for its time, and remains so in some of its Scriptures. They contend that Islamic law has evolved in ways that are inimical to gender equality not because it clearly pointed in that direction, but because of selective interpretation by patriarchal leaders and a mingling of Islamic teachings with tribal customs and traditions. Islamic feminists now seek to revive the equality bestowed on women in the religion's early years by rereading the Koran, putting the Scriptures in context, and disentangling them from tribal practices.

She points to the multiple interpretations of the Qur'an in areas such as marriage where some scholars view it endorsing polygamy and some monogamy. Similarly in the case of veiling:

Progressive Muslims point out that nowhere does the Koran actually require the veiling of all Muslim women. Veiling was simply a custom in pre-Islamic Arabia, where the hijab was considered a status symbol (after all, only women who did not have to work in the fields had the luxury of wearing a veil). When the Koran mentions veils, it is in reference to Muhammad's wives. The "hijab verse" reads, "Believers, do not enter the Prophet's house … unless asked. And if you are invited … do not linger. And when you ask something from the Prophet's wives, do so from behind a hijab. This will assure the purity of your hearts as well as theirs." In the Prophet's lifetime, all believers (men and women) were encouraged to be modest. But the veil did not become widespread for several generations – until conservatives became ascendant. Coleman (2006: 27)

With this she suggests that it is important who actually interprets Sharia in areas such as gender equality where the letter of the law is ambiguous or vague.

Ali (2002) writes on the opposing 'fundamentalisms' of the Islamic Jihadists and the, then, Bush presidency and its foreign policy, and notes how extreme forms of Islamic fundamentalism have been used for political power and in the service of imperial ambitions. One such case is that of Wahhabism. Like Christianity, Islam has had its puritan strains. One such was initiated by Muhammad Ibn Abdul Wahhab in the eighteenth century (CE). Ibn Wahhab sought to return Islam to its former 'pure beliefs'. He denounced the worship of the Prophet Muhammad, prayers at the shrines of holy men, the marking of graves and denounced all non-Sunnis, and what he saw as the more corrupt Sunnis, and advocated jihad again the Shia 'heretics' and the Ottoman Empire. Yet what brought objections from religious leaders and his ultimate expulsion from his home town of Uyayna in 1740 was his advocacy and then practicing of punishment beatings, stoning of adulterers, the amputation of the limbs of thieves and public execution of criminals. Over four years he travelled in the region, and through his charisma and message, gaining followers and ending up in Deraiya. Here he was taken in by a notorious bandit-emir Muhammad Ibn Saud who recognized in him an ally for his own political and military ambitions with a theology that justified everything that Ibn Saud wished to achieve. This involved a permanent jihad against other Muslim settlements, ignoring the caliph and imposing a rigorous discipline on his own people. His ultimate goal was to unite the tribes of the peninsular under his rule. The two, emir and preacher, signed a binding exclusive contract which excluded Ibn Wahhab allying with any other emir in the region. The agreement was sealed with Ibn Wahhab's marriage to Ibn Saud's daughter. Ali (2002: 75) adds that 'Thus was laid the basis for political and confessional intimacy that would shape the politics of the peninsula. This combination of religious fanaticism, military ruthlessness, political villainy and the press-ganging of women to cement alliances was the foundation stone of the dynasty that rules Saudi Arabia today.'

The neighbouring tribes were unable to resist the onslaught of this partnership which led to the takeover of the region by Ibn Saud's forces, including the two holiest cities in Islam, Mecca and Medina. It was only in 1811 that the Wahhabis were defeated by an Ottoman force led by Muhammad Ali. After the fall of the Ottoman Empire and the end of World War I, the winning side, Britain and France, shared out the Middle East between them, with Britain mandated to run Iraq and Palestine and watch over Egypt, with France keeping control of the 'Maghreb' and gaining Syria and Lebanon. Rebellions ensuing in Iraq and Syria were crushed by the imperial powers, leaving resentment in the Arab world. The Russian Revolution then came, with the promise of international communism, oil became important, and the United States began its international ascendency. The British enlisted the help of Emir Abdal Aziz Ibn Saud, and armed him. Despite heavy residence he took control of Central Arabia, and to seal the agreement of resisting neighbouring emirs, force-married wives of these now defeated rivals. Many people fled to Iraq, Syria and Yemen out of fear of the Wahhabi dictatorship. Britain, and then America, who then challenged Britain's monopoly in the area by signing oil deals and then paying millions of dollars in aid to the kingdom, had secured a highly conservative 'confessional despotism' as a bulwark against communism, secular nationalism and dissent in the Arab world, as well as a major source of oil, while ignoring what went on within its borders (the issue of human rights and the United States has been discussed in Chapter 5)

Changes in the workforce

Today, there is no doubt that Saudi Arabia is one of the most conservative nations in the Arab world. This is true of gender issues as we saw above, where women account for only 4.8 per cent of the workforce (Mellahi, 2006). Yet this is changing as more progressive policies encourage women into the workforce, to meet pressures from an increasingly dwindling skills base, and an overreliance on cheaper expatriate labour and a move towards greater 'Saudization'. Metcalfe (2007) suggests this is also in response to increased global competition for the Middle East particularly in relation to new players such as China and India. The increasing importance of the banking and finance sectors and a lower dependency on an oil economy also contribute to this trend.

Whiteoak *et al.* (2006) suggest that the pressure to increase the number of women in the workforce is common to many Arab countries. In the United Arab Emirates (UAE), for example, the percentage of women in the workforce increased from 5.3% in 1980 to 16.3% in 1990, with more recent figures estimating 20%. As in Saudi Arabia, a higher proportion of women is to be found in the government sector (40% of the workforce in UAE), but they tend to be in lower positions than men. These authors admit that there is little evidence to suggest attitudes are any more conservative towards women than in Western countries such as the United States. Similarly it might be assumed that with influences of modernization and Westernization on countries such as UAE, attitudes of younger generations may be less conservative than those of older generations. Although their own research in UAE does not support this supposition overall, it does support a more progressive attitude of women (more so for women under 30 years of age) towards their own abilities and place in the workforce, against men's more conservative attitudes, which the authors suggest might harden as women begin to surpass them in terms of educational qualifications and having better access to work opportunities.

Other Arab countries have seen dramatic increases in the participation of women in the workforce including Bahrain, Kuwait and Yemen. Bahrain for example had a female labour participation of 25.8 per cent in 2002. Yet Metcalfe (2007) suggests that as in other Arab states the workforce is still strongly gender segregated, with women predominantly in education and roles concerning female health. Much of the increase in women's participation in the workforce is due to their greater involvement in government employment.

Yet the role of women in Islam is too often interpreted, by the West, from a Western perspective, when perhaps we should see this as culturally embedded and try to understand gender roles from a culture-specific context. This is the view taken by Metcalfe (2007) who points to the common Western perspective that depicts women in the Middle East as oppressed, with this becoming a political issue in international relations. The United States' criticism of Yemen, Iran, Afghanistan and the new constitution of Iraq is an example of this. She asserts that the nature of gender difference and equality is more complex than simply assuming women in Islamic countries are in a position of subordination. Some of her arguments reflect the previous discussion in this chapter, on the nature of paternalism in Arab cultural space. They also reflect the nature of the types of cultural space that Arab/Islamic cultures might occupy regarding their interface with Western and other cultural influences.

The role of women at the interface of cultural/religious influences

Metcalfe (2007) argues that patriarchal relations are the product of cultural practice rather than of the teachings of Islam. However, this does rather beg the question, how is it possible to separate 'culture' and 'religion'? Surely the latter is part of the former? As it is difficult to write a text on ethics without referring to religion, as is the case in this and preceding chapters, it is obviously necessary to understand the relationship between culture, religion and values/ethics. However, as with all social science, it depends on who is the teller, as to the story told. This does not suppose that social science is a branch of the humanities. It supposes that the scholar/researcher plays a key role in formulating questions of enquiry, and indeed how evidence is produced, and how evidence is interpreted in order to arrive at answers to our questions.

If one assumes that God precedes humanity, then religion could be assumed to be a cultural antecedent. If, however, one assumes that religion and the construction of a deity or deities is a product of society, then obviously religion is a cultural product, which itself constructs culture as it evolves. Islam appears to have played a key role in constructing the types of cultural space discussed above. Yet it has also been adapted, first by the Arab societies out of which it first grew, and subsequently by such puritan forms including Wahhabism in Saudi Arabia which may have been used for political means, and adapted accordingly. Yet the current author believes that religion is a cultural product, just as any other social institution. It provides a set of values which are adhered to, adapted, come into contradiction with other value sets, adapted, opposed to other world views, asserted, adapted and interpreted. This is an ongoing social interactive process that depends as much on geopolitical power relations as it does on whether or not one believes the Qur'an is the word of God.

Metcalfe (2007: 59) tells us that 'the interpretation of labour laws are guided by *urf* (custom) and Sharia law which reflect the need to protect women and create a moral work environment ... The concept of *diwan* and *wasta* ... are strongly gendered since these relationships are channelled through male connections and networks.' She defines *diwan* as 'a style of decision making which represents a process of achieving balance (*adl*) and justice (*adalah*)' (2007: 57). It is fundamentally consultative but often based on personalism and sometime autocracy. She refers (2007: 57) to *wasta* as the 'recognition that power in society is related to tribal and familial structures, and that working relations in the Arab world are facilitated by recognizing how to move within relevant power networks. The national business system [within Arab countries] is thus largely characterized by an interlocking structure that stretches across, and between, networks in families, organizations and political life.'

Hence within Arab society, which is fundamentally influenced by Islam, informal and family relationships are important, together with patronage, trust building and open relationships which come from this strongly patriarchal system. Metcalfe (2007) also refers to gender and employment reports from the UNDP and World Bank that emphasize the importance of the family, rather than the individual, where men and women have complementary roles and men are seen as the breadwinners of the family; and where a code of modesty exists that stresses the dignity and reputation of women and where interaction between the sexes is restricted, together with an unequal power balance in the private sphere which is premised on family law based on Sharia.

Metcalfe believes that perceived from a Western perspective *diwan* and *wasta* appear to create inequalities, yet these principles also support balance and equilibrium (*adl*) in work and social relationships, with the idea of *qiwama* (protection) relating to the responsibility of men to protect and care for women, including her dignity, modesty and honour, and protect the family. Yet she is keen to stress that this does not suppose superiority of men over women. Also the stress on modesty, including veiling, does not suggest a 'gender hierarchy through control ... but is concerned with acknowledging markers of sexual difference as a sign of respect and reverence' (2007: 60).

She believes that although globalization and expanding markets have created more opportunity for women in Arab countries, the rise of Islamic revivalism may be having a counter effect. As was mentioned above, geopolitical processes are important in the evolution of the influence of Islam. We have already seen that ahhabism was put to work politically first by Ibn Saud, and then by the British in achieving imperial ambitions, and more latterly by the Americans. Yet the backlash is perhaps something that, even before and perhaps after 9/11, was unexpected.

An enduring memory of the current author of the attacks on the twin towers of the New York World Trade Centre on 11 September 2001 are the words of an American journalist living in London on the BBC news that evening. She said that the Americans simply cannot believe that anyone in the world could see them as the bad guys. Rather than heralding a phase of intense introspection and examination of how America could be cast in this role, it appears to have led to quite the reverse. Through the subsequent 'war on terrorism', and the wars in Afghanistan and Iraq, the image of the Arab/Islamist/Middle Eastern became even more a subject of suspicion. The backlash, after years of Western imperialism, has come in the form of terrorism, and the subsequent reaction from at least two powers in the West, to invade Iraq and Afghanistan and to rattle sabres towards Iran against its nuclear programme. This may not have fundamentally changed the way Muslims and Arabs are seen from the historical perceptions explored in Said's (1978/1995) account of Orientalism, but it has certainly made the 'objective' study of Arab and Muslim cultural space more difficult from a Western perspective. While politicians, as well as academics, are condemning the perceived values of Islam (including those that relate to the role of women), many Muslim women, in the West, and secular states like Turkey, appear to be reasserting their cultural identity by adopting *hijab*.

Certainly, Metcalfe's (2007) own research findings in business organizations in Bahrain indicate a move towards women wearing *hijab* in professional situations as a sign of respect, among remarks in interviews such as 'a woman who wears *hijab* is treated as a human being not as a sexual object' (2007: 66). As the *hijab* was a practice that was borrowed from the elite woman of Byzantium, Greece and Rome, it was seen as a sign of high status and respectability not as an indication of oppression against women.

Schech and Haggis (2000: 102) focus on a postcolonial analysis of Western feminist discourse of the 'Third World woman', among them the veiled woman, as a sign of oppression. They refer to Mohanty's (1991) work as she explores how 'Western and feminist authors universalize their own particular perspectives as normative, and essentialize Third World women as tradition-bound victims of timeless patriarchal cultures'. In so doing she suggests that they reproduce and continue 'the colonial discourse of mainstream, male-stream scholarship'. This involves a 'twinning of a binary model of gender, which sees "women" as an a priori category of oppressed, with an "ethnocentric universality" ... which takes Western locations and perspectives as the norm'. This has the effect of creating the 'Third World woman' stereotype, which completely ignores the diversity across class and ethnic boundaries within the 'Third World'. So, within 'a first/third world balance of power' (Mohanty, 1991: 73) this produces and reproduces a set of universal images of the 'Third World woman' such as 'the veiled woman, the powerful mother, the chaste virgin, the obedient wife, etc' (1991: 73). Mohanty adds that these images set in motion 'a colonialist discourse which exercises a very specific power of defining, coding, and maintaining existing first/third world connections'.

Schech and Haggis (2000) add that this also involves a practice of 'blaming culture' or a submission to medieval systems, and suggest the way that Western feminists have viewed veiling is an example of this, and regard it as oppression of women. These authors are concerned with the role of culture in development, and suggest that as part of the development discourse veiling is seen as an indication of backwardness, and that what is necessary is to throw off the veil and renounce Islam in order to liberate women. Yet they add that perhaps what confounds this is when educated, professional Muslim women adopt the veil 'claiming it as a mark of agency, cultural membership and resistance' (after Hirschmann, 1998: 345). Indeed, they see a big difference between Muslim women voluntarily adopting the veil and defending this, and for example the Taliban's 'draconian laws regarding women's veiling and public visibility' (Schech and Haggis, 2000: 103).

Closing case: the Savola Group

Previously in this chapter we have looked at the role of Islam in formulating principles that should be adhered to in relation to the various stakeholders of an organization. Although Beekun and Badawi's (2005) work was useful in gaining an idea of how this should work, as a manifesto, they were not very helpful in terms of demonstrating how this is achieved in practice. Little research has been undertaken on this in Arab and Middle Eastern countries, yet Beekun and Badawi (2005) suggest that the large Saudi group Savola adheres to these Islamic principles. It does this by publishing a detailed code of ethics, almost along the lines of American companies. Although without further research it is difficult to say how effective this is in terms of internalization and behaviour of the group's managers and staff, it does provide an example of how Islamic principles are adopted into the way a company professes to do business.

According to its website (www.savola.com/SavolaE/About_The_Savola_Group.php, accessed 20 September 2010) the Group

is one of Saudi Arabia's leading industrial companies ... established in 1979. Savola's first business was in the edible oil industry in Saudi Arabia. It is now one of the most successful and fastest growing multinational food groups in the Gulf and the Middle East Region, also penetrating North African and Central Asian countries, with a wide portfolio of businesses including Edible Oils, Sugar, Noodles/Pasta, Packaging, Real Estate and Franchising. Savola currently has market shares of 62% of the Edible Oils market and 68% of the Sugar market in the Kingdom as well as 79 Supermarkets/Hypermarkets retail outlets throughout Saudi Arabia with one Hypermarket in Dubai, UAE.

The Group sees its ethical principles (subtitled 'The Balanced Way') not just as guiding principles, but also as providing a 'balancing force among competing interests both within the individual and among the contending stakeholders'. The belief is that these principles help individuals in the organization to function more efficiently and that the organization consequently functions in a more coordinated manner. This is asserted, firstly because 'individuals are moral creatures' and a system of ethics congruent within their own morality mitigates against possible conflicts, and a higher job satisfaction; and, secondly because it is 'our belief that despite all efforts ... success in business needs a blessing from Allah' and 'to reiterate words from our vision "we firmly believe that Allah's help and blessing will always be there supporting those who maintain good and sincere intentions"'.

Rather than prescribing specific actions, the principles address the nature of relationships:

Specifically, we engage in three classes of external relations – with **partners**, with our **third party customers** (customers, suppliers and the community at large) and with our **colleagues**. At the same time, we are in constant touch with **our own selves**.

These relations are governed through four 'ethics':

- Honesty (*Amanah*). This involves honouring the trust that others have given to the company, such as providing the highest possible return for the funds entrusted to the company. This involves traits that encourage transparency, trustworthiness and fairness in dealings with others. It also involves telling the truth, fulfilling promises and obligations, honouring pledges to others, and commitment to resolving conflicts with 'respect and objectivity'.
- Conscientiousness (*Taqwa*). This concerns the relationship to external parties and the idea of being a good citizen, including aspects such as not making misleading statements about products or polluting the environment. It involves making a decision by checking its legality, and checking with public opinion in the sense of would you be proud of the decision in front of others, and with regard to one's own personal opinion and feeling comfortable with the decision. Above all it concerns making the right decision in regard to the relationships with external stakeholders.
- Caring Justice (*Birr*). This is the responsibility towards colleagues and employees within the company. This goes beyond simply fair play and justice. It involves 'genuine care and concern for people and their welfare', and being sensitive to people's material and family needs. 'Birr, at its basic level, is about love. It is concerned with doing what we would have liked to be done to us.'
- Personal Control (*Mujahadah*). This is the 'drive within us towards self-improvement and towards progressively increasing self-discipline'. It requires evaluating oneself. This includes having the time to contemplate our own behaviour and being aware that we are in need of self-improvement. This includes aspects such as avoiding doing activities that waste one's time, not being bothered with what others are doing when it does not concern us, not looking for information about the actions or problems of others, nor being involved in gossip. It is about 'controlling our tendencies, and directing our effort towards developing our ability to ensure fulfilment of our ethical responsibilities towards all stakeholders'.

These four principles relate to the conclusions drawn by the Muslim scholar Abu Daoud, following a lifetime of studying some 500,000 *Hadith*. It reflects the essence of Islam as revolving around the four *Hadith* that relate to these four principles which form the framework of Savola's business ethics. For example, for the principle of *Mujahadah* the following is given in support: 'The Messenger of Allah said: Part of someone's being a good Muslim is his leaving alone that which does not concern him.'

The principles conclude by stressing the need for balance:

We recognize and believe that the first three values, which deal primarily with the external relationships, are inherently consistent. Even though it may appear that the immediate Birr obligation to employees conflicts with Amanah obligation to shareholders, in reality they re-enforce each other. Birr raises the morale of the employees and leads to improved productivity. This in turn improves shareholder value and consequently constitutes Amanah. Similarly, Amanah focuses the attention of the employees on their responsibility for the growth and success of the company. That, in turn, secures employee welfare, thus constituting Birr.

From this, the balancing principle is that of *Mujahadah*. This 'plays a balancing role at two levels: Balancing the values that govern our relationships with the external world; and balancing us internally between contemplation and action.'

In some respects, these principles provide an example of how Islamic principles may be integrated into a code of ethics. At the same time, it could be questioned to what extent an Islamic company needs to codify such principles if religion, as was argued above, is so pervasive in the life of Muslims, where such principles should be internalized: hence the arguments for not having a codified *habeas corpus* within Islamic principles, and not having a concept of employee rights. It may be that Savola also employs non-Muslims, which was certainly indicated by Beekun and Badawi (2005). The other explanation may well be that this Saudi company has adopted the practice of publishing a code of ethics from Western influences. There are distinct parallels between, for example, the principle of *Taqwa*, in ensuring a decision is legal and will stand up to public scrutiny, and one feeling comfortable about the decision, and the principles contained in the Americans Blanchard and Peale's (1988) book, *The Power of Ethical Management*.

Implications for international managers

The issues dealt with in this chapter include what an Islamic ethics of social partnering might look like. Clearly, as a major world religion, Islam has much to say about the relationships between people, and people with the natural environment. As Islam appears to be pervasive in Muslim countries, much of this can be applied to conduct in business and other work organizations. The work of Beekun and Badawi (2005) and the example of the ethical principles espoused by the Saudi group Savola have indicated how religious principles may be manifested in organizations, as they concern relationships among different stakeholders. There do appear to be stakeholder principles working here, yet these are far from the social partnership principles operating in some European countries. What appears to distinguish organizational relationships in the Arab world, and perhaps other Muslim countries in the Middle East, is paternalism. This type of leadership may well pre-date Islam within the Arab world, yet appears to run parallel with Islamic principles. This chapter has not posed this as a negative attribute, but has attempted to view this within its context, and with a positive inflection.

Much of the work on *Power Distance* by Hofstede (1980a/2003) and others suggests that it is relatively easy for a manager to move from a low *Power Distance* society to a high power one, but difficult to move from a high *Power Distance* country to a low power one, because the leadership competences needed in a high power culture are easier to learn. It is easier to move from an influencing position to a telling situation, and difficult to move from a telling situation to an influencing one, because it is more difficult to acquire the necessary skills. Yet this tells us nothing about a manager moving into an organization where the predominant societal cultural values favour paternalism. Although strictly this is moving into a higher *Power Distance* situation, the type of nurturing and protecting ethos needed may be difficult for an individual manager to acquire, particularly out of his or her own context. It may also be difficult for a Western manager to understand that a paternalistic style of leadership is no worse, and no better, than say a more participative one, or that the Western manager has anything to learn from the paternalistic manager. Of course, this represents an oversimplification, and we should also take on board Aycan's (2006) distinction between benevolent paternalism and exploitative paternalism. Not all paternalistic behaviour is good, and not all is bad. This could equally apply to some of the types of consultative leadership found in Western countries.

There may be two upshots of the type of paternalistic leadership described in this chapter that may be ethically problematic for Western managers: *wasta* and gender relations. *Wasta* can be seen as nepotism from a Western perspective, and simply part of a paternalistic protection and nurturing of a shepherd for his flock. Similarly, veiling may be seen as oppressive to women, and the low employment of women as discriminatory. It may, again, be seen as protecting one's own in a paternalistic relationship, with the *hijab* as a sign of modesty, respect and reverence.

Questions for managers

1. In assessing the ethical code of Savola, are there any aspects of this that could be adopted in your organization? Is there anything there that you would like to see in your organization?
2. Are codes of ethics such as this effective? Are they likely to be more effective in an Islamic company than in a Western company?
3. How can a Western company operating in a Muslim country conform to Islamic principles concerning gender relations, given that there may be different interpretations of what this involves?

An agenda for research

Ghorbani and Tung (2007) provide an approach to researching some of the issues discussed in this chapter by exploring 'myths and reality' in a Middle Eastern, non-Arab Islamic country: Iran. A preamble decries the still continuing 'glass ceiling' for women professionals and executives in countries such as the UK, USA and Canada, despite supposedly progressive equal opportunities legislation. The myths they set out to investigate in Iranian organizations are as follows:

1. Women do not participate in the labour force nor occupy professional and/or managerial positions.
2. Women are excluded from higher education.
3. Women must wear the *chador* [full veil without face covering or *burqa*, equivalent to *jilbab*] in public and are segregated from men, thus limiting their interaction/activities in societies.
4. In general the government, legislation and society discriminate against women.
5. Islam in general is biased against non-Muslims.

Despite recognizing limitations to their methodology which includes only including a small number of interviews (twelve interviewees: five men and seven women) with Iranians, some by telephone and some no longer living in Iran, they recommend the approach to exploring myths, as myths often lead to the 'formulation of misguided policies that govern action' (Ghorbani and Tung 2007: 378). They are often the result of stereotyping, particularly based on religion, which has particularly gained in significance after 9/11.

Their findings indicated that women and men get the same pay for the same job, particularly in the government sector, yet more men get better-paying jobs and there is a tendency to promote men. A majority of the respondents thought also that women were lacking in confidence. Another factor for men ending up with better jobs is that as head of households they need more money, and they talk to the boss about this who may take this into consideration. Men also appear to have better social connections. It did appear that women do not have any problems with access to higher education, and that despite some segregation in classrooms and workplaces, the wearing of headscarves is often relaxed in private companies where women are not in the public eye. In the major cities the wearing of a small headscarf normally suffices in the street. Yet in government employment more modest dress is required: a bigger headscarf and loose manteaus or a raincoat.

Findings also suggest that women do not enjoy full equality with men despite the gradual reinstatement of rights to pre-revolutionary levels, and the constitution guaranteeing gender equality. Interviewees generally see the government as neither encouraging nor discouraging women into the workforce, that some employers prefer men, but treat women equally once recruited. Some women respondents had difficulties dealing with government agencies; they thought because they were women. Also, findings from this study suggest little if any discrimination towards non-Muslims, although, for example, Christians tend to be in the private sector rather than work for government. There also appears to be tolerance towards non-Muslims' use of alcohol in a country that prohibits its sale.

Although very limited, this study may indicate a possible way of studying Islamic countries, where it may be possible to cut through the perceived 'ethical' issues by first identifying the 'myths' that exist from the Western perspective, and then exploring those myths (as hypotheses) empirically. It would also be useful to do this more extensively among both Western managers and Muslim managers, and to bring the two together in dialogue in order to more thoroughly explore perceptions, myths and reality, and to attempt to understand the 'other' in constructive dialogue. It may also be possible to borrow from some of the principles of discourse ethics explored in Chapter 6 in order to engender a 'good conversation' (Bird, 1996).

Questions for researchers

1. What are the different influences on ethical values and practices in a country such as Saudi Arabia, where not only a particular type of Islam prevails, but also where Western influences appear such as in the Savola ethical principles?
2. How effective are such codes of ethics in terms of the connection between values and behaviour? In the face of a lack of research in Middle Eastern Muslim countries, how might this be investigated?
3. What myths regarding management ethics in Middle Eastern Muslim countries could be explored using Ghorbani and Tung's (2007) approach?
4. Postcolonial theory alerts us to some of the problems of conceptualizing non-Western cultural space, particularly that of the Arab and Muslim world. What are the associated ethical problems of working across cultures, and how might they be investigated?

8 Reconstructing indigenous values and ethics: the South speaks back

There is an anecdote about Christianity entering Africa, attributed to Archbishop Desmond Tutu (although the current author has also seen it attributed to Jomo Kenyatta), which goes like this.

When the white man first came to our lands he had the bible and we had the land. He said, 'close your eyes and let us pray'. When we opened our eyes again, we had the bible and he had the land.

The introduction of Islam to Africa (eighth and ninth centuries) certainly predates Christianity's introduction, and, although the dynamics of its introduction may differ in detail, the basic process of its being introduced alongside political, economic and military ambitions is likely to have been similar. As was seen in Chapter 7, Islam was also disposed towards trade and enterprise, and perhaps towards a proselytizing zeal, like Protestant Christianity, to spread the Word alongside the acquisition and protection of trade routes, the spread of commercial interests, the subjugation in some form of indigenous populations, and assimilation and taking over of existing religious beliefs.

Yet it is unlikely that the 'foreign invader' was able to forcibly introduce a foreign religion on local people, if there did not previously exist some predisposition towards religiosity: although Britain's failure to introduce Christianity into India certainly challenges this assumption, so clearly other factors had to be in place. As Deegan (2009) also points out, there were instances of tremendous resistance to the introduction of both Islam and Christianity to parts of Africa, where people were very happy with existing religion, such as the Goemai of modern-day Nigeria whose religion was based on the desire to protect the lives and welfare of the people. They saw Christianity as concerned with life after death rather than of the living. This may be a key difference between African 'humanistic' religions and Christianity and Islam. Deegan (2009) suggests that such a new religion had little meaning to them beyond any material benefit that might accrue. There is also much evidence to suggest that many Africans have held on to traditional beliefs and simply incorporated them into Christianity or Islam. For example, in the 1990s Christian missionaries were reporting that the Ibo of Nigeria, who had largely converted to Christianity, were becoming more occultist, performing magical rituals and searching for an 'authentic spiritual identity in keeping with their culture' (Deegan, 2009: 30). Again, there is a concern with the here and now, not the hereafter.

European colonial expansion in Africa and other southern climes, in the words of David Livingstone, involved the introduction of commerce, Christianity and civilization, and according to Pakenham (1991: xvii) 'it was in Protestant Britain, where God and Mammon seemed made for each other, that Livingstone's words struck the deepest chord'. The connection between commerce and the spread of Christianity and 'civilization' appear to have gone hand in hand, but certainly in Britain, this connection came quite late in the country's dealings with Africa. Ferguson (2003: 113) tells it thus:

In the eighteenth century the British Empire had been, at best amoral … Native peoples were either taxed, robbed or wiped out. But paradoxically their cultures were largely tolerated; in some cases, even studied and admired.

The Victorians had more elevated aspirations. They dreamt not just of ruling the world, but of redeeming it. It was no longer enough for them to exploit other races; now the aim became to improve them. Native peoples themselves would cease to be exploited, but their cultures – superstitious, backward, heathen – would have to go. In particular, the Victorians aspired to bring light to what they called the Dark Continent.

Thus the modernization project began, and still continues today in various forms. Imperialism (or 'globalization') still sees Africa in particular, but also other southerly regions, as resource rich (and resources there for the taking); but this goes hand in hand with a civilizing/modernizing/developing and often proselytizing mission. In many respects, in terms of Christianity, this mission has been accomplished, and is often not an issue. Indeed, Desmond Tutu's anecdote seems insightful in that Britain, as well as France, appears to have lost much of its religiosity, while Christianity for many Africans is still a major life factor. In the case of Islam, there does not appear to have been a straight swop between land and holy book. The Arab lands, from which the early traders and proselytisers came, have largely not embraced secularism, nor have they actively acquired African lands. They have left a legacy in the Sahel, North West Africa and East Africa in particular. African nations in modern times were not under the direct control of Arab countries, yet as

Deegan (2009) points out Arabs had settled in East and North East Africa, establishing strong trading ties with Yemen and Oman before Islam emerged as a religion. Conquests in North Africa appeared only after this with the spread of Islam, and the extension of the Arab Empire in 656 CE, with Islamic states also emerging in Ghana and Mali. Apart from North Africa, Mauritania, Niger, Mali, Senegal and Gambia are predominantly Muslim, whereas Ghana today is predominantly Christian.

If Islam came to Africa along trade routes, with the acquisition of both human resources (in the form of slaves) and natural resources, Christianity followed similar acquisitions but, following a momentum directed towards abolishing the slave trade, took on a particular moralistic turn.

Ferguson (2003: 114) refers to the early missionaries as the equivalent to modern-day NGOs: 'Like the non-governmental aid organizations of today, Victorian missionaries believed they knew what was best for Africa.' Far from being a government project, the nineteenth-century missionary organizations were part of what is known today as the voluntary sector. Yet it is not just this voluntary sector today that perpetuates the modernization project. Government agencies, international supra-governmental agencies like the World Bank, IMF or WHO, together with large commercial MNCs, and an increasing new subsector spanning the commercial and voluntary sectors, namely the 'new philanthropists' such as the software magnate Bill Gates and pop superstar Madonna, with completely different types of motives, all have a part to play in 'doing what is best' for Africa and 'the South'.

This chapter focuses predominately on sub-Saharan Africa, yet many of the areas covered could equally be applied to other 'developing' regions such as South America and South Asia, and reference will be made to these as appropriate. Yet the Indian subcontinent in particular is different in that it has a long and well-documented civilization, and is also dealt with in Chapter 9. Sub-Saharan Africa also has a long history of different civilizations, but it is largely unrecorded in any written form. This is not because Africa south of the Sahara was in some way more 'primitive' than other civilizations. Mostly societies relied on oral traditions, passed through many generations. There have been attempts to document this, or indeed to reveal it to the eyes of an outside world that was never intended to see it (Mutwa, 1964).

What unites 'the South' that justifies the inclusion of many regions in one chapter is the perception of these countries as 'developing' and historically more primitive than the 'developed' world. Similar ethical issues arise in terms of the perceptions of the West, in terms such as corruption, and cronyism or nepotism; the interaction of power relations; and the framing of the 'indigenous' and how this is understood. Yet the dynamics of North–South relations, and indeed South–South relations are changing. In a way, after years of domination, the South appears to be 'speaking back': both economically and ideologically. The Indian manufacturing company Tata now owns two of the most iconic of British car brands, Land Rover and Jaguar, which it bought from the US giant Ford. It owns Corus, previously British Steel. India, Brazil and China all have major investments in Africa. In particular China is beginning to change the traditional dynamics of Europe's and the USA's interaction with Africa, particularly their policy of conditional aid to the 'developing' continent.

However, there are still relationships between 'developed' and 'developing' countries that appear to hark back to Livingstone and the Victorian era (for example, doing what's best for Africa and the African) perhaps with some religious motivation, but also within an attitude of taking what one wants from a resource-rich land, including human resources.

Opening case: Madonna and Malawi

In the Channel 4 documentary broadcast on British television in June 2009, *Madonna and Mercy: What Really Happened?* journalist Jacques Peretti reported that on 13 June 2009 the Supreme Court in Malawi granted an adoption order allowing the 50-year-old single mother, New York resident Madonna, to adopt the four-year-old Malawian child Mercy James. Peretti questioned whether Madonna is 'saving' the child or depriving her of her culture and country: an extraordinary act of charity, or immoral and wrong? A Malawian judge had in April of that year previously denied the adoption order, saying that Madonna might not be the only international celebrity wanting to adopt the children of Malawi. The concern was that it would 'open the flood gates, and even encourage child trafficking' according to Peretti. Madonna immediately launched an appeal.

Peretti interviewed Mabvuto Banda, a local journalist who had been investigating Madonna's activities in Malawi for Reuters and *The Times*. He reminded Peretti that three years previously Madonna had adopted a boy named David Banda. Far from Madonna adopting him on the spur of the moment when she went to Malawi as the world media assumed, the adoption was a result of her then husband Guy Richie going to the country on her behalf. Twelve children had been lined up for him to choose from. Later he was walking through the orphanage and came across David, a child not in the line-up. He took some pictures, sent them back to Madonna, who 'went crazy about him'. And, according to journalist Banda, 'that is how it happened'. So, before Madonna set foot in Malawi, it was a 'done deal'. But according to Banda, 'why should they in the first place line up twelve children? It was like slavery, you chose who you want.' Peretti adds, 'So David got the golden ticket, he was flown out on Madonna's jet. But he wasn't actually an orphan at all. As Banda discovered, he had a father who loved him, but was unable to look after him.' The mother died after childbirth, and her village was not able to provide care including breastfeeding for the child, so they took him to the orphanage to arrange for someone to feed him. The father walked or cycled every day to see the child and take him presents.

But the plot thickens even more. When Madonna went to the orphanage to see David, according to Peretti's report, she saw another child whom she decided was the one she really wanted: a little girl called Mercy. Like David, she also had a family: 'But unlike David's father, Mercy's family stood in Madonna's way' according to Peretti. The grandmother said that she was 'not interested in Madonna taking Mercy away'. Hence, adds Peretti, 'these adoptions aren't what they seem'.

He discovers that in Malawi, families do not give up their rights to the child they leave in an orphanage. They are more like foster homes. When the family cannot take care of a child for reasons such as a bad harvest, they may leave their children to be taken care of by the orphanage. In the case of Mercy, the deal was that the orphanage would keep her for six years, then she would be returned to her village where her grandmother could take care of her. Mercy's grandmother, Mary, had delivered her into the world, but soon after the birth the mother had died. 'For three years, ever since Madonna set her eyes on Mercy, Mary has been the only one stood in her way, refusing to let Mercy go,' according to Peretti. Eventually, after three years the grandmother was persuaded by the rest of the family that it would be better for Mercy to go with Madonna to get an education, and then she would be in a position to come back at a later stage to help her family. This is with the background that Mercy's mother had been paid by the village to get a good education. She was to become a doctor so she could help the village. But she got pregnant and died in child birth. The village said she was cursed. The father left the village. Mercy, with this opportunity, was now seen as the 'salvation of the village' according to Peretti, with the expectation that she will return. Yet he doubts if Madonna knows anything about this.

He adds that there is a whole number of celebrities who are adopting children from Africa. He asks, if they really want to help can they not just donate money? Yet, as he points out, Madonna is giving a lot of money to Malawi through her charity Raising Malawi. This, as the local journalist Banda points out, is an organization set up by one of the heads of the Kabbalah organization and Madonna, who is a member of this organization. Kabbalah was originally a branch of Jewish mysticism, which has more recently attracted the following of some very rich patrons such as Madonna and Britney Spears. According to *The Telegraph* (2005) 'The Kabbalah Centre sells copies of its sacred texts and other 'spiritual tools', such as Kabbalah Water. Among the best-selling items is the red string bracelet, said to protect the wearer from the evil eye. The Beckhams, Paris Hilton, Britney Spears, Demi Moore and Madonna have all been seen sporting one.'

This is the same bracelet that Madonna has put around the wrist of her adopted son David. According to Mabvuto Banda, the Kabbalah organization Spirituality for Kids trains Malawians in the United States to become trainers of Kaballah in Malawi, and these are the same people who run the orphanages set up by Madonna and the Raising Malawi charity. Perelli points out that their website says that 160,000 children are benefiting from Raising Malawi, and asks if this comes with Kabbalah attached. With all orphanages and childcare being run by foreign Christian and other religious organizations such as Madonna's, in a country where schools are only for the very rich, he asks if a whole generation of children are being handed over to people like Madonna and her way of thinking.

He goes on to investigate a school that Madonna is building in Malawi where the local village, which owns the land it is being built on, knew nothing of the project. Raising Malawi says that the village was happy to give the land for free, yet neither the village nor the chief, who should have been the first person consulted, knew anything about it. Perelli suggests to the villagers that this arrogance is rather like nineteenth-century colonialism, to which they seem to agree. He suggests that a great deal of secrecy exists around Raising Malawi's activities, and his attempt to gain any information from the Executive Director, Philippe van den Bossche, who was sitting outside the courtroom that was hearing Madonna's appeal to get her adoption order, led to nothing.

The revelation that the journalists had located Mercy's natural father, a penniless night watchman, who said he wants to take care of the child, may count for nothing against the fact that Madonna is rumoured to have put £12 million into Malawi, with much political support and having personal interviews with the President. When Perelli had an interview with the government spokesman for the ministry responsible for adoption, and asked if

Madonna coming to Malawi was not like the rich white missionaries coming in the nineteenth century and bringing a new religion which would be
the salvation of the people, the minister said no, because the missionaries,
such as David Livingstone, declared themselves and their religion. Perelli
concluded that this well summed up the difference. He further concluded
that the government appear just as unable as Mercy's family to stop the 'jug-
gernaut' of Madonna.

After visiting one of the orphanages supported by Madonna's charity,
which has Western-standard accommodation, Peretti can see the attraction
to the Malawian government, if this could be brought to every village. This
could never be afforded by the government. He says, 'the price they may have
to pay is to buy into Madonna's loony religion as well, but maybe that is a
small price to pay compared with the benefits to children'. Yet he concludes
that what they are doing in the orphanage is fantastic, but 'like 19th century
colonialism', and 'history repeating itself'. He adds, with the programme
closing by showing images of Madonna on a cross from one of her recent
performances, that 'Madonna is not just a woman who has adopted a child,
maybe she believes she is the messiah, if not the messiah then the saviour
of the future generation of the children of a nation' (see also *The Guardian*,
2009).

The readers may ask, as a management scholar, or practitioner, what has
this got to do with management ethics in 'developing' countries? The current
author, as a management scholar, has taken an interest in this case, going
back at least two years on a visit to South Africa. In the guesthouse in Cape
Town where he was staying were two German couples. Each had come to
South Africa to collect their African babies they were adopting, to take them
back to Germany. One couple had already adopted a baby from South Africa,
and this was their second adoption. This was just one guesthouse out of the
thousands of hotels and guest accommodations in South Africa, and indeed
sub-Saharan Africa, and the author was wondering how widespread adoptions from Africa had become, particularly with such a high-profile figure as
Madonna showing the world the possibilities. McLaughlin (2003) writes in
the *Christian Science Monitor*, that:

in Ethiopia, Americans adopted 114 orphans during the US government's 2002 fiscal year. In fiscal 2003, 190 were adopted. In 2004, some 400 to 500 adoptions are
expected. That could put Ethiopia in the top 10 countries from which Americans
adopt. In 2001, Liberia became the second sub-Saharan African country to be in
the top 20 US adoption spots, with 51 adoptions. One agency alone has placed about
140 Liberian kids in the US and Canada since 1996. Sierra Leone is the only other

African country that allows American agencies to facilitate adoptions. (Others allow them on a case-by-case basis.)

Africa's numbers are just a fraction of the total. Most adoptees come from China (5,053 in 2001) and Russia (4,939 in 2001). Overall, 20,099 orphans got US visas in 2002.

It may well be that the figures have changed considerably since 2003, and are far more substantial when European countries are also included, and now Africa is becoming more popular for adoptions. Many countries, such as Malawi, have a residential qualification. In Malawi, the law states that adoptive parents have to live in the country for eighteen months. Madonna, in the case of David Banda, managed it in eighteen days (*The Guardian*, 2009).

Yet surely this is providing opportunities for very poor children who would have a hard life in Africa, to enjoy the benefits of a comfortable life in the West? As we might see from the case of Madonna in Malawi, there is more to this, particularly at the macro level. This raises two issues. The first one is the belief that Africa (and other 'developing' regions) is a 'basket case' and in need of help. The second is that there are 'resources' in Africa (and elsewhere) that are there for the taking (and it is a charitable act of 'Christian' kindness). Both are controversial, when stated in this way, and represent perceptions of Africa and other 'developing' areas that are pervasive and persistent and colour the attitudes that scholars take to their studies and managers take to work. The spirit of David Livingstone and the Victorian colonists may be far from dead and buried. These are areas that the current chapter will be exploring in relation to an examination of ethical issues in sub-Saharan Africa in particular and 'developing' countries generally, and how local views, values and knowledge might be beginning to answer back. One such issue, which affects managers directly, is that of corruption.

Africa and corruption

In the field of business and work organizations, the modernization project appears to continue into the twenty-first century, but rather than this going hand in hand with the type of colonialism experienced in the nineteenth century that simply saw savages in need of civilization, this may involve issues such as the levels of inefficiencies at best, but corruption at worst, as a result of the legacy of colonialism. The modernizing project is to introduce 'modern' management, including Western (commercial) values, and getting rid of inefficiencies and corruption. Corruption certainly is seen as one of the major ethical issues in developing countries, and not least in sub-Saharan Africa. For example, quoted in Ayittey (1991: 121–2), and alluded to in Chapter 5 of the current text:

President Mobutu's fortune approached $5 billion in a Swiss bank account, a fortune larger than Zaire's [now Democratic Republic of Congo] $4.4 billion foreign debt ... The President's official salary alone amounts to 17 percent of the annual budget, while the country's foreign debt amounts to 70 percent of GNP (*West Africa*, November 30, 1981, p. 2881).

This is perhaps one of the most notorious cases of state corruption by a regime that was supported for many years by the United States. Yet Ayittey (1991: 122), an authority on African indigenous institutions, tells us that:

One of the recurrent myths about Africa is the notion that corruption is culturally ingrained among Africans. The traditional practice of offering a 'dash' has often been used by scholars to provide a 'cultural' explanation to the pervasive incidence of bribery and corruption in Africa. In most West African countries, a bribe is often called a 'dash'. This appellation, however, is a misnomer that reflects a confusion or misunderstanding of the traditional practice ... the 'dash' constituted an advance payment for a service to be performed by the chief, who was not paid for his judicial services. By contrast, today's bribe is demanded or extorted by civil servants, prior to the performance of a service they are paid to render.

He goes on to state that (1991: 123):

In southern Africa, where indigenous legal systems were more developed than elsewhere, the legal code on corruption, bribery and extortion by public officials was explicit. The Rolong, the Hurutshe and the Kwena of Botswana prohibit bribery in order to protect communities against corruption by the use of public office to further private interests.

He also provides a number of examples where the chief was often 'destooled' where corruption in traditional societies was proscribed, and where the chief was caught and became answerable to his people. In fact, rather than the chief being autocratic, where perhaps he could get away with corruption, there were numerous checks and balances built into indigenous political systems. Traditional government was almost always built around consensus, and not, in the common view of modern commentators on Africa, on autocracy. Modern-day autocratic state presidents such as Mobutu, and Robert Mugabe of Zimbabwe are almost certainly going against the traditions of indigenous systems of government. It is worth quoting the assertion within a

Kenyan government Sessional Paper (No. 10 of 1963/65, paragraph 9), which appears to have been forgotten in recent Kenyan politics:

In African society a person was born politically free and equal and his voice and counsel were heard and respected regardless of the economic wealth he possessed. Even where traditional leaders appeared to have greater wealth and hold disproportionate political influence over their tribal or clan community, there were traditional checks and balances including sanctions against possible abuse of power. In fact, traditional leaders were regarded as trustees whose influence was circumscribed both in customary law and religion. In the traditional African society, an individual needed only to be a mature member of it to participate fully and equally in political affairs. (quoted in Ayittey, 1991: 503–4)

So, why now do political institutions, which are criticized by the West as being corrupt at worst, or giving rise to poor governance at best, seem so divorced from the more consensus-seeking institutions of pre-colonial times? The point here is not to glorify everything that predated colonialism, and to denigrate everything that came with colonialism and remained, it is merely to try to understand the current context of a post-colonial Africa, in relation to the type of ethical issues managers may have to deal with. It is futile trying to understand these issues ahistorically, if one is to get to the roots of modern African societal and organizational cultures. Dia (1996), for example points to the 'disconnect' between indigenous communities and colonial institutions that were imposed on local societies. It is instructive to understand how this was done.

Ayittey (1991) reminds us that kinship was the main facet of political organization in pre-colonial Africa. Authority was derived from this kinship system as a main component of what is referred to as 'collectivism' in cross-cultural management theory today (see Chapter 3). Hence political structures could be destroyed, but authority was continuous and could be substituted. That is, it was not dependent on one person or one structure. Hence authority to rule was needed from the people. Without this consensus, anyone who usurped the throne (or stool) was not regarded as legitimate. The colonial authorities often removed traditional leaders, and replaced them. But the new incumbent lacked the traditional authority and respect of the people.

Origins of corruptions: from consensual to autocratic governance

Out of the two types of political organizations indigenous to Africa, states and stateless societies, Ayittey (1991) asserts that it was the stateless societies that the colonists had the most difficulties with. These included the Igbo and Fulani of modern-day Nigeria, the Somali, and the Ga of modern-day Ghana. As there were no chiefs or central authorities in these societies, the 'leaders' that the colonists created simply were regarded as illegitimate: they were shunned and rejected by the people. Even worse, relates Ayittey, the designated 'canton chiefs' in French West Africa and the 'warrant' chiefs in southern Africa became autocratic as they knew they had colonial backing, thus creating a type of leader and leadership institution that was in fact completely foreign to the local community. As an illustration he refers to the example of the Ga Kingdom, a federation of six independent republics with no paramount chief, and each town governing itself, and each with its own *mantse*: not a chief, with no political authority, and not part of the government of the Ga, simply having magical use during war. Yet like many chiefs, he had a stool. This was only used when he carried it to the battlefield, never entering into the battle, but being guarded to one side by a special bodyguard.

Not normally regarded as colonists in Africa, it was in fact the Danes in the nineteenth century who arrived in the Ga independent republics and insisted on dealing with a chief. Not having any chiefs, the *mantse* was the only one to whom the colonists could attribute what they could identify as a chief. When they started dealing with him as such, the people deserted him and created a *mankralo* to whom they transferred allegiance. Similarly other Ga independent republics started de-stooling their *mantse* when the colonial authorities insisted on dealing with them as 'chiefs': in Accra (one of the six Ga republics) for example the *mantse* was de-stooled by the people because he started selling off town land and appropriating money and privileges for himself which were not customarily due to a *mantse*. His successor also acted in such an arbitrary way with the backing of the colonists that he too was de-stooled.

The British colonialists went on to invest yet more authority in the Ga *mantse*. This position became quite sought after because of the privileges that came with it. With the authority of the colonial government the *mantse* often attempted to extend his authority, often leading to bribes being proffered to gain favour of the decision he was now in a position to impart. Yet frequently the elders would refuse to en-stool the government appointee, with respectable people ignoring him and taking their affairs to the elders. Similar stories are told of the Somali and their government-appointed *akils*, and of the *akida* appointed by the German colonialists in East Africa. In the Belgian Congo, the colonial authorities made such appointments from the ranks of

African soldiers serving in the state military. They were given the authority to enforce quotas on rubber collection, became petty tyrants with the authority to punish anyone on the spot with whipping, or in the case of collective resistance, destroy complete villages or punish whole districts through punitive expeditions.

These are just examples of the way the colonists usurped traditional leaders, not really understanding, or wanting to understand their role, and developing from these quite different types of institutions that may have had the look of indigenous institutions, but may well have encouraged authoritarian and often corrupt ways which were certainly far from the stateless societies over which these institutions were superimposed. Of course there were many differences across Africa, and between colonists. The British tended to treat each territory differently, while all French colonies were regarded as part of France rather than a separate entity; did not use traditional leaders as any form of intermediary, but simply neutralized them and finally disposed of them. Those that did remain were merely regarded as agents of the state and had no authority in their own right. Traditional authority based on kinship ties, and consensus of the collective, was broken, and replaced by more authoritarian authority based on the power of the colonists, while having some degree of resemblance to traditional institutions.

Ayittey (1991), however, contends that many indigenous institutions did survive, particularly in British territories and French West Africa where, in the latter, assimilation into France simply did not work. Yet it is perhaps unfortunate that after independence, rather than Africans gaining their freedoms that they had lost to the colonists, and rather than no longer being drained for resources, the new nationalist African leaders continued with authoritarian rule, draining countries' resources. Ayittey (1991: 416) asserts that many Africans are less well off than under colonialism, and that rather than this statement being a 'veiled justification for colonial rule' he contends that 'the fixation with past colonial exploitation blinds many to the grotesque exploitation and treacherous oppression of the people of Africa today'. He goes on to say (1991: 418): 'Independence did not herald the era of prosperity trumpeted by the nationalists. Rather, the economic exploitation of the African people intensified – at the hands of the same elites and nationalists who denounced the colonial powers for exploiting Africa to develop their European countries.'

This is the background to the Africa we see today. It is the background to the Africa that MNCs, international NGOs and private 'benefactors' such as Madonna see today. As noted by Ahluwalia (2001: 133): 'The very signifier

"Africa" is one that was constructed by the West, and one that is currently being reconstructed through Western institutions that decide and exert their power by "knowing" what is best for Africa – namely development and modernity. It is through their amassing of statistics and surveillance that an underdeveloped, primordial, traditional and war-ravaged Africa is (re)produced.'

Certainly, the huge industry of international aid appears to perpetuate the image of Africa as a 'basket case': a sector that not only is self-perpetuating, but also appears to contribute to and, seemingly unknowingly, to support the type of corruption that was exemplified by Maputo in the extreme. Yet the modernization process still appears to go hand in hand with recognizing Africa as resource rich. It may be ironic that the first resource that was recognized by foreigners (mainly the Arabs, and Britain) was human slaves. Since the (almost) abolition of the slave trade,[1] natural resources have been sought and exploited in Africa by foreign powers. Now, with a shortage of healthy babies for adoption in the West, and the expense of doing this in the USA (McLaughlin, 2003), attention appears again to be turning to Africa.

So, how is this represented in organizations and management in Africa, and what are the ethical issues that international management should be concerned about?

The dynamics of leadership, organization and ethical values in Africa

One of the big problems in studying Africa, even from a cross-cultural perspective, is this very appropriation of 'Africa' described by Ahluwalia (2001). It is the pejorative and obstructive influences on scholarship of the 'developing–developed' world paradigm (itself a cultural construct, and one defined by the 'developed' world and also adopted by intellectuals and elite in the 'developing' world) which still seems to persist, and certainly hampered research well into the 1990s (see for example in Jaeger and Kanungo, 1990; and to a lesser degree in Blunt and Jones, 1992) and is probably still doing so. It also colours what managers 'see' when they look at how to work in Africa or with Africans. It is the perception of negatives such as levels of corruption. Certainly if we look at the figures published by Transparency International (TI) on perceptions of corruption, many of Africa's countries appear at the

[1] For an overview of modern slavery see: www.antislavery.org/english/slavery_today/what_is_modern_slavery.aspx, accessed 30/09/09.

bottom of the list with other more 'corrupt' countries of the 'developing' world. Yet TI's Bribe Payers Index also shows that many of the 'developed' countries are not averse to paying bribes to facilitate business. Particularly keen, also, to pay bribes appear to be the so-called BRIC countries of Brazil, Russia, India and China. It is exactly these countries (particularly China and India) that over the last few years have been challenging the West's domin-ance in Africa.

The 'developing–developed' world dichotomy is indicative of the power relations that exist on a global basis in Africa and influence the way we see organizational dynamics such as leadership and management behaviour. The disparaging of African culture is but one example of such power relations, and the 'developing–developed' world dichotomy is an articulation of this. There does appear to be a view that African indigenous thought has little to offer. In some ways it is difficult to know, in a globalized world, what 'indi-genous' actually is (see Jackson *et al.*, 2008). The convergence thesis suggests that world cultures are coming together, while the divergence thesis sees cultures as remaining distinct. The current author subscribes to the cross-vergence view that different globalizing/localizing dynamics lead to hybrid forms of knowledge, organization and action (see Priem *et al.*, 2000, for an overview; and the discussion in Chapter 2 of the current text), but a process that is driven by geopolitical power relations. Yet it is still important, in order to analyse that crossvergence, to try to conceptualize what goes in and what comes out.

These dynamics can best be understood by focusing on three 'ideal type' organizational systems that, through historical, modernizing and localiz-ing processes appear to represent the types of organization present in sub-Saharan Africa and other 'developing' regions, and stemming from the types of colonial/post-colonial and indigenous processes described above in con-nection with corruption and the nature of political governance. These are conceptual categories, used for analysis purposes, and described previously by the current author (Jackson, 2004). Although conceptual categories, they provide the basis for understanding management ethics in Africa.

- Post-colonial systems, arising through the historical and political legacy of colonial Africa, and represented often by negative assertions of autocratic and even corrupt management. Seen as what constitutes 'African' man-agement in the sense used above by Ahluwalia (2001) as a Western-created signifier.
- Post-instrumental systems, arising from modernizing economic and struc-tural influences. This is driven by (neo)liberal economic policies, as well as

by Western multinational companies operating in Africa, and is often seen as the solution to the problems of Africa (knowing what is best for Africa), but is driven by instrumental values and a form of neo-colonialism, which may be at variance to local humanistic values. It may even perpetuate aspects of corruption through bribe paying: seeing this as a means to an end, and having a teleological justification. At national policy level, the liberalization of the economy often has led to downsizing of organizations, with a reduction in services and jobs.

- African 'renaissance' systems, arising from an embryonic cultural and political indigenous revival, focusing on humanistic values and represented by people-centric leadership and policies. At the national policy level it could be represented by the ill-fated South African Reconstruction and Development Programme (RDP).

These three influences often vie for position with one another. Hence Western systems, which appear to be instrumentally motivated, attempt to 'reform' what is seen as 'African' institutions, policies and organizations, while 'cronyism' particularly in the public sector persists in post-colonial styles of management and forms of organization (often consisting of formal, and informal, systems, the latter holding the reins of organizational power). Sometimes African 'renaissance' forms creep through like RDP, only to be met by often Western pressures or market forces, and to be put on hold in favour of more neoliberal policies such as the GEAR (Growth, Employment and Redistribution) strategy, a turnaround from the South African socially oriented policies towards achieving open markets and privatization, with negative implications for service delivery and employment.

One more largely unresearched influence that is achieving ascendency in Africa currently is that of China. Whether this is a benign influence or simply a new form of colonialism will be more fully discussed at the end of this chapter. Certainly a new South–South dynamic is changing things in Africa, and challenging the old North–South dynamics.

However, there is one more theoretical category that should be taken on board in order to understand the nature of management ethics in Africa. This is the *instrumental-humanism* distinction introduced in Chapter 3 of the current text, within the concept of *locus of human value* (Jackson, 2002a). In other words: what value is placed on human beings in organizations in Africa, and how can this be conceptualized in these three different organizational systems? Conceptually the alternatives can be represented as follows:

- An *instrumental* view of the utilitarian value of people in organizations (managing people as a resource), whereby people are seen as a 'resource' and a means to an end: human resources are used to meet the executive objectives of the organization (Jackson, 1999), and;

- A *humanistic* view of the intrinsic value of people in their own right (developing the potential of people in organizations as an end in itself), whereby people are seen as having a value for what they are, rather than what they can do for the organization (Koopman, 1991; Lessem 1994, Saunders, 1998; Jackson, 1999).

As we saw in Chapter 3 the Western cultural perception that human beings are a resource to be used in the pursuit of executive goals and shareholder value may be challenged by a view that people have a value in their own right (Jackson, 1999). This is not the distinction made in Western management theory between 'hard' and 'soft' approaches to human resource management. It actually challenges the foundations of regarding a human being as a resource. Tayeb (2000) has pointed out that the concept of human resource management is itself a product of a particular Anglo-American culture.

The 'hard' and 'soft' approaches taken within Western organizations are both a reflection of an inherent cultural concept that sees human beings in organizations as means to an end (Blunt and Jones, 1997, use the term 'functionalism'). The two approaches are simply two poles of a continuum from high to low instrumentalism. Hence Lobel (1997), arguing for the 'soft' side of human resource management (integrating partnership building with communities, and balancing work and personal life) does not break out of the paradigm. She simply makes out the business case for bottom-line consequences. That is, if the hard approach does not work, namely, an overt task-focused approach, then use the soft approach of the human relations school to influence and bring people in. Often in mature human resource management systems, in such countries as the United States and the UK, the soft side of HRM is used, rather than a hard instrumentalism. Hence the term 'post-instrumental' has been used to describe the Western influence on management in the current context.

As with any other value systems that organizations use when making decisions about human beings, the instrumental-humanistic dichotomy does have implications for ethicality. For example, in transferring Western HRM systems to Africa, it is relevant to talk about both their efficiency and their appropriateness. Appropriateness in this context refers to its acceptance within the local values systems: that is, if it is seen as an ethical way to regard people.

We now focus on the three ideal types, how they value people within the organization and implications for our understanding of management ethics in Africa.

Post-colonial organization, and corruption

Descriptions of management in Africa have largely been informed by the developed–developing world dichotomy as was noted above, and exemplified in the work of Blunt and Jones (1992), one of the most thorough descriptions, and that of Jaeger and Kanungo (1990) of management and organization in 'developing' countries in general. This is particularly in the distinction made between 'Western' leadership and management (for example, teamwork, empowerment) and 'African' styles (for example, centralized, bureaucratic, authoritarian) (Blunt and Jones, 1997).

However, the current text postulates that the forms of management identified in the literature as 'African' (Blunt and Jones, 1992; 1997) or as 'developing' in the wider literature on management in developing regions (Jaeger and Kanungo, 1990) are mostly representative both of a post-colonial heritage, and a post-colonial perspective from the West.

Focusing on the first of these assumptions, that such management and organization is inherited from the colonial past, institutions have been identified in the more critical literature as being 'tacked on' to African society originally by the colonial powers (Carlsson, 1998, and Dia, 1996), and being perpetuated after independence, perhaps as a result of vested political and economic interest, or purely because this was the way managers in the colonial era were trained. The type of process that brought this into being was discussed above, providing among others the example of the Ga of Ghana (Ayittey, 1991). The upshot of this appears to be as follows.

Organizational structures, in terms of their governance and decision making are characterized as authoritarian and sometimes paternalistic decision styles with centralized control and decision making (Kiggundu, 1989). This is also reflected in Blunt and Jones's (1997) view that leadership is highly centralized, hierarchical and authoritarian. They also add that there is an emphasis on control mechanisms, rules and procedures rather than performance (and a high reluctance to judge performance), a bureaucratic resistance to change and a high level of conservatism, and importance of kinship networks.

The character of such organizations may well reflect public sector, state-owned enterprises or recently privatized organizations that are not foreign owned. Some of the inadequacies which Joergensen (1990) draws attention to in relation to state-owned enterprises in East Africa, include lack of clear objectives, overstaffing, lack of job descriptions and job evaluation, lack of incentives, and political interference, as well as poor infrastructure and lack of management systems. Part of the inefficiency of post-colonial organizational systems may be the levels of corruption and 'unethical' behaviour. (e.g. de Sardan, 1999). It is often this crisis of governance, reflected in the state sector, which international organizations such as the IMF and World Bank point to as in need of reform.

Internal policies may be discriminatory as a result of preferences given to in-group or family members. Kanungo and Jaeger (1990) suggest that because of the 'associative' thinking in developing countries, there is a tendency for behaviour in organizations to be context-dependent, rather than the 'developed' country orientation towards context-independent behaviour orientation where explicit and universal rules apply to a situation rather than the situation and context determining the responses to it. This may lead to decisions based on relationships rather than the application of universal rules, and may therefore be regarded as discriminatory. This was met, for example, in Cameroon by Jackson and Nana Nzepa (2004) where the 'unofficial' or 'informal' organization played a key role in the public sector in promotions and other favours to in-group members. Although this may reflect a general collectivism or communalism in traditional African cultures, its distortion during the colonial era, and after independence into 'cronyism' may perhaps be seen here.

There is an indication of a commitment to 'business' objectives involving the pursuit of end results at the expense of means, although not reflecting an achievement orientation, but rather cutting corners perhaps (Montgomery, 1987 noted a regard for internal aspects of the organization rather than policy issues, development goals or public welfare, remarking on an aloofness of managers in the public sector). A mistrust of human nature, and a belief in the undisciplined nature of African workers to industrial life may be part of an autocratic management style and also, at worse, leads to the regarding of Africans as 'lazy': a sentiment found in the literature well into the 1980s (Abudu, 1986).

A number of authors have also perceived decision making in the 'developing' world generally as focused in the past and present rather than the future (Montgomery, 1987; Kanungo and Jaeger, 1990). This may indicate a deontological orientation, but is more likely to indicate a short-term focus, with a curious moralistic focus mixed with self-interest.

We can now focus on the second assumption posited above, that this perception of 'African' management and organization is a postcolonial creation from the West, in the same way that Ahluwalia (2001) contends that 'Africa' is a Western construct. The perceptions created by this conceptualization of

'African leadership' within a developed–developing world paradigm (fatalistic, resistant to change, reactive, short-termist, authoritarian, risk reducing, context-dependent, associative and basing decisions on relationship criteria, rather than universalistic criteria) when directly contrasted with management in the 'developed' world, implies that the developing world should be developed to become more like the 'developed' world. Hence 'modern' management techniques provide a 'solution' to the problem. As we saw in Chapter 5, both dependency theory, from an economic perspective, and postcolonial theory provide critiques of the modernization project: the latter from a perspective of the West's construction of the East, largely within a developing–developed world paradigm, which is not only internalized by Western scholars and managers, but also by local (indigenous) scholars and often managers. This of course is partly through the education systems that mostly have disparaged the indigenous culture, and within the profession itself, through Western textbooks and MBA programmes. It is often difficult therefore to obtain a proper account of management and organization in Africa and other developing regions, as postcolonial theory suggests that these (mostly pejorative) perceptions are deeply entrenched for both Westerner and indigene. For the social science researcher, postcolonial theory is very difficult to operationalize, as was noted in Chapter 5.

The developing–developed conceptualization often fails to recognize other (sometimes embryonic) management systems operating in Africa. It is also not sufficiently underpinned by cross-cultural theory, yet must surely influence what cross-cultural researchers investigate and how. The developing–developed world paradigm reflects a paucity of cultural analysis, and in management theory reflects the traditions of the convergence thesis (from Kerr *et al.*, 1960).

Where this view of management in 'developing' countries is explained by cross-cultural theory, reference is often made to Hofstede's (1980a/2003) value dimensions. Hence Kanungo and Jaeger (1990) depict the organizational situation in developing countries as relatively high in *Uncertainty Avoidance* (low tolerance for risk and ambiguity), low *Individualism*, high *Power Distance* (reflected in a lack of consultative or participatory management), and low in *Masculinity* (a lack of competitiveness and achievement orientation, and a low centrality of work). Hofstede's (1980a/2003) own data is not very helpful on African cultures as he had low sample sizes from West and East African countries that he combined into two regional samples, and a whites-only sample from South Africa. The more current results from the GLOBE study (House *et al.*, 2004) are more comprehensive but also somewhat limited in their analytical use.

The popular South African management literature supports a view that African cultures have a collectivist propensity (Koopman, 1991). The academic work of Blunt and Jones (1992) indicates from the now somewhat dated literature that African societies are low on individualism. More recent studies that include African countries suggest lower levels of values associated with individualism (Munene *et al.*, 2000), and higher levels of those associated with collectivism (Smith *et al.*, 1996; Noorderhaven and Tidjani, 2001). Yet these say little about the nature of African collectivism, and provide little explanation of the 'disconnect' thesis of Dia (1996) that postulates a separation between the individualist institutions of the colonizers (such as the firm) and the more communalistic local populations. They also fail to 'unpick' the different influences on management and organization (such as the post-colonial, Western and humanistic/renaissance 'systems' postulated here) and their different values and implications for our understanding of management ethics within 'developing' regions such as sub-Saharan Africa. For example, if we are to accept that 'African' management ethics is represented by the post-colonial management 'system' presented above, then from a Western perspective we could point to the overly autocratic style of management, the lack of accountability and often corrupt nature of management. We could see mostly self-serving leaders who took a highly instrumental view of their employees who were used to serve vested interests, yet who would be favoured if part of the in-group, but would be overlooked if from the wrong village, or clan, or ethnic group.

In fact little has been written on management/business ethics in Africa that is not concerned with such negative practices as corruption, and by implication this literature directly reflects a perception of what has been called here post-colonial management. If one sees, from the West, that 'African' commercial organizations are inefficient, government organizations are unaccountable, and institutions generally are weak and not able to support a liberal, modern economy, then clearly this is seen as being in need of change and modernization. So, what is the solution?

Post-instrumental organization and CSR

A belief, within the developing–developed world paradigm, reflecting the convergence theory of Kerr *et al.* (1960) and contingency theory of Hickson and Pugh (1995; and see also Cray and Mallory, 1998, for an overview), is that the developing world, through industrialization, should become more like the developed world. This is reflected in the trend for 'Western' approaches to management to be imported into African countries and other 'developing' regions, through multinational companies, and 'Western' approaches to be sought out by managers who are increasingly being educated within Western or Western-style management courses, and being trained in Western traditions. This may not only affect organizations in the private sector, but also those in the public sectors including state-owned enterprises, and those recently privatized enterprises which are in the process of refocusing as a result of downsizing and other major organizational change. This may reflect also a disparaging of 'African' (i.e. post-colonial) ways of organizing and managing. This disparaging is reflected in much of the literature reviewed above.

Within the confines of the instrumental (as opposed to a humanistic paradigm discussed above) and a contingency hard/soft approach to human resource management, the Western 'ideal' is seen as a concern for performance, drive for efficiency and competitiveness and participative with a relative equality of authority and status between manager and subordinate, delegation, decentralization, teamwork and an emphasis on 'empowerment'. This is within a context of acceptance of change and uncertainty, with high levels of trust and openness and the support of followers being essential with a drive to secure commitment and high morale. More recently, there is also a major concern for corporate social responsibility (CSR).

There is evidence in the literature that over the last decade or so organizations in Africa are moving more towards this type of Western or post-instrumental approach particularly in the area of human resource management (see for example Kamoche, 2001, with regard to Kenya). The current author's surveys across fifteen sub-Saharan countries (Jackson, 2004) suggest both a move towards a Western-type results-oriented style of management, and a desire to see more of this among managers, although there are differences among the various countries which suggests, for example, that both the current situation and the desire to move towards this is far less in the Democratic Republic of Congo (DRC) or the Côte d'Ivoire than in South Africa, Botswana or Namibia. Yet this is compounded with a corresponding desire to move towards a people-centric approach that managers generally over the fifteen countries see is missing from their organizations currently, albeit with some differences among the countries (for example managers in DRC, Botswana, Burkina Faso and Nigeria see their organizations as low on people-focus and high on control-orientation, compared with managers in Mozambique and Rwanda who see their organizations as far more people-centric) (Jackson, 2004: 112).

Mellahi *et al.* (2005) believe that many Western corporations operating in 'developing' regions such as Africa have re-evaluated their policies regarding the relationship between business and society in the aftermath of major issues regarding environment protection and disruptions to local communities with Shell's oil exploitation in Nigeria's Delta region. Following organized protests by the local Ogoni people about environmental damage within their homelands (their suffering all the problems associated with oil exploration, but receiving none of the benefits) Shell withdrew from the area, only for the Nigerian government to execute eight leading protestors and the high-profile critic of Shell, Ken Saro-Wiwa. Certainly this type of exploitation of natural resources, with the cooperation of the national government, appears to have been a major feature of Western corporations' activities in Africa and other 'developing' regions. Yet such operations are increasingly coming under scrutiny, not always from local community groups who often have little international 'voice', although this certainly is a factor, but from international NGO pressure groups such as Greenpeace.

Mellahi *et al.* (2005: 105), after the World Business Council for Sustainable Development, define CSR as 'the commitment of business to contribute to sustainable economic development, working with employees, their families, the local community and society at large to improve their quality of life'. This implies taking a stakeholder approach that goes beyond serving the narrow interests of the shareholders. Or does it?

As Mellahi *et al.* (2005) point out; the traditional position of the firm is that it is there to make profits. They suggest that the extreme view represented by Milton Friedman is that the firm has no responsibility beyond profit maximization. Yet there is another *raison d'être* of the firm: to stay in business. Under the latter rationale there may be two main arguments for CSR and the stakeholder approach. The first is that CSR is good business, in a world where consumers are more sensitive to these issues, and that commercial organizations will lose popular support, customers, and in the longer term their business if they do not show a level of social responsibility. That is, not to implement CSR initiatives may be against the interests of the shareholders. Hence CSR as a concept may be well within the instrumental paradigm discussed above. Secondly, not to take cognisance of the different stakeholders in a context such as sub-Saharan Africa, which can be complex and difficult to understand for a foreign company, and to not include them in at least some form of decision-making process, may simply be inept from a management point of view. Environmental scanning is fundamental in strategic management theory. That is, it is necessary to scan the business environment by involving views from different stakeholders such as local communities, governments, trade unions and consumers, in order to do good business. Again, it is easy to see the instrumental rationale for this.

The current author has previously pointed out the approach of companies in 'developing' countries, such as Colgate Palmolive in South Africa (Jackson, 2002b). In a published case by Beaty (1998) the company, with a turnover of US$100 million and workforce of 600 employees, allocated some US$3 million to set up a Colgate Palmolive Foundation. The funding allocation was then managed by a company-appointed management rather than representatives of the different stakeholder communities that would stand to benefit from projects. It was criticized by the trade union for not involving them. It was also criticized for funding projects in part, such as dental-related projects and others, in the areas of their product lines. This was because they appeared to be doing this out of 'enlightened self-interest' rather than through altruism or a sense of what is required to develop communities and people within them. Other companies, which the current author studied in South Africa (Jackson, 2004) appeared not to be contributing substantially to the local labour market, and were actively downsizing, to an extent that one such company operating in one of the poorest provinces in South Africa, removed its operations and consolidated its activities in the country's main commercial centre, Johannesburg. Certainly travelling within poor and rural areas in South Africa, it is not unusual to see large signs on schools indicating international companies such as Coca-Cola as a main sponsor.

Mellahi *et al.* (2005) asserts that CSR should go beyond public relations exercises, yet they also state 'The stakeholder view of the firm undermines the notion that a firm should only maximize profits for shareholders. Rather, the goal of any firm should be to satisfy the aspirations of all of the main stakeholders' (2005: 107). One could contend that if a firm did anything to undermine shareholder interest, shareholders would withdraw their investment in the company, with a corresponding plunge in share value; or would see a change to the executive. Within a purely instrumental (and capitalist) view of the firm, CSR would have to be in line with shareholder interests, at least in the medium to long term.

Jackson *et al.* (2008) contend that the firm is an alien construct in the mainly agrarian and communalist context of Africa, and by implication other such communities in other parts of the world, and perhaps is yet to be entirely assimilated. The Anglo-American concept of the firm may be different to that of co-ordinated markets:

In the neo-liberal capitalist philosophy, firms are considered as market artefacts with the primary responsibility of providing decent returns to their shareholders within the 'rules of the game' (Friedman, 1962). This liberal market orientation is largely characteristic of the Anglo-American business model. It is less characteristic of the co-ordinated markets of Western Europe and South East Asia where business concerns traditionally go beyond shareholders to include other stakeholders such as employees and suppliers (Whitley, 1999). Jones (1999) refers to these as property rights capitalism and stakeholder capitalism, respectively. In the former, firms are constructed as private actors, with private rights mainly embedded in contracts (licenses of operation), while in the latter, firms are construed as fabrics of the society with the purpose of providing some social benefits (i.e. employment, productivity, economic growth, sustainability) (Fannon, 2003). Although firms in coordinated markets operate on the basis of contracts, they are expected to adhere more to the spirit than the letters of contracts. (Jackson *et al.*, 2008: 405–9)

It is likely that firms that are actually African, rather than Western or post-colonial, may have appropriated the capitalist model of the firm in a particular way that is quite different to that of, say, a UK company. There is evidence to support this (Jackson, 2004). Yet some are struggling with the ideal of an African indigenous approach, and what this might look like. This is because what may be regarded as 'indigenous' knowledge, values, ethics, has been either submerged among the crossvergence processes, and among these different influences (post-colonial, post-instrumental/Western), or has been appropriated (e.g. 'African' ethical values incorporate corruption). This, and other aspects of what may constitute 'indigenous' management and business will be explored in the next section.

African renaissance organization, back to the future

To have any chance of reconstructing the 'indigenous', it is necessary to understand what has led to where we are today. However, understanding that is far from harking back to the past. Cultural identity is about the future. It is about what we are to become. Homi Bhabha, quoted by Ntuli (1999), puts it thus: 'Our existence today is marked by a tenebrous sense of survival, living on the borderlines of the 'present', for which there seems to be no name other than the current and controversial shiftiness of the prefix 'post' – postmodernism, postcolonialism, post-feminism.'

Ntuli (1999: 185) goes on to point out that '[t]his signifier [i.e. post-] points to the continuation of the past, reinscribing itself in the present, while struggling to reconcile the two moments', and adds '[t]hat something can be alive and dead at the same time can create conceptual violence if one is social-ised into the Western binary mode of thought … A 'traditional' African or Asian will not find this concept of the 'dead-alive' absurd or mind-boggling. Traditional African world views permit for the world of the living, the dead and the living dead.' Ntuli (1999) goes on to add:

Africa has entered into the era of postcolonialism with its multiple discourses. The issue of identity is of crucial importance, since this affects the direction(s) in which Africa must traverse and who determines this direction(s). In the postcolony we do not encounter singular pristine identities determined by a singular organising prin-ciple. (1999: 186)

restoring the African as subject of his [sic] own history is not the search for an ori-ginal pristine, authentic past to be venerated but a search for guidelines for future programmes. As a people we have been interpellated into the Western ideological machinery, hence the need for decolonising our minds. (1999: 189)

The author goes on to explain that:

the success of the Western powers in effecting world domination was predicated on its use of culture as ideology. Christianity was used as a subtle battering ram to gain hegemony over the rest of the world. It portrayed a religion based on perfection. A perfect God against pagan gods … Mission schools forbade the native from the use of 'their' language … where complementarity existed, binary thought was intro-duced [with the] … Cartesian imperative [leading] to instrumental reason. And how capitalism used it! (1999: 191)

As with the case of the Ga of Ghana, and other instances where the colonial power distorted institutions, so they also 'invented' African religion, such as ancestor worship, animism and totemism, which the 'educated' classes then accepted as a result of Western education in schools. As Ntuli (1999) points out, the 'uneducated' African knew very well that the *idlozi* or shade/ances-tor was not worshipped, and that the praise songs addressed at animals were addressed at preserving the animals and in being conservationists.

African religion is more about the here and now (and how everything relates to that), rather than the hereafter, as is the case with Christianity and the other monotheistic religions. And it is perhaps exactly because African thought systems do not make binary distinctions (either/or) that Africa was able to absorb the new religion of the colonizers with the old, humanistic, reli-gions. Christianity makes a (binary) distinction between the material world and the spiritual world, between life on Earth, and life after death; whereas African religions do not. This is expressed, at least partially, by Mutabazi

(2002: 208), when he says that 'In African countries, life cannot be conceptualized and compartmentalized (into professional life, family life, life on Earth, afterlife, etc) as it can in the West'. He goes on to add that life is rooted in the distant past, and branches out into the distant future, and 'is quite naturally lived in continuity'. He contends, as a result of research in over thirteen countries, that throughout Africa there is a great deal of commonality regarding beliefs and value systems. One such belief is that there is no dichotomy between the natural world and the supernatural, or the material and spiritual worlds. 'God is the Father of fathers, the Ancestor of ancestors' (2002: 207) and that 'Heaven and Earth are inseparably linked by ancestors'. Pityana (1999: 145) believes that 'The ancestors are the connecting mechanism between an ordered objective world and the spirit world, the world of the past and the future. The present world or the objective reality bears a relationship to the world of the spirits. This reality is able to ensure a moral equilibrium through the principle of *ubuntu*'.

Ubuntu is fundamentally a humanistic construct, which is now heavily used in South Africa, including in management studies and practice. African beliefs and values (including traditional religions) are fundamentally humanistic, non-instrumentalist, and based in the here and now, with no contradictions seen in this being linked with the past and future, and in the link between the spirit and material world. Long before *ubuntu* arrived as an all-singing, all-dancing concept to be appropriated by management consultants, Steve Biko (1984: 27) tried to explain this humanistic concept thus:

A visitor to someone's house [in the Westerner's culture], with the exception of friends, is always met with the question, 'What can I do for you?'. This attitude of seeing people not as themselves but as agents for some particular function either to one's disadvantage or advantage is foreign to us ... we believe in the inherent goodness of man. We enjoy man for himself. We regard living together not as an unfortunate mishap warranting competition among us ... We always refrain from using people as stepping stones.

This brings us back to the distinction previously made in this chapter between instrumental and humanistic values, which may be a far more useful distinction than the collectivist-individualist dichotomy (see also Chapter 3). Mutabazi (2002: 209) points out that, as a result of his extensive studies:

Western notions of individualism and collectivism did not exist in any of the communities we observed ... These communities' fundamental method for managing human relations ... is cosubsistence – among individuals and among the concentric circles that make up a clan or community. As for newcomers to this system, they are not rejected or dominated but are welcomed and perhaps even integrated into the community.

Again, a work that predates the current use of the word *ubuntu* is that of Binet (1970) who provides an account of the values that make up this humanistic perspective, and is cited by Dia (1996). A fuller elaboration of these key values can also be found in Jackson (2004).

- *Sharing.* A need for security in the face of hardship has provided a commitment to helping one another. However, it is likely that this value is not based on simple exchange, but as a result of a network of social obligations based predominantly on kinship. This reflects a wider community-orientation which also includes elements of family and other outside involvement, and a character that involves the development and well-being of its people, with a general people-orientation and a sense of belongingness, trust and openness.

- *Deference to rank.* Dia's (1996) assertion that this refers to *Power Distance* (in Hofstede's, 1980a/2003, conceptualization), particularly within the organizational context between employer and employee, is too simplistic. Although traditional rulers were such by their title to the senior lineage, they had to earn the respect of their followers, and rule by consensus, as was discussed earlier in the current chapter. It also includes the senior person showing humility towards the younger person, and to the educated person not looking down on those less educated.

- *Sanctity of commitment.* Commitment and mutual obligation stems from group pressures to meet one's promises, and to conform to social expectations.

- *Regard for compromise and consensus.* This certainly involves the maintenance of harmony within the social context, but also qualifies a deference to rank discussed above.

- *Good social and personal relations.* This stems from many of the aspects discussed above, particularly the commitment to social solidarity. Dia (1996) observes that the tensions of management–labour relations that have been a feature in (Western and post-colonial) organizations in Africa can be attributed largely to a lack of a human dimension and the adversarial attitudes of colonial employment relations.

Yet when we look at this 'idea type' of humanistic or renaissance management values, are we looking back, or are we looking to the future? The word 'renaissance' suggests both: 'revival or rebirth, especially of culture and learning, from Latin RE- + *nasci* to be born' (*The Collins English Dictionary*).

In search of 'indigenous' values and ethics

Identifying what is indigenous, and what is not, is in some ways a pointless task. It is a harking back to 'what we were'. The concept of 'renaissance' is a useful construct in terms of trying to understand where we came from (what constituted 'indigenous' in the first place), the dynamics that got us to where we are today (colonialism and globalization), and what we are to become (the South 'speaking back'). The following is an attempt to synthesize some of the above discussion.

Where we were, and who we were

It is very difficult, in sub-Saharan African countries, to conceptualize and identify the 'indigenous' or an 'indigenous' people. For example, in the context of South Africa, the Khoisan peoples are generally regarded as the original occupants of the southern part of the continent, although now mostly obliterated by successive Dutch and British colonists (Sparks, 1990; Beinart, 1994). The 'Bantu' people more recently moved into this part of the continent from much further north and are now regarded as the 'indigenes' (Reader, 1997). The extent to which 'Afrikaners' established a 'tribe' within South Africa, as quite distinct to their mostly Dutch origins, could be thought of equally as colonists and as indigenes some three centuries after the first settlements were established. If indigenous 'blacks' suffered under apartheid, so did the Afrikaners suffer under British rule. Yet to what extent can a white African 'tribe' be thought of as indigenous? Clearly Afrikaners have no other home, other than in South Africa. Similar issues could be raised within the context of the UK and USA in terms of successive waves of immigration and migration, and who are the indigenes, and what constitutes the 'indigenous'.

For example, Marsden (1991) describes the use of the term 'indigenous' in three ways. First is the reference to 'indigenous' people. In this sense, often applied to marginal peoples such as Native Americans or Australians, it is difficult to apply to African countries. In colonial times, the whole black population was often marginalized, and given second or third class status. The dispossessed today are a result of rapid urbanization and the breaking up of traditional agricultural rural communities and movement to the large cities.

His second use of the word is in the context of 'indigenization', for example following independence from colonial rule, and is not directly relevant here other than noting that this may have led to discrimination, for example against Asian groups in East Africa, or perhaps currently in South Africa against white males, or indeed in Saudi Arabia against non-Saudis (see Chapter 7).

His third sense of the use of 'indigenous' (Marsden, 1991) is in 'insider knowledge': that of local approaches to management that reflect knowledge of the local context and local communities. Marsden (1991) gives the example of insider knowledge systems in farming. This therefore does not assume an 'indigenous people', rather a distinction between what can be regarded as 'local' as distinct from 'global' (read 'Western', but could also be 'Eastern', but has the characteristic of imposition by, or adoption of the 'foreign'). It is a knowledge of the 'local', by local people 'who know what will and will not work', to quote Marsden (1991: 31).

Perhaps a way of linking these different concepts of 'indigenous' may be to introduce a factor of social solidarity: that is, identifying one's self as part of a local community, which has its own networks and 'insider knowledge' and favouring one's fellow group members. In other words, taking a lead from the literature on collectivism, where one's identity is based in the belongingness to a social group or network (Triandis, 1990; Hofstede, 1980a/2003) to the extent that the solidarity of collectivism is target specific: aimed at in-group members, and exhibiting different behaviours and attitudes towards out-group members (Hui, 1990). Here, insider knowledge may well be guarded and kept from out-group members (as Hui's, 1990, discussion of Chinese family businesses suggests; and as the lack of knowledge on successful informal African micro-businesses suggests).

An understanding of the indigenous as 'insider knowledge' should therefore be qualified to reflect the multiple influences on the management of organizations in sub-Saharan Africa.

The dynamics that got us here

What we consider indigenous knowledge, attitudes and values, as well as organization and management, carries issues of who identifies what as 'indigenous', and this is dependent on the dynamics of colonization and globalization, but also other aspects such as the politics of cultural identity.

As we saw above, within 'indigenous' African institutions the chief is seen through Western eyes as an autocrat and his institutions reflect this high Power Distance, in much the same way as we saw that 'African' organization and management values are identified with a post-colonial construct.

This is a view contested by Ayittey (1991) who describes many African societies' chiefs as ruling by consensus. However, as we discuss below, a view that
African organizations can somehow revert back to indigenous values and
structures is, as Human (1996) suggests, slightly naïve. Unravelling the 'indigenous' from the long history of colonial occupation, intercontinental and
intracontinental migration and settlement is a complex project.

For example, Thomson (2000) has argued that many current ethnic groups
in Africa are a creation of colonialism. The Hausa-Fulani, Yoruba and Igbo
of Nigeria are the dominant groups in three regions of post-independence
Nigeria: northern, western and eastern respectively where 'tribes' were
encouraged to develop in order to work with the colonial authorities for
distributing resources. He suggests that ethnic groups that had previously
only had loose and changing affiliations came together as 'tribes', otherwise
they had little power in dealing with the authorities and gaining resources.
The Yoruba is one such example of a modern social and political construct.
Previously to colonial rule the term Yoruba did not exist. People of the region
identified themselves as Oyo, Ketu, Egba, Ijebu, Ijesa, Ekiti, Ondon or members of other smaller groupings, although they were aware of each other and
had links through trade, social contacts or war. They had a common language, but with different dialects that were not always mutually understand-
able. The colonial authorities wanted larger communities to deal with, as did
the missionaries who consequently invented a standard Yoruba vernacular
based on the Oyo dialect, and printed a Yoruba bible. If people wanted access
to Western education they had to adopt this common language.

This identification with a larger or more important group can be found
active in pursuit of better job opportunities, and involves a politics element
in cultural identity. Nyambegera (2002) points out the impact of ethnicity
on areas such as recruitment and promotion opportunities. This is bound up
with power relations within interethnic interactions in the workplace, where
an ethnic group tends to predominate. The process of ethnic *phagocytosis*
(smaller groups being swallowed up by dominant groups) that this stimulates
may actually be having an effect on the apparent ethnic composition of the
country in Cameroon, as pointed out by Jackson and Nana Nzepa (2004). It
is therefore not unusual in the private sector of the economy, for a Bakoko or
Yabassi (both minority ethnic groupings) to present themselves as the more
prestigious and influential Douala in the commercial city and port of the
same name. Similarly, within the public sector, members of the various small
minority groups around the Central Province may present themselves as the
politically dominant Beti.

This provides a picture of the fluid nature of ethnicity, and its relationship to power dynamics. Yet modern-day processes such as urbanization and intermarriages may also pose other dynamics which confound a simplistic understanding of the 'indigenous'.

In particular, in the management context, it is useful to analyse the different influences on organization and management values by using such 'ideal type' categories as post-colonial, post-instrumental and humanistic/renaissance. The difficulty is always going to be with the latter. This is because of the interpretation of what constitutes indigenous, and indigenous values. The chapter opened by looking at the processes and dynamics of power that made modern Africa, and how these processes, including attitudes and assumptions, with some religious proselytizing thrown in, continue and affect the continent today. It also looked at 'corruption' as an assumption of an 'African' value, and how this has informed much of what has been written on management ethics in Africa and other 'developing' regions. By identifying the various influences on 'developing' countries, using sub-Saharan Africa as our main example, it is possible better to understand where this is all leading.

What we are to become

Integral to the concept of an African renaissance is the idea that Africa, and other 'developing' countries that have experienced similar colonizing/globalization dynamics, has something to offer that is uniquely African. This appears to be a pervasive humanism that is to be found in traditional communities, religion and ways of life, that stand in distinction to the instrumentalism that appears to be more pervasive in 'The West'. It appears to assert that whatever has been constructed on our behalf, with some collusion by ourselves, and construed as 'African', we now wish to try to break free from and assert an identity as Africans (Makgoba, 1999). This may sound idealistic, but any social scientist working in Africa, and one could assume other regions of the world that have been designated 'developing', would have to understand this, and the dynamics and influences that have led to this.

Closing case: China in Africa

However, again things are changing, as we alluded to above, in a new set of dynamics: South on South.

The more recent interest shown by China in the continent of Africa is causing some consternation among the Western powers. The German Chancellor Angela Merkel is reported to have said: 'We Europeans should not leave the continent of Africa to the PRC. We must take a stand in Africa.' The IMF (and World Bank) is concerned about the implication of China's apparent policy of non-conditionality of loans and aid in Africa, with a reported view that China's unrestricted lending has 'undermined years of painstaking efforts to arrange conditional debt relief'. Yet China's involvement in Africa is not new, and goes back to the Han dynasty (206 BCE to 220 CE), and during the Tang dynasty (960–1279) when trade grew intensely. Modern-day involvements go back with agreements with Ghana signed in 1960. However, China–Africa contact appears to be qualitatively different from European plunder in the wake of the slave trade. It also appears to be part of a grand plan with deals with ASEAN, Latin America/Caribbean and Africa from 2006. A major motivation of course seems to be the securing of Africa's (and other 'developing' areas) natural resources to feed the growing economy of China. Yet at the same time there appears a genuine desire to provide other resources for Africa, and to do so on the basis of cooperation and friendship. Hence the President of Botswana is quoted as saying 'I find that the Chinese treat us as equals; the West treat us as former subjects'. There is also the view that from the experience of transformation in China, there are lessons to be learned in Africa. Evidence also appears to exist of a sense of 'Third World Solidarity' towards China's relations particularly with Latin America, drawing on its socialist heritage and anti-imperialist discourse, and as a reaction to the IMF's neoliberal policies and government alignment with the United States (Shaw *et al.*, 2007; Campbell, 2008; Kaplinsky, 2008).

The Centre for Chinese Studies (2008), at the University of Stellenbosch in South Africa, reports that:

China's approach has been one of mutual respect, also awarding small African countries with relatively little economic or political significance, with aid and investment support. However, it is likely that resource-rich countries such as Angola, Sudan, Nigeria and Zambia, as well as more politically strategic countries, such as South Africa, Ethiopia and Egypt, are priority countries in China's broader African engagement.

... 2006, the PRC Government announced its intention to develop between three and five special economic zones (SEZs) on the African continent, to serve as enclaves for Chinese investment in key African states. So far, the location of two zones has been announced; the mining hub in Zambia and the Indian Ocean Rim trading hub in Mauritius. Three other zones are in the process of being established in Nigeria, Egypt, and possibly Tanzania.

Yet the exact nature and amount of aid and/or investment is not known. Either secrecy and/or the Chinese government simply not knowing owing to the number of actors involved may be possible reasons for this.

There is involvement of Chinese organizations in a number of African countries, the three highlighted below are significant examples:

In Ethiopia involvement goes back to the 1980s when construction companies initially dominated. This activity was overtaken by the manufacturing sector a decade later. Products including steel, chemicals, pharmaceuticals, textiles, machinery, paper and glass comprise 50 per cent of Chinese investment. There were sixty active businesses in 2007 valued at US$60 million. However, Chinese companies are not allowed, under Ethiopian law, to engage in retailing the products they produce.

Involvement in Ghana goes back to 1960. Today large Chinese state-owned enterprises predominate, but also smaller private Chinese entrepreneurs have established a footprint in Ghana. There are approximately 250 Chinese companies registered in the country, largely involved in huge construction and manufacturing projects. Also China has made investments in infrastructure, education and social welfare, and more recently ICT.

China's presence in Zambia is also longstanding, going back to 1964. Mining and construction predominate in this natural resource-rich country that is well known for its copper. Very large organizations such as China Overseas Engineering Company (COVEC) and Shanghai Construction Company are present.

However, as the reports of the Centre for Chinese Studies points out (2008): 'There is at times a stark contrast between the Chinese rhetoric of brotherhood with African people, and some of the criticism coming from African citizens.'

It is unfortunate that most of the literature on China's involvement in Africa remains at the macro level and within discipline areas such as economics, development studies and international relations. The management literature seems as yet uninterested in exploring these South–South dynamics and their implications for organizations and their stakeholders. It may be that the implications are far reaching, particularly if they are indeed upsetting the traditional North–South dynamics. Yet whether China (and indeed other rising southern powers such as India) is a benign force, or simply another imperial power, remains to be seen. The way China is operating at organizational level should be the subject of management research projects, and the relations between Chinese and African management and staff should be the subject of research into ethical values and their implications. We know much about Chinese organizational values and management (explored in Chapter 9), less about African values and organization, but little if anything about the interaction between the two. What cultural Third Spaces are being socially constructed, through what type of power dynamics, where will this lead, and is this desirable? Only through further research will we find these things out.

Implications for international managers

One of the biggest ethical challenges for managers in Africa, whether Western or African, is the ethicality involved in the transfer of knowledge. This is not a simple issue that can be solved by referring to Hofstede's (1980a/2003) value dimensions as was discussed in the first three chapters of the current text. The problem is how managers should conceptualize those differences between 'Western' and 'African'. Are 'Western' principles and values an appropriate 'solution' to the ills of African organizations? To put this in the realm of the concrete: what should managers do about corruption? It is perhaps one thing to understand that corruption may not be an indigenous phenomenon, but is part of a post-colonial management system; it is another to have to deal with it. For example, Utomi (1998) argues that the way organizations and managers respond to such issues actually inputs into the environment in which organizations are operating in. He provides the example of a bank that chooses in its strategy to make ethical conduct central to delivering quality service to customers. He argues that service delivery is weakened by banks where 'playing according to the market' by making questionable payments has resulted in the corruption of bank staff and a lowering of morale of others. This policy can then be a major advantage as the environment changes and customers turn to what they perceive as the more reliable banks. This can then influence regulations as stronger institutions evolve to maintain these standards of ethics in banking.

CSR is another big issue involved in the transfer of management knowledge and values from the West. It is unlikely that CSR is a local invention in Africa, and it would normally be Western MNCs, such as Colgate Palmolive, that would institute such policies. CSR appears to be just a side-line, and not integral to developing or contributing to the community. Surely the concept of a humanistic, renaissance, African organization would be more integral to the community. There are a number of examples of this, for example Afriland First Bank (Jackson, 2004) which set out to develop entrepreneurship in Cameroon and the case study described by Mutabazi (2002) of a company in Kivu, Democratic Republic of Congo that trained a wider circle of associate workers in the community to provide stand-ins for when workers were absent and eventual replacements for current workers. These do not reflect Western concepts of CSR. Their policies and practices, indeed their business, is more central to the communities they seek to serve, and reflect more a social concept of entrepreneurship discussed by the present author (Jackson, 2004).

Questions for managers
1. How are issues of corruption dealt with in your organization, and how might this be more widely applied to issues of corruption in sub-Saharan Africa?
2. How relevant is CSR to communities in Africa?

An agenda for research

The main challenge for researchers in Africa is to get past the pejorative views of the post-colonial conceptualization of Africa as a 'basket case', and it is hoped that the discussion at the beginning of the chapter, and that around the case of Madonna in Malawi provided some initial thought in this area. However, the question still remains from previous chapters, how does one get around the issue of mimicry of the colonizer by the colonized? So many current texts on management in Africa almost glorify the use of Western modes of management, and Western management theoretical concepts as some kind of salvation of Africa's organization, and in so doing denigrate what Africa might have to offer (two such examples written or edited by African authors are Waiguchu et al., 1999; and Ugwuegbu, 2001). This has been a theme running throughout the current text, and Chapter 9 discusses some of the other issues involved in looking at an apparent contradiction of denigration and at the same time approbation of 'the other'. This applies to China and India in Chapter 9. The concluding chapter will then try to pull the pieces together and make some suggestions as to how we might overcome the lack of operationalization in postcolonial theory.

In regards to Africa and the 'developing' South, the problem can be conceptually overcome by focusing on the 'ideal type' constructions of post-colonial, post-instrumental and renaissance models of management. At least this builds an awareness of the historical and current roots of management and management values in organizations and some of the ethical implications. It challenges issues such as corruption and cronyism. As 'ideal types' they serve as a priori conceptual categories into which research findings can be sorted. In so doing they can be refined and developed. Similarly the construct of instrumental and humanistic 'locus of human value' can be used as a basis for research questions and analysis of findings. Yet empirically, neither of these constructs are 'clean'. The notion of hybridization almost guarantees this. Hence managers may show a mixture of humanistic and instrumental values (Jackson, 2002a), and organizations may show often a complex fusion of post-colonial, post-instrumental and renaissance-type organization and management culture.

Yet this also begs the question, what other ideal type management systems can we conceptualize and/or discover? For a number of years Japanese management has appeared to offer another type of model for organizations in Africa. This seems logical as the Japanese societal culture appears to also reflect a collectivism and a form of humanism (Jackson, 2002b), and may be more appropriate to African cultures than those alternatives from the West. Yet this appears only to have marginally influenced organizations and managers in Africa, despite the presence of some Japanese multinational corporations, such as Toyota, in sub-Saharan Africa (Jackson, 2004). So, what of Chinese organizations? As mentioned above, this is still uncharted territory. Yet as we know so much about Chinese management, values and management ethics, it may be possible to construct an ideal type that can then be empirically investigated. The next chapter may help in that task.

Questions for researchers
1. How can 'ideal types' be used in research in management ethics in Africa to transcend simplistic (pejorative) conceptualizations of 'African' management and organization?
2. What types of Third Space are being created through China's involvement in Africa?

9 The resurgence of ancient civilizations: a taste of the exotic

Although India and South Asia, and East Asia (except Japan) are often lumped together with Africa as 'developing' or at least emerging countries, there is often almost a reverence (from the West) towards these regions as being the successors of ancient civilizations. This reverence does not exist for Africa, which is seen as being without history. Nonetheless, much has been written, particularly on China and India, on the problems of business ethics. For example, similar arguments are given for China, as an economy in transition, as they are for say Russia (see Chapter 6), that 'China today has business ethics issues primarily because its economy is in transition … As the old command economy is replaced by a market-based economy, the rules of the game become less clear, and central authorities have less control' (Hulpke and Lau, 2008: 59). That this may be an oversimplification is taken up later. In some ways these regions of Asia are seen in the same light as Africa: corruption, nepotism and so on. Yet Said (1978/1995) had pointed to this ambivalence of the West towards the East: not only seeing the 'Orient' as backward and primitive, but also seeing it as exotic. He alludes to 'Oriental despotism, Oriental splendour, cruelty, sensuality' (2008: 5). However, as Said says, the *Orient* may mean different (geographical) areas to the Americans who may associate it with the Far East, particularly China and Japan, and the Europeans, particularly the French and British, who have

a way of coming to terms with the Orient that is based on the Orient's special place in European Western experience. The Orient is not only adjacent to Europe; it is also the place of Europe's greatest and richest and oldest colonies, the source of its civilizations and languages, its cultural contestant, and one of its deepest and most recurring images of the Other. (Said, 1978/1995: 1)

As a result of this, one of his meanings of Orientalism is as a profession. A fascination with the Other has led to 'a very large mass of writers, among whom are poets, novelists, philosophers, political theorists, economists, and imperial administrators, [who] have accepted the basic distinction between

East and West as the starting point for elaborate theories, epics, novels, social descriptions and political accounts concerning the Orient, its people, customs, "mind", destiny, and so on' (1978/1995: 3). Hence: 'many Eastern sects, philosophies, and wisdoms domesticated for local European use' (1978/1995: 4). While Britain and France were dominating the *Orient*, this meant particularly the 'Bible lands'. Following World War II and America's dominance of the *Orient*, this had largely meant the 'Far East'.

There is therefore no shortage of literature on the 'East', and this also applies to the management literature. There has been a fascination by management scholars, firstly of Japan, then more recently of China. With the emergence of the Indian economy, it is likely that interest in the near future will be as intense as that of China.

Opening case: a Singaporean company in China

Begley (1998) tells the story of Chang Koh Metal, an international organization based in Singapore and producing metal stamping precision parts. In the mid 1990s it expanded its operations to Putian in the People's Republic of China. The founder's parents had emigrated from Putian. Andrew Teo, the founder's son, was appointed general manager in change of the Putian operation. He had an engineering degree from the National University of Singapore and had previously worked for an American multinational company in Singapore where he had gained significant responsibility, training and grounding in the methods of the multinational. He now joined his father's company as he felt he could now make a contribution as a senior member through ability rather than family connections.

A relative from Putian, Jian Wei, was appointed plant manager, to help Andrew as his father felt it was important to have someone with local knowledge in place. Apart from a shared heritage and culture, a reason for starting the operation in Putian was a ready supply of labour, and in Singapore it was getting difficult to recruit suitable people due to full employment. Another reason was the lower operating costs. However, after a year, although the operating costs were lower, productivity was disappointing to Andrew. There was also a problem with the way he saw Jian Wei doing business.

Andrew had learned from his previous employment that it was important to identify the appropriate competences and qualifications needed for a particular job, and to recruit the best person who matches the specifications.

However, to fill open positions Jian would contact city officials and friends and relatives and ask them for recommendations. Quite often the people hired did not have the necessary skills needed to do the job well.

Andrew protested to Jian and instigated formal recruitment and selection procedures through systematically advertising positions, evaluating candidates and hiring based on qualifications and identifiable competences.

Jian became upset and argued that the practice was necessary in order to keep channels of communication and mutual exchange open with important officials. The company might need their help in the future. It is also worth mentioning that often skilled people are to be found in state-owned enterprises where it is difficult getting such (good) staff released.

Guanxi as a double-edged sword

Much has been written about *guanxi* in China. Chan *et al.* (2002), for example, define *guanxi* as 'a special type of relationship which contains trust, favour, dependence and adaptation, and often leads to insider-based decision making in the business world'. They claim that this can turn into highly complex networks comprising an intricate system of overt or covert, and formal and informal social subsets based on reciprocity. Yet, they assert, Westerners often see *guanxi* as related to unethical behaviour and perceive personal *guanxi* as possibly leading to corruption. Chan *et al.* (2002) describe *guanxi* as being based on trust leading to reciprocal obligations that are almost impossible to refuse under conditions of poor legal infrastructure and that *guanxi* might result in such unethical business practices as rendering privileged treatments to members within the same *guanxi* network, as well as undertable dealing. Yet they go on to say that although some Westerners regard *guanxi* simply as corruption, the Chinese, from their own cultural perspective, may perceive it as ethical: a *guanxi* network represents the only efficient means to conduct business in countries such as China where the distribution and legal systems are not fully developed.

Encapsulated in the (interpretation of the) term *guanxi* is a curious mixture of denigration and approbation, almost mirroring Said's concept of the Orient. *Guanxi* is perhaps no different to the familial nepotism and corruption viewed negatively in African countries by the West, but it has become encapsulated within a mystique of wonder and almost admiration, particularly helped along by international management scholars who have taken a particular interest in China over the last decade. This exoticism may exist because *guanxi* can be traced back to ancient civilizations; back to Confucius who lived from 551–479 BCE.

Gu *et al.* (2008: 18) explain what they call the dark side of *guanxi*, saying that these negative aspects could offset the benefits for individuals and organization:

Among the negative bundles of *guanxi*, two aspects have been noted. First, the ties that bind may turn into the ties that blind. A strong *guanxi* network may create overembeddedness that reduces the flow of new ideas into the network ... and limits the openness to alternative ways of doing things ... In this way, *guanxi* may produce collective blindness to the firm within the network. Second, *guanxi* may overload a firm with obligations to its network members.

Among *guanxi*'s most ardent critics is Fan (2002: 376) who says the acid test of whether or not it is ethical is if there are any victims of such a transaction:

These victims may be known as the competitor of the firm, or the customer, or even unknown in some cases. But the truth remains that such guanxi transaction produces gains for individuals or firms but social loss to the whole society. A guanxi action is right from the ethics point of view only if there is no third party either known or unknown that is adversely affected as a result of this guanxi action. Unfortunately, the vast majority of guanxi cases would fail this test.

His main concern is that while it may bring benefits to individual firms, it is the wider social costs that are detrimental. He asserts that 'the majority of business guanxi practices ... are totally unacceptable even by the current Chinese ethical standard. That is why business guanxi has a notorious reputation inside China' (2002: 376). He goes on to add that 'It is rather strange to see that something detested and condemned in China has found its popularity in the Western business literature. While China is attempting to move away from the guanxi-based system to a rule-based system ... advocates of guanxi in the west appeared to have found a new business model with a Utopian enthusiasm' (Fan 2002: 379).

Similar modes of social networking exist in Arab countries as we saw in Chapter 7, and most certainly in India. As Budhwar (2001: 81) notes in India 'low social and intellectual mobility forces owners to recruit managers from their own families, castes and communities, reinforcing old customs, values, beliefs'. He goes on to add that 'top Indian industrial houses (such as Tatas, Birlas) are good examples of this'. This presents a similar situation to that described in the opening case of Chang Koh in China, where without this social connectivity it is difficult to get qualified employees. Yet we still do not have an Indian equivalent to *guanxi* in the management literature (and the popular management imagination) that demonstrates the descent from classical tradition. That may explain why the exotic is not quite as exotic in India. Yet India, like China, can trace its social value systems back to the classical traditions of religious and philosophical thought. These are well documented in ancient written languages such as Sanskrit, unlike sub-Saharan African traditions which are mostly oral and inaccessible to Westerners. Yet having well-documented traditions may be a double-edged sword, in view of the vast Orientalist industry in the West. The extent to which 'oriental' traditions have been invented and reinvented, interpreted and reinterpreted by Western and Eastern scholars, policy makers and leaders, and perhaps sold back to the West as an authentic tradition in the case of Japanese management (see Chapter 5), or perhaps the various strands of Buddhism adopted in the West, may indicate a certain wisdom in keeping these to oneself (or a lack of entrepreneurial flair). Management consultancy and religious proselytizing hold much in common (not to mention a common word: guru).

Of ancient civilizations and religions

Buddhism originated in India (in modern-day Bihar), and spread north and west, and then mainly to East Asia, where today some estimates put adherents to Buddhism in China as high as 80 per cent (some 1.1 billion) of the population,[1] although simply from the personal experiences of the current author's students and colleagues in and from China, this would appear to be an exaggeration. Although it declined in India in the thirteenth century, it left an impact on Hinduism where the Buddha is regarded as the ninth-century incarnation of the god Vishnu. Since the late nineteenth century Buddhism has enjoyed a revival in India, although it has had far more impact on East and South East Asian countries, including Japan and, perhaps surprisingly following the communist years, in China. Hinduism, a much older religion, is far more prominent in India today. Yet in Eastern religions syncretism is common. In China it is not unusual for a family to have a small shrine in the home with statutes and icons from Daoism (Taoism), Confucianism and Buddhism.[2] Yet perhaps rather than this being syncretism, it may be that these three press different buttons: they meet different social and spiritual needs.

---

[1] http://thedhamma.com/buddhists_in_the_world.htm, but see also US State Department, 2006.
[2] http://thedhamma.com/buddhists_in_the_world.htm.

Hansen (1993) reminds us that there are major differences between Chinese and Western traditions in that the latter, largely inherited from the Greeks, divides the ego into rational and emotional, explaining mental processes through belief and desire. Morality is related to the faculty of reason. Chinese thinkers do not take this approach, nor do they take beliefs or desires as reasons for action. He suggests that the Chinese approach is more social, on the basis that humanity is social, and that a social 'way' (*dao* or *tao*) guides actions. Ethical thinking is concerned with how to preserve or transmit this way, or to change it as a public, guiding discourse. 'Ethics' is translated into Chinese as *dao de*, providing a composite of ways and virtue. The former, *dao*, is a concept of public and objective guidance, whereas *de* is the realization of *dao*. It comprises character traits or skills that are induced by exposure to a *dao*. Through *de* (virtue) a *dao* is realized through and by a family or state institution or individual. This virtue is obtained either by internalizing a way, or it could be innate. Yet there is no one *dao*. Hansen (1993) suggests that it is a common translation error to write *dao* as 'the way'. The different schools do not agree on what is *the* way.

Confucius offered one such way, and has subsequently had tremendous influence even on modern-day thinking in China. For example, describing Confucianism as a 'resilient Chinese cultural tradition' Ip (2009: 464) explains that its 'ethics is basically humanistic, obligation-based and collectivistic in nature'. He suggests that it is humanistic because its primary concern is the human condition and is 'this-world-oriented'; it is collectivistic as it puts collective values and interests above individual ones. Therefore harmonious social relationships are paramount in human society, with the family the most revered form of relationship. As human conduct is articulated in terms of obligations requiring extensive practice of virtues, Confucianism is obligation-based. Human moral traits are consciously acquired. These virtues comprise the 'moral capacity for compassion (*ren*) and sense of rightness (*yi*), and reciprocity (*shu*)' (2009: 464).

Ip (2009) tells us that there are three elements, or mega-virtues, in Confucian ethics defining what is morally acceptable:

- *Ren*: a capacity for compassionate or benevolent acts towards one's fellow human beings within social relationships (Hansen, 1993, defines it as 'humanity'). It is also described as a *de*, or virtue, in this case what Ip describes as a mega-virtue from which other virtues are derived.
- *Yi*: a sense of moral rightness or a capacity to appreciate what is appropriate, or the right direction, in acts, relations and human matters in general (Hansen, 1993: 70, defines *i* as 'morality', and as a conventional

morality – *li i*, as against Mozi[3] utilitarian morality: yet rejecting a deontological interpretation as 'duty' as 'the Chinese do not individualize obligations and duties as we do', and 'do not segment their systems of guidance into sentential rules',). Ip notes that *ren* and *yi* work together in defining morality and guiding actions.

- *Li*: the norms, conventions and etiquettes involved in personal and institutional daily lives. *Li* is based both on *ren* (humanity) and *yi* (morality) in terms of its legitimacy. If it is not thus legitimate people are not obliged to follow it. Hansen (1993: 71) adds that '*ren* ('humanity') is the intuitive ability to interpret the *li* correctly. We may apply *ren* either in our own action or in guiding others'. Ip (2009: 464) suggests that 'though *li* is not in itself a virtue, *observing li* is a basic virtue'.

From *ren* (humanity), the human capacity for compassion was articulated, according to Ip by the notion of *zhong shu*, which in its 'soft version' is the Confucian version of the Golden Rule or Kantian categorical imperative that one should do unto others what they would want others to do to them. Yet Ip asserts that in its 'hard form' it goes beyond what might be met in other cultures by this Rule. It also encourages people not only to morally develop themselves but be actively involved in the moral development of others, so that one's moral development, far from being undertaken in isolation, should be undertaken in synchrony with others. The three 'mega-virtues' together with wisdom and trustworthiness, we are told by Ip, comprise the five cardinal virtues in both traditional and modern Chinese culture. *Junzi* is the model moral person who possesses these five virtues.

The Confucian concept of the person is essentially a social person, through familial collectivism. The person is defined by his or her relationships. A person's identity cannot be understood as something separate from his or her social attachments and place in the hierarchy of social relationships. A person is shaped by this social embeddedness in terms of their interests and goals, and also constrained by the same relationships. The social bonds thus created are a source of indebtedness and obligations. Ip (2009: 465) adds that 'there is no individual in the egoistic sense as conceived in some versions of liberal thinking in the West'. He asserts that this concept of the person fits well with the virtue of *ren* and with 'the family as the person's nurturing collective entity'. This explains well 'the modern day version of Confucian relationalism': *guanxi*.

[3] Mozi (also Mo, and Mo Zi, and giving rise to the Mohist school, the first rival to Confucius' normative scheme) provides an alternative Dao which basically rejects traditional customs which Mo says can be wrong, relying rather on a benefit-harm criteria (Hansen, 1993).

Yet although relationships of mutual obligation are built together with the notion of social embeddedness, and harmony is also regarded as a cardinal value within relationships, Ip (2009: 466) reminds us that filial piety holds a very strong position within Chinese culture, often with family patriarchs, or indeed state patriarchs, demanding filial piety from their children, or subjects. This implies 'a *hierarchical* structure of human relationship in society'. Social exchange and obligations may therefore be asymmetrical, which Ip sees as in contrast to *zhong shu*. Reciprocity appears as an ethical principle in Western theory, including that of Kant, Mills and Rawls, as Chan (2008) points out. Yet he also points out that Confucian ethics differ from these in that the reciprocity principle is qualified on the basis of familial relationships, as well as hierarchy and *li* (rules of propriety). Firstly, he points out that Confucius appears to suggest that favouritism should be shown to family members, even to the extent of concealing misconduct on the part of another family member. This is similar to Trompenaars' (1993) concept of particularism-universalism, and also allied to the situational/relativist ethics described by the current author (Jackson, 2001) in relationship to empirical findings of the attitudes of Chinese managers (this also concerns the concept of maintaining 'face' as well, and possibly the lack of an equivalent of the Western concept of absolute truth: see Chapter 4).

Within this context, Chan (2008: 354) explains that the 'concept of *guanxi* is based on and reflects the principle of reciprocity and interdependence as well as hierarchy in society'. He goes on to say:

Guanxi involves social exchange for mutual benefit which favours parties superior in the hierarchy. The notion of reciprocity (*bao*) is significant amongst Chinese people. If favours given by one party are not reciprocated by the other party, the latter may suffer a 'loss of face' (*mianzi*) or may be regarded as ungrateful, thus resulting in estrangement by others ... *Guanxi* and *mianzi* are part of the Confucian social rituals (*li*).

An interesting example of how this might apply is explored by Chan (2008). He suggests that Confucian values of loyalty, respect for authority and hierarchy, and maintaining harmony may present obstacles to a potential whistle-blowing within an organization. This particularly involves an examination of the concept of reciprocity and whether this is embedded in the notion of loyalty. If loyalty is a matter of mutual obligation then from a perspective of rational loyalty, the company can expect from the employee what the employee expects from the company. This may involve explicit company mission statements, goals and codes of conduct. If a company expects rational loyalty from employees then the company has to reciprocate that by institutionalizing whistle-blowing. Yet as Chan (2008) points out, and as we have seen above, Confucianism does not advocate equal reciprocity. An employee is expected to show filial piety towards the employer, yet not expect the same to be directed by the employer back at them (in the context of the influence of Confucianism in Japan, Ornatowski, 1999: 388, describes this thus: 'the prime virtue of the superior is benevolence and of the inferior is loyalty'). The reluctance of Chinese employees to report the wrongdoing of employers, as compared to a willingness to report their peers, has some empirical support, and Chan (2008) points to a study by Zhuang *et al.* (2005) in this regard.

Confucianism appears to provide a highly systematized social framework model which governs relationships, recognizes the social embeddedness of people, provides rules within a hierarchy and virtues that people should aspire to, and prescribes the human capacities needed in order to conduct oneself in a moral way. It provides a different model of social partnership to that explored in Chapter 6 in the context of Europe, and although it has similarities with the paternalistic relationships described in Chapter 7 in Arab/Islamic countries, it provides a secular and perhaps more finely honed social nexus.

Through invention, and reinvention, perhaps mostly by Western, or Western-educated scholars, Confucianism and its modern interpretations in Greater China have taken on a certain mystique. This, not the least, applies to the concept of *guanxi*, which Fan (2002) points out has almost acquired the status of a new Utopian business model. This may be also a result in the decline in the status of Japanese management in the West, and management consultants simply looking for the next mystical tool in their international armoury (to mix metaphors).

Yet mentioned above also was the supposed syncretism of Chinese cultures and an ability of mixing 'religions'. Confucianism may meet one particular need. Some argue that it has provided the basis of the powerhouses of the East Asian economies. What of Daoism and Buddhism? The latter will be briefly returned to a little later, via a discussion of India and an analysis of the influence of Hinduism.

Cheung and Chan (2005) argue that there are four main foundations of Chinese culture that influence Chinese leadership including Confucianism. The other three are Daoism, Mohism and Legalism. Mohism has already been referred to as a challenger to Confucius' formalism. Cheung and Chan (2005: 50) refer to this philosophy stemming from Mo Zi, who lived 468–376 BCE, as 'altruistic utilitarianism'. It advocates loving and serving others while keeping oneself thrifty. They further assert that it is a philosophy that favours the masses or working people, craftsmen and engineers. Incidentally, Mo Zi's other talent lay in his engineering work. Although favouring the common people, he also advocated centralization and authoritarianism, in the sense that common people should be submissive to the 'talents and sages'. Yet this authority is only legitimate if leaders are both altruistic and 'productive', in such a way as to take care of the masses. Although having some consistencies with the Communist leadership, the authors explain that it became unpopular because it proclaimed the authority of 'gods, ghosts, and other supernatural beings' at variance to the atheism of Confucianism. Hansen (1993: 72) refers to Mohism as the 'utilitarian Dao', adding that Mo Zi was outspoken against what he regarded as wasteful Confucian ritual practices, including 'elaborate funerals, expensive concerts and especially aggressive warfare'. He reckoned that the resources could be better used to benefit the people. The utility of Mo Zi, Hansen (1993: 72) explains, is not related to subjective individual states such as pleasure, happiness or desire satisfaction. It is rather a matter of 'objective, material well being'. As such this perspective is less individualistic than Western utilitarianism.

Cheung and Chan (2005: 50) also assert that Legalism has an influence today on Chinese culture and on leadership. They present it as a 'philosophy of state utilitarianism', as it promotes the welfare of the state. As such the lawyer is the archetypal leader as one who is 'impartial, honest, thrifty, independent, and efficient, legislating and building trust among people'. This is a view based on 'self-control, prudence, and honesty'. It also advocates leaders not being honest with the people and being tactical to manipulate followers. At the same time it favours 'generous reward and severe punishment'. It proposes 'strict job differentiation and distrusts bureaucrats who claim general skills'. Yet perhaps because of this advocacy of specialization it emphasizes innovation, and that 'rules change in response to changing conditions'. The ultimate goal is to be 'a strong state with a well-off populace', and downgrades personal virtue or vice as a consideration.

Daoism is literally the philosophy of the way, although Daoism as a philosophy/religion advocates a natural way, hence it is normally regarded as a 'Chinese philosophy of naturalism'. This natural way is universal and permeates physical and social worlds. In this respect it could be regarded as transcending other advocated 'ways' such as those of Confucius and Mo Zi. The view is that human action cannot change this natural way. Human wisdom, cunning or trickery cannot have an effect on the natural way.

The founder of Daoism is believed to be Lao-Tse (604–531 BCE), a contemporary of Confucius, although it is disputed whether he was a real person, a composite of several persons, or simply a myth. More than any other Chinese philosophy/religion Daoism has captured the imagination of the West, adding to the mystique and exoticism of the Orient. From Daoism we get yin and yang, tai chi and feng shiu, as well as associated holistic and alternative therapies such as acupuncture, martial arts and meditation. In some ways Daoism is difficult to define, and has a number of manifestations. Common principles in popular appreciation of Daoism[4] appear to be as follows:

- The Dao of Daoism refers to a force that flows through all life and is the first cause of the universe. As it surrounds everyone, everyone must listen to find enlightenment. As such the goal of Daoists is to harmonize themselves with the Dao.
- In religious Daoism the many gods are seen as manifestations of the one Dao. Therefore, the concept of a personified deity does not exist. Similarly the creation and a creator of the universe is not a concept in Daoism. Hence Daoists do not pray as Christians do, as there is no God to hear their prayers or to act upon them. Rather they seek answers to life's problems through inner meditation and outer observation.
- There is an apparent distinction between the Daoism of the priesthood, and popular or folk Daoism of the 'laity' where the various gods and spirits act in much the same way as officials where those in heaven act like and were treated like the officials in the world of men. Worshipping the gods was seen as rehearsal of attitudes toward secular authorities. The demons and ghosts of hell acted like and were treated like the bullies, outlaws and threatening strangers in the real world; they were bribed by the people and were ritually arrested by the martial forces of the spirit officials.
- Time is seen to be cyclical, not linear as in Western thinking.
- Health and vitality are strongly promoted. Each person must nurture the *ch'i* (air, breath) that has been given to them.
- A main task of Daoism is to develop virtue by means of the *Three Jewels*: compassion, moderation and humility.
- Daoists follow *wu wei*, which is letting nature take its course (action through inaction). One should allow a river to flow towards the sea unimpeded rather than erecting a dam which would interfere with its natural flow.
- One should plan in advance and consider carefully each action before making it.

[4] I am indebted to www.religioustolerance.org/taoism.htm, accessed 16/09/09, from which this is adapted.

- Daoists should be kind to other individuals, in part because such an action tends to be reciprocated (the Golden Rule that occurs in many manifestations including Confucianism).

Cheung and Chan (2005) add that this universal, natural way is the way of flexibility and reversion. The former principle is that nothing is absolute as there are many alternatives and opportunities. The latter is premised on the principles that things can turn into their opposite. A soft thing such as water can also be powerful and can penetrate rock. This together with *wu wei* suggests that in leadership inaction or doing nothing that may deviate from the natural course is considered to be the most effective course. For these authors, this suggests that leaders can gain support naturally by inaction and non-coercive means.

A contribution that Cheung and Chan's (2005) work makes to our understanding is their synthesis of these various traditions, arising between the seventh and third centuries BCE, how they differ from Western philosophies, and the influence they have had on Chinese culture, and ultimately on Chinese ethical leadership. They explain as follows:

> The integration of Chinese thoughts distinguishes Chinese culture from other cultures even though each Chinese philosophical view may have its corresponding part in another culture. Considered in isolation, Confucianism is similar to Kantian and Christian ethics because they are formalist doctrines and Aristotelian virtues; Daoism is similar to the theories preached by Rousseau and Thoreau, which are naturalist doctrines; Mohism and Legalism are similar to Millian works [i.e. that of John Stuart Mill] in that they are utilitarian doctrines ... The Chinese doctrines, nevertheless, differ from those of other cultures in their focus and thereby the extent of emphasis on each essential value. For instance, Confucianism differs from Christianity in the emphasis on interpersonal solidarity in the former and brotherhood through piety to God in the latter ... Harmony and benevolence, which apply mostly to the in-group and gentlemen in Confucianism, are therefore different from agape [i.e. Christian love or charity], which emphasizes sacrifice for God, brothers, and even enemies in Christianity. The collectivist flavour of Confucianism clearly distinguishes it from individualist and liberalist doctrines held in the West ... Chinese culture, however, tempers Confucianism with Legalism and Mohism, thereby introducing utilitarian reasons for maintaining social relationships, that is, *guanxi* ... The utilitarian and universal concern in *guanxi* prevents it from becoming cronyism. Chinese culture further tempers the rule-based, formalist tenet of Confucianism with the flexible, situated view of Daoism ... (Cheung and Chan, 2005: 50–1)

These authors report the influence of these ancient philosophies on Chinese leaders in Hong Kong where they undertook a study of five eminent CEOs.

Rather than being entirely based on Confucian principles they found that the ethics of Chinese leadership within their limited study was also influenced by the 'Daoist ethics of non-intervention, the Mohist ethics of altruism, and the Legalistic ethics of impartiality' (2005: 58). They add that the Confucian ethic of benevolence is vulnerable to cronyism and nepotism, yet these other influences counter this. Similarly Confucian ethics can be moralistic, impractical and conservative; the other philosophies appear to counteract this.

Confucianism remains an influence on business leadership not only in the greater China (PRC, Taiwan, Hong Kong SAR, Singapore and other Chinese communities) but also in Japan and Korea. Similarly Daoism appears to have widespread appeal that extends well beyond the East Asian communities, and has gone through various stages of popularity in the West together with its association with traditional therapies, tai chi, martial arts and feng shui, which appear to have perpetuated the appeal of the Orient in the Western imagination. Yet as we have seen above, Buddhism appears to be popular in China. It has had influences on Daoism, and appears to have commonalities with it, including a concept of achieving the correct path through self-reflection. It also has left influences on Hinduism in India, although Hinduism predates Buddhism and remains one of the major influences on Indian culture, and perhaps ethical leadership. We now turn to Hinduism and the influence of the Vedantic tradition, which again relates to ancient civilizations and systems of thought.

Chakraborty (1995) makes a distinction between Indian culture and Indian ethos. It is difficult to speak of a homogenous culture because of the endless diversity of local customs and deities even within the Hindu fold, let alone the other religions in India. In addition to the indigenous Vedantic, Buddhist, Jaina and Sikh traditions, the country has absorbed traditions from Islamic, Christian and Parsi (Zoroastrians, originally from current-day Iran) sources. Yet, he asserts, despite this diversity of cultures and many influences brought into India, there is one Indian ethos 'at the level of the vedantic "deep structure"' (1995: 4) that has its origins specifically and uniquely within the India land mass.

Budhwar (2001) points to this ancient inheritance, as well as the cultural diversity of modern-day India, when he says (2001: 75):

India is the birthplace of three of the world's main religions: Hinduism (about 7000 years BC), Buddhism (487 BC) and Sikhism (1699 AD). Indian society comprises six main religious groups: Hindus (83.2 per cent), Muslims (11 per cent), Sikhs (2 per cent), Christians (2 per cent), Jains and Buddhists (less than 1 per cent). There are over three thousand castes.

He goes on to explain that in addition, India has 179 languages and 544 dialects and that the constitution recognizes sixteen languages with Hindi and English being the two official ones. Yet it is surprising that spirituality, which appears so important to India in the non-management literature and some of the ethics literature such as that of Chakraborty (1995), does not seem to have a prominent position in the management literature such as the work of Budhwar. It is interesting that one of the first observations made in the current author's 1923 copy of S. Radhakrishnan's *Indian Philosophy* is as follows (1923: 25):

Philosophy in India is essentially spiritual. It is the intense spirituality of India, and not any great political structure or social organization that it has developed, that has enabled it to resist the ravages of time and the accidents of history. External invasions and internal dissensions came very near crushing its civilization many times in its history. The Greek and the Scythian, the Persian and the Mogul, the French and the English have by turn attempted to suppress it, and yet it has its head held up.

The leaders of India have often been deeply spiritual. One obviously can point to Ghandi, but also corporate leaders such as the founder of Tata Industries, J. N. Tata, who was a Parsi priest (Worden, 2003). Radharkrishnan goes on to say (albeit in 1923: 25) that the 'spiritual motive dominates life in India. Indian philosophy has its interests in the haunts of men, and not in supra-lunar solitudes', and the 'hard task of interesting the multitude in metaphysics is achieved in India'.

In modern-day works on Indian management, how is it therefore possible to ignore 7000 years of civilization? As mentioned with China, above, although recent history (Communalism and then globalization) may have more recently shaped the trajectory of corporate and business life, there are strong indications that the forces of ancient civilizations have survived, and are currently prospering. As with Africa, recent imperial history has no doubt had its effect on India, as has recent economic liberalization. Yet such ancient civilizations have brought and maintained both a reality and a mystique, which in part has been the theme of the current text. Said (1995: 150) describes this as the paradox of Orientalism. Particularly in connection with India he says:

The Orient was overvalued for its pantheism, its spirituality, its stability, its longevity, its primitivism, and so forth … Yet almost without exception such overesteem was followed by a counterresponse: the Orient suddenly appeared lamentably underhumanized, antidemocratic, backward, barbaric, and so forth. A swing of the pendulum in one direction caused an equal and opposite swing back: the Orient was undervalued.

Said (1995) asserts that it was out of these opposites that Orientalism, as a profession, grew, mainly out of inequality. Orientalism 'enshrined' this inequality and the paradoxes it engendered. One wonders to what extent modern-day cross-cultural management studies reflect this paradox through inequality. Certainly the mystique of 'the other' is still there. Why else would we want to study other cultures? Yet at the same time we attempt to tame 'the other' by wrapping it in 'universal' (Western) rationale, rather than asking the question 'What do you make of your own culture?' Is this because we have little confidence in 'the other' to present an understanding of their culture? Yet this lack of confidence may be justifiable. If we are to accept what postcolonial theory has to say, the 'subaltern' is at worst incapable of speaking, or at best very limited in what he or she can say. As we saw in Chapter 5, Bhabha's (1994) concept of 'mimicry' applies to a colonizing power's ability to get the colonized to mimic the colonizer, in order better to control the unfamiliar, and to gain acceptance of the colonizer's view. It would seem that if the Orientalist project is characterized by the paradox described by Said (1978) then so will the image that 'the other' will hold of himself, and that will be reflected in whatever theories and concepts he or she develops about the indigenous. This must particularly apply to management theorists, where very few Indian academics publishing in international academic media do not reflect a Western or Westernized approach. The richness of the inheritance from ancient civilizations is sanitized or simply forgotten.

Chakraborty (1995) may be an exception. Yet it is more difficult to ignore such a heritage when focusing on ethics, and perhaps this is another reason why ethics should be more central to international management studies.

In Hinduism the concept of 'God' appears to be integrative to the human person, rather than in monotheistic religions where a supreme being stands above humanity and creates 'man' in His image, as in Christianity. In this aspect it appears to share a naturalism with Daoism, which is particularly articulated in Buddhism many millennia later. Hence Bilimoria (1993: 44) tells us that

the higher good ... is identified with the total harmony of the cosmic or natural order, characterized as *rita*: this is the creative purpose that circumscribes human behaviour. The social and moral order is thus conceived as a correlate of the natural order. This is the ordered course of things, the truth of being or reality (*sat*) and hence the 'law'.

Chakraborty (1995) refers to evolutions also needing involutions, and this also forms the basis of attaining harmony with the natural order. Hence, the way forward (perhaps again reflecting the concept of Dao in Chinese phil-osophy) is not solely to press ahead on the secular route, nor to be isolated from worldly affairs. Chakraborty (1995: 5) presents this as a four-goal 'systems view' or *chaturvarga* of human existence. Bilimoria (1993: 47) refers to these as *purushartha* or 'human ends', who unlike Chakraborty does not see these as continuous with each other. These are as follows:

- *Dharma*: rectitude, rightness, social and individual duties;
- *Artha*: material interests, money and wealth;
- *Kama*: pleasure and affective fulfilment, desires and needs; and
- *Moksha*: liberation of the spiritual core.

In Chakraborty's estimation the two secular goals are integrated into the 'model' within the bounds of *dharma* or 'ethico-moral propriety' and *moksha*. Perhaps in a slightly moralistic tone, that may or may not reflect any type of 'Indian management' he says that 'the key task of management in any secular aspects of life is to transform and elevate it into a sacred process'. Bilimoria (1993: 47) remarks that this

conception of human ends provides the context and criteria for determining the rules, conduct and guidelines in respect of the institutes of class and life-cycle stages. For an individual will want to strive towards achieving the best in terms of these ends within the limits of his or her temperament, circumstances, status and so on. Sometimes it is a question of balance; at other times it is a question of which interests get priority.

He positions *purushartha* (or, 'things sought by human beings') as the fourth of four principles or 'institutions' of the Vedas, which also include *ashrama* (life-cycle), *dharma* (as an overriding concept of duty) and *karma* (action-effect). These, together with the caste system in Hindu life, contextualize an understanding of Hindu ethics which may have implications for modern corporate life and management ethics.

- *Ashrama*. Life progresses through various stages in concentric circles, each with its own code of conduct: *studentship* requiring dedication to a teacher and discipline; *householder*, with marriage, family and obligations; *semi-retreat* entailing gradual retreat from worldly pursuits and pleasures; and *renunciation* or total withdrawal and involving preparation for liberation shedding both egoistical and altruistic tendencies in a state of extreme disinterestedness.
- *Dharma*. An all-embracing concept which Bilimoria (1993: 46) believes is unique to Indian thought and conveys the idea of maintaining a 'fixed order and coherence to any given reality'. It also suggests a 'form of life'

which goes beyond individual or group preferences, but has an essential human dimension. It forms the basis of a comprehensive social and moral system of regulation for each different social group including castes. Hence different '[v]ocational niches, duties, norms, and even punishments are differently arranged for different groups, and the roles and requirements also vary in the different life-cycle stages for the different groups'. He goes on to say that *dharma* provides a 'frame' for what is ethically proper and desirable at any one time, and relieves the burden of *karma*.

- *Karma*. In some ways this may be an alternative to the Golden Rule, as it does not simply ask that people treat other people as they would like to be treated, it provides a natural law that says that every conscious action by a person will have an effect that transcends the visible. It suggests the idea of retribution, also carrying this over to a further existence in another birth. In other words, actions have consequences. The connection with *dharma* suggests that there are no 'accidents of birth' that determine social iniquities as there is no social mobility within one lifetime. One has one's *dharma* as an endowment and a social role. One therefore can accumulate an improvement through *karma* in order to aim for a higher position in the next rebirth. One can also strive for the best in terms of *purushatha* within the limits of one's caste and life-cycle stage as we saw above.

Budhwar (2001: 80) notes that:

Hierarchy and inequality are deeply rooted in India's tradition and are also found in practice in the form of unequal caste and class groups. Indian organizational structures and social relations are therefore hierarchical and people are status conscious ... Such inequalities have persisted and remain in equilibrium because of organic links between them and ingrained inter-dependence of the different socio-economic groups.

Invented traditions

The caste system may today be one of the costs of the endowment of 7000 years of civilization. Yet this endowment is a contested area. In India, understanding this from the point of view of invented traditions may shed some light on how we might consider the ethicality of the caste system. It also qualifies much of the modern discourse on globalization as purely a modernization process. If the colonizers invent or reinvent traditions as we saw in Chapter 8 in relation to Africa, so does the nationalist project reinvent it again. In one respect this is in order to challenge the ideology of the ruling colonial power, but on the other hand, the new nationalist elite has mostly been educated in the schools and universities of the colonial powers, where 'indigenous' traditions were mostly suppressed or denigrated. In India, with what amounted to only a handful of military personnel compared with the millions of the populace, in order to gain and retain control the colonial authorities 'were able to draw on the complex traditions of previous rulers and well established hierarchies of caste, ethnicity, and religion' (Schech and Haggis, 2000:130). The ensuing ideology of the globalization of the colonial era was a mix of 'a taste for the exotic', denigration of ancient civilizations as barbaric, and an appropriation of social traditions and structures as control mechanisms.

Drawing on Chatterjee (1993: 237) Schech and Haggis (2000: 134) explain how the nationalist project seeks to supersede this (the words in double quotation marks are Chatterjee's):

One of the ways in which the indigenous intelligentsia claims cultural leadership is through incorporating the popular into national culture. While the popular is taken to be "the repository of natural truth, naturally self-sustaining and therefore timeless," it must be mediated by an enlightened leadership so that "all marks of vulgarity, coarseness, localism, and sectarian identity" can be removed. Thus the popular can be controlled, and "its capacity for resolute endurance and sacrifice and its ability to protect and nourished" can be harnessed.

Schech and Haggis (2000) refer in particular to Ghandi's construction of tradition where he alludes to a return to traditional village life of self-sufficiency and that there is no need for modernization and change because Indian tradition 'had found the true principles of social organization' (Chatterjee, 1986: 103). Yet at the same time, in order to bring in the whole of the people it was also necessary for Ghandi to cut through social divisions. He did this by denying caste divisions. He says: 'Caste has nothing to do with religion. It is a custom whose origins I do not know and do not need to know ... But I do know that it is harmful both to the spiritual and national growth' (quoted in Chatterjee, 1986: 95, and cited in Schech and Haggis, 2000: 134).

As Bilimoria (1993) points out, Ghandi provides an example of a curious mixture of radical and conservative. Although he rails against the iniquities of the caste system, he later defends the *varna* class structure on the basis that it is different from the caste system as it provides a sensible division of work and that complies with a law of nature and hence a part of *dharma*. The *varna* (meaning 'colour') system of the Vedas prescribes four classes, namely Brahmin (religious teachers), *Kshatriya* (administrators and military), *Vaishya* (agricultural and commercial production) and *Shudra* (menial labourers).

Schech and Haggis (2000) point out that this version of nationalism against the caste system clearly contradicts another influential version which argues that caste is an essential element in Indian society: one that distinguishes it from the West, and maintains a stable and harmonious social order, where each person has a specific place. They argue that the Gandhian version of national culture reflects the socio-cultural position and experience of the nationalist elite, while mobilizing the peasants as an anti-colonial force, but at the same keeping their distance from them, and remaining suspicious of their backwardness and inability to participate in the institutions of the state.

It is likely that in China also, the Communist Party played a significant role in reinventing tradition. However, by the turn of the twenty-first century, global dynamics were beginning to shift, as we briefly explored at the end of Chapter 8. Both China and India were emerging from their post-colonial pasts, to perhaps be in a future position of usurping America's role of grand imperialist of the twentieth century. This may not be the perceived traditional realm of the management scientist, the organizational behaviour or cross-cultural management specialist, yet the social, cultural and ethical aspects of this global dynamic may have fundamental implications for the way cross-cultural studies are conceptualized and conducted.

Resurgence of civilizations and a new world order

Through the 1980s most of the world appeared to lurch towards the political right. These were the Thatcher and Reagan years, the time of Structural Adjustment Programmes and conditional aid imposed first on 'developing' countries, and then on the countries of the former Soviet bloc. The conditionality involved moving formerly state-protected economies of the Third and Second Worlds towards liberal free-market economies, and emulating those of the First World. There was a lifting of protectionism from the economies of countries such as India (Rohmetra, 1998). China began to open its doors first to international joint ventures and, moving into the 1990s and then the twenty-first century, to more direct means of investment and membership of the World Trade Organization. The 'Iron Curtain' came down in 1989. Potential new players such as South Africa rejoined the global economy after sanctions were lifted, Mandela was released from prison, and democratic elections held, all in the first half of the 1990s. The concomitant was that communism was dropped from the agenda, not only from the policies of the African National Congress, but globally. There was no challenger to the free-market economy agenda. Even Northern European countries, formerly the bastions of social market economies and social democratic politics, were moving to the right. Germany, from 1982, had sixteen years of the conservative chancellor Helmut Kohl.

The binary distinction between the 'free world' and 'communist' countries fell away. America and its allies, represented by the countries of NATO, but mainly the UK, no longer had a natural antithesis: no known enemy (neither Cuba nor North Korea commanded the same kind of kudos as enemies, but the latter is now in the process of being upgraded). Now the USA was trading with and investing in Russia and China. America apparently had a free rein. Chomsky (2003: 11) for example offers compelling arguments that America has had a deliberate 'imperial grand strategy', which has intensified post-2001 to maintain hegemony, if necessary through military means, quoting a White House release of 17 September 2002 on the National Security Strategy that 'our forces will be strong enough to dissuade potential adversaries from pursuing a military build-up in hopes of surpassing, or equalling, the power of the United States'. He goes on to add, by quoting John Ikenberry, a prominent international affairs specialist, that this 'grand strategy begins with a fundamental commitment to maintaining a unipolar world in which the United States has no peer competitor'.

Yet one of the arguments put forward in the current text is that national (and cultural) identity is defined also by who you are not (see Chapter 5). If one has an economic, militaristic and hegemonic identity as a world power, one almost has to invent an enemy from whom to protect the integrity of such an identity as well as being seen to protect one's citizens from the outside world. It is perhaps therefore coincidental and fortuitous that an enemy presented itself in such an overt and dramatic way on 11 September 2001. However, this was not an enemy that one could easily fight back at in a conventional militaristic way. One could therefore venture the opinion that it was necessary to convert the situation back to a conventional militaristic situation that both the military and one's citizens understood: that is to be able to identify a known enemy. It may be because George W. Bush and his advisors chose this route into attacking two countries many thousands of miles away from the United States (on the argument that one country had 'weapons of mass destruction' and that both were harbouring terrorists) that actually turned the tide on the United States' future prospects of world hegemony. However, the process of the ascendancy of former ancient civilizations, India but particularly China, had already started.

Already, in 1993, Dobbs-Higginson was popularizing the issues of the ascendency of the Asia-Pacific region and its role in the 'new world disorder', pointing particularly to China and to what he called 'Greater China', incorporating PRC, Hong Kong, Taiwan and the Chinese Diaspora, as 'the most powerful regional and global force in the making?', and characterizing India as 'counterbalancing the Greater China threat'. The so-called 'threat' of China should be understood in terms of what Dobbs-Higginson (1993: 86) called the 'arrogance' or 'confidence' of the Chinese when he says:

China's history has moulded a people whose confidence is difficult to overstate, a nation whose emperor in 1793 proclaimed to a British envoy that since his 'celestial empire' had all things in prolific abundance, he had no need for 'the manufactures of outside barbarians'.

The Chinese claim to have invented everything from gunpowder to paper, some say even pasta. Outsiders conclude that the Chinese are arrogant. Possibly they are. However, things just look different when you have five thousand years of recorded history.

Dobbs-Higginson's (1993) analysis to the background of such aspects as corruption, which includes this confidence and also touches on the discussion in Chapter 5 on human rights, highlights the restrictive view of Hulpke and Lau (2008), posited at the beginning of the current chapter, that much can be attributed to China's rapid transition. He refers to the idea that China can and should become democratic as nonsense, suggesting that Western notions of democracy, if introduced to China, have the potential to divide the country. Certainly, he suggests, this would not benefit the 1.2 billion Chinese in the near future. He explains that China has always been threatened by anarchy in such an expansive and geographically diverse country, and that centralized, autocratic governments have ruled China for thousands of years. However, the tradition of highly centralized government has also been countered by a strong tradition of 'provincial insubordination' (1993: 85). Provincial warlords challenged the authority of the emperor in the nineteenth century, with more recent 'socio-economic warlords' flouting the central authority of communist bureaucrats in Beijing. He believes that giving each person a vote could potentially reduce the situation to disintegration through warring economic factions throughout the provinces, or the military stepping in to impose authoritarian order. He goes on to say (1993: 85) that:

When the Chinese government ordered the army to fire on demonstrators in Beijing in June 1989, the world reacted with naïve, and in some cases hypocritical, horror. This event became known around the world as the Tiananmen Square incident.

Virtually no one seemed to realise that China's leaders were trying as best they could to control the divisive forces that, if left unchecked, risked splintering their country. Vigilance against anarchy has been an absolute throughout Chinese history.

Perhaps unlike the colonial legacy of African countries, authoritarian government has not led to economic decline. Within the context of China, the move towards economic development and China becoming a major international player may even be premised on its centralized authoritarian mode of government, as was touched upon in Chapter 5. The human rights expounded by the Declaration of Human Rights is not necessarily commensurate with economic and social development (Schech and Haggis, 2000).

Yet despite China's spectacular rise onto the world stage, writing in 1993, Dobbs-Higginson reminds us that in the early 1990s almost 200 million in China were semi-literate peasants and that the illiteracy rate among the adult population was 27 per cent. The social and cultural-linguistic diversity of such a vast land almost makes a mockery of studies such as GLOBE which tries to capture the essence of the cultural values of China in relatively small sample sizes. Although having one written language, there are some fifty-seven spoken dialects, many unintelligible to speakers of other dialects. Dobbs-Higginson points to Shanghainese and Hakka as examples of this. In addition there are some fifty minority groups with their own languages. The main defence for studies such as GLOBE is that there may be an identifiable commonality among this diversity, in particular an identity that defines itself in terms of what it is not. That is, the confidence of a people inhabiting the 'Middle Kingdom' vis-à-vis the barbarians who have often threatened and sometimes humiliated the Chinese over the last two centuries. Yet still Dobbs-Higginson reminds us that with 75 per cent of the population living in small, scattered villages with little national infrastructure and exposure to the outside world, it is difficult, despite this national pride, for people to have a sense of sharing in the larger Chinese nation and feeling loyalty to over a billion fellow compatriots.

It may be, as Dobbs-Higginson suggests, that the unifying mechanism has been the Communist Party with its highly developed political infrastructure. Child (1994: 29), perhaps as a prominent representative of management scholarship in this area, takes what may be regarded as a more romantic position. He takes the view that communism is a mere veneer, quoting Redding (1990), also a prominent China management scholar, where he refers to an 'elderly professor in Guangzhou' commenting confidentially that "the thing you must remember about China is that for the last thirty years we have all been acting". Child goes on to side with Shenkar and Ronen (1987) that it is

Confucianism that provides the foundation and cohesion of China's culture, society and the way relationships are conducted and regarded. It is interesting, however, that *guanxi* does not appear to have one mention in Child's 1994 book. It is only later that this concept appears to have been introduced to the world of management scholarship, and have taken on an aura of mystique.[5]

It is likely that the centralized planning and managing, to keep a grip on the potentially disintegrating forces, and enforcement through centralization and authoritarian means, which have driven China through intense industrialization, are now assets in a carefully managed integration into a global capitalist world. Fanciful ideas that China will now embrace a free-market economy and universal suffrage may be misguided, and fail to understand what is driving China. It may well be Confucian dynamics, tempered by Mohism, Legalism and Daoism, and highly effective (*guanxi*) networks throughout the world that are driving China's globalization.

That China has managed to get itself into a global position where it is able to challenge the economic might, and influence, of the United States, has major implications for globalization itself, and the ethical implications of this, and for international management ethics.

Closing case: a Confucian firm

Chapter 8, in connection with Africa, discussed the use of 'ideal type' management systems in order to first conceptualize, and then investigate the different influences on organizations, and what might go into the hybrid forms of management that could be identified. Ip (2009) uses a similar device to try to identify what a Confucian firm might look like, as an ideal type. This may be extremely useful when looking at the 'Confucian' elements that might remain in a Chinese firm operating abroad. As was discussed in Chapter 8, Chinese presence in 'Southern' regions is largely an unknown from the organizational perspective: there is still scant literature and reports of empirical studies undertaken in regions such as sub-Saharan Africa. Does the Confucian firm present another 'ideal type' in Africa and other regions where Chinese companies are gaining influence? Are Chinese firms indeed operating according to what may be regarded as Confucian ethics?

---

[5] Although there was an article in Forbes, appearing as early as 1985 (Smith and Gilbert, 1985); and in the academic press as early as 1990 where it is introduced: the latter as '*guanxi* (influence peddling)' in Wall (1990). It was only in the mid-1990s that it appeared more widely and more prominently.

Ip (2009: 467) defines the core principles of the Confucian form in terms of *ren* (a virtue or capacity of benevolence and compassion: humanity), *yi* (a sense of moral rightness) and *li* (conventions, etiquettes or norms) as discussed earlier in this chapter, as follows:

- Goals, strategies and practices defined by the principles of *ren-yi-li*;
- Structures, processes and procedures conform to *ren-yi-li*;
- Stakeholders treated with *ren-yi-li*;
- Leaders conform to thoughts and deeds of *Junzi*; and
- Members of the organization are virtuous and act in accordance to *ren-yi-li*.

Hence in terms of strategy and goals, the profit motive would be acceptable for corporate leaders but would be morally constrained and consistent with *ren*, *yi* and *li*. However, other legitimate goals of the organization would be looked at, such as doing good for the community and society. Business leadership would be defined by Confucius's distinction between *Junzi*, or the superior moral person, and ordinary people. The former is conscious of rightness, whereas the latter more aware of self-interest. *Junzi* would use *yi*-constrained or guided self-interest. Within this sense profit is morally legitimate. Business leaders should then emulate the characteristics of *Junzi* and strive to conduct a virtuous corporate life and virtuous leadership, and continuously morally improve themselves while strengthening their *Junzi*-defining virtues including *ren-yi-li*, and setting a good example to others. At the same time they should use the principles of *zhong shu* (the Golden Rule) in managing relations with stakeholders.

If the strategic direction and leadership of the corporation has to be guided by *ren-yi-li*, so do the power structures, relationships, decision-making and management processes have to be also consistent with these concepts and principles. Hence all stakeholders of the firm would be treated with rightness and humanity. This would involve providing fair wages and safe working environments, fair-dealing with customers, providing benefits to the community, being a good corporate citizen, promoting social good generally and protecting the environment. Furthermore it should be *de* (people's moral virtues) that drive people's moral actions within the firm rather than rules and regulations (as in a code of ethics, perhaps). There may still be rules, but these are secondary to virtues in motivating and directing actions. Hence conflicts are resolved by appealing to virtues rather than rules and regulations. Ip (2009) in fact makes the point that the Confucian Golden Rule is not a rule but involves the virtue of reciprocity and a reflection of the capacity of *ren* (humanity).

Yet, even though an ideal type, Ip's (2009) concept building of the Confucian Firm still needs qualification in terms of its existence in the real world, and particularly with regard to familial collectivism. Hence:

- Collectivism/familialism: family interests and goals overshadow individual corporate members' interest. There should be harmony between individual and family interests. Similarly the well-being of individuals can only be realized within the overall well-being of the family collective.
- Particularism: practice is based on personal relations rather than people's qualifications or abilities. Opportunities and benefits are therefore allocated in this way. This includes in hiring. This is also connected with *guanxi*, as Ip (2009) suggests, and is seen as critical to a company's success.
- Paternalism: this works on the principle that the father knows what is best for the children and is an extension of familial collectivism, Ip claims. It also goes with authoritarianism, he suggests, with the patriarch at the top of the relationship hierarchy deciding on what is best. He is seen to possess wisdom, knowledge and benevolence. There is therefore no need for consultation and no place for dissent. 'People are not equal in the hierarchy, and males are more equal than females' (Ip, 2009: 470). Ip sees this as a negative, stifling genuine harmony.

Yet surely the leader as *Junzi* should counteract these features of the Confucian organization that Ip perceives as negative. The problem with this, he says, is that leaders aspire to, but often fall short of being a *Junzi*. Hence in the real world leaders often lack all the good features of Junzi, and therefore sometimes cause harm to the weak, abusing powers and overlooking corruption. It is the difference between what leaders might aspire to and what is in the organization that fosters contradictions between the good and bad aspects of the Confucian firm. Yet surely this is what ethics is all about: the difference between *what is* and *what ought to be* (see Chapter 2).

Implications for international managers

Despite the abstractness of Ip's (2009) ideal type Confucian firm, it does provide an indication of the kinds of aspects that could influence Chinese firms both at home and abroad. As mentioned above, this might also help identify some of the influences (good or bad) on China's relationship with Africa, (and other countries in developing regions). Surely if Confucian concepts are being adhered to, or even strived towards, this must be a benign influence. Yet the fact that the contracts that China funds for construction in Africa, for example, go to Chinese organizations may be an indication of *guanxi* relations at work, or might simply indicate that the necessary capacity does not exist in local firms.

A similar exercise could be undertaken for the 'ideal type' Indian or Vedic firm. There are many similarities between Vedic and Confucian or Daoist concepts, not least the idea of a 'path' along which the virtuous person strives in order to reach the ideal of, for example, the Confucian *Junzi*, or the more abstract Vedic concept of *purushartha* (or, 'things sought by human beings') which is qualified by one's life position.

The problem that international managers face is distinguishing between the myth and reality, the 'exotic' and the 'backward': namely, trying to negotiate the ambivalence of the West towards the East, as was discussed in the early part of this chapter. In the same way that the concept of ideal type was useful in trying to understand influences in Africa and 'developing' countries (Chapter 8), in cutting through some of the mystique and prejudice, so it can be used in the context of 'the East' where the contradictions between the pejorative and the exotic have historically reached a high point.

Within the current discussion of the 'Orient' there seems little room for discourse ethics, and the 'good conversation' that theoretically could provide some element of agreement and understanding, and which appear to be useful in a social Europe. Although reputedly India is now one of the biggest democracies on Earth, it still appears to retain the rigidly hierarchical structure, if not of the caste system, the *varna* class structure that even Ghandi appeared to have endorsed. In China, the strictures of paternalistic hierarchy, within a familial collectivism, appear to persist. As Dobbs-Higginson (1993) has noted, Western democracy seems highly inappropriate for China, and may even do it considerable harm.

Given these factors, what can international managers learn from China and India? At the time of writing (2009) China is celebrating sixty years of communism. At the same time it is poised to be the second-largest economy on Earth. India, as a global economic power, is showing that its corporations can compete with those from the more established capitalist economies of Europe and North America. They must be doing something right. Yet is this at the same time as infringing human rights? And, as discussed in Chapter 5, what are human rights? Are they Western in concept, and why do Western powers appear sometimes to infringe them so readily?

Some of the comparative studies explored in Chapter 4 do not show German managers in a good ethical light compared with American managers. Even more so, managers from the 'greater China' countries do not appear in a good ethical light compared with European or North American managers. Some authors have pointed to the situational ethics of East Asia, of the importance of virtue and 'face' rather than of an absolute truth. Eastern philosophies and religions, as discussed in the current chapter, seem to have a concept of striving, or finding and following a path. This appears quite different to both deontological and teleological philosophies of ethics (although commentators have distinguished the apparent deontology of Confucius and the teleology of Mo Zi). The idea is of the virtuous person, or perhaps the virtuous firm, as an ideal. Perhaps the business leader or the corporation will never reach the ideal, but at least there is a concept of taking a path towards this. Sometimes this is naturalistic, as in Daoism, where there is a striving for a person to achieve harmony with a naturally defined path, or there is an element of choice in terms of defining that path in terms of striving to be virtuous. This is all tempered by one's position in life and what one can achieve within the confines of that position, and by one's obligations in terms of predefined hierarchical relations where, for example, the boss will protect and do what is best for an employee, while the employee will reciprocate by showing loyalty, and for example not blowing the whistle on one's employer. Obligations and networking are also defined by one's family connections, and this ensures harmony within the social structure.

This is indeed a different view of ethics, or even of values (the foundations of so many cross-cultural management studies). Many parts of what has appeared to be exotic in the East have been appropriated by Western scholars, and at the same time been denigrated as, for example, authoritarian or even despotic, without a clear understanding of the contributions that five or seven thousand years of documented history of civilizations have made, and what can be learned from them. The moral concepts that leaders still strive for today in China or India, have not been invented on a whim by the latest management 'guru'. Yet there is always the problem that concepts such as the Confucian firm, may be distilled, reinterpreted, reinvented, and then served up as the latest offerings to the corporate world in the West, in much the same way that so-called Japanese management was two decades ago.

Questions for managers
1. What elements of Indian philosophy and values could be integrated into an 'ideal type' model of the Vedic firm?
2. Is *guanxi* a positive or negative influence on the conduct of business in the greater China?
3. If your firm developed good *guanxi* connections in China, would you consider this good or bad? What are the wider implications for Chinese society?

An agenda for research

There may be a number of different influences on the actual nature of management values and ethical conduct of firms operating in China. Confucianism may be just one. Throughout the current text a picture of process and results of cultural hybridization has been developed that comes about by the interfaces of different cultural spaces, and the development of a Third Space. Different actors interact, but not simply on an interpersonal level. They are actors in a global nexus of power relations. This has developed through centuries of geopolitical interactions, and in the case of ancient civilization maybe many millennia. It is our job as researchers to try to understand and unpack these influences, and to be aware of processes such as mimicry, which makes it extremely difficult to directly, empirically research the influences and effects of these relationships. India has been heavily influenced by the West. First this has been through a couple of centuries of occupation by the British. More recently this is through the ingestion of Western management education. China may not have had the same types of influences, yet there is no doubt that globalization will be having its effects. Many thousands of Chinese students come to the West for their university education, and a large proportion of these are on business and management courses. It is very unlikely that many of these students meet the concept of the Confucian firm in a British or an American university business school.

Rather than trying to compare China, or India, with a Western country by reference to such concept as Hofstede's value dimensions, the job of the researcher should be to identify the different influences that contribute to the Third Spaces that are occupied, for example, by the Chinese organization in PRC, Hong Kong, Singapore, Brazil or Zambia. A device for doing this is to conceptualize different ideal types, and then trying to identify their influences in the organization. Much more will be discussed regarding this in the concluding chapter of this text.

Questions for researchers
1. What ideal types could be constructed for Chinese firms operating in India?
2. How is it possible to research Chinese business students' 'what ought to be' against 'what is' in Chinese organizations, given that the researcher understands the concept of mimicry? What are the issues? What are the problems? And, how can one get around these problems?

Part III

Managing ethically across cultures

10   Looking forward, looking back

In Chapter 1 I alluded to Neil Brady's book *Ethical Managing: Rules and Results*. The cover of his book portrays an image of the Roman god Janus. Indeed he uses a 'Janus-headed view' as a metaphor for his *rules* (looking back – deontological) and *results* (looking forward – teleological) approach to ethics. Janus is the god of doorways, beginnings and endings. The month of January, the beginning of the new year, is named after him. He is always depicted with two heads, one looking backwards, the other looking forwards. Brady (1990: 62) tells us that 'this view portrays the social process of resolving ethical issues simultaneously looking to the past as well as to the future'. His distinction between utilitarians as the forward-looking ethicists and the 'formalists' as the backward-looking ones, may still be slightly too simplistic, yet does provide the basis for viewing how tradition links with change, and how we must incorporate these two fundamental views when making an ethical decision. Ethical decision making is all about making sense of ambiguity, by trying to understand what has led to where we are; then taking risks, making a leap in the dark almost, by taking some kind of action based on what has worked in the past, and your estimation of what the results of your action will be. Often, the making sense of ambiguity might involve considering religious precepts, as we saw in Chapter 7.

These are the aspects that perhaps do not travel well across cultures, yet attempts have been made to lay down universal standards of ethics as we have seen with such prescription as the Universal Declaration of Human Rights in Chapter 5. The precept of the sanctity of the person as an isolated individual comes out strongly in this attempt, and is challenged by, for example, the African Charter of Human and Peoples' Rights, and Cairo Declaration of Human Rights in Islam. Balancing individual human rights with national development issues is something that, for example, China has constantly had to contend with.

The way that countries such as the United States can then essentially ignore human rights in terms of expediency and results, such as in the case of Guantanamo Bay, may be indicative of the conflicts between a rules and results approach. In a management situation, Hosmer (1987) attempted to show how these two approaches might be combined in his model of ethical management. Cultural experiences, ethical belief systems and the economic and social situation combine to influence 'moral standards of behaviour'. This is what feeds into what he calls the 'content of management dilemma'. Content comprises the financial, legal, organizational, social and personal consequences of managerial actions. Although highlighting aspects that should be taken into consideration when making ethical decisions, including highlighting differences in 'cultural experiences', it still does not help very much in making decisions across cultures. Donaldson (1989) tried to solve this issue by devising his 'algorithm' for international ethical decision making. This begins with what he calls a conflict of cultural norms, namely: Is the practice permissible for the multinational company when it is morally and/or legally permitted in the host country, but not in the home country? He then goes on to describe type 1 conflict and type 2 conflict. The former is when the reasons for the host country's view being different are related to the level of its economic development. For example, this may be the case where regulations relating to levels of pollution may be more lax. The resolving of the conflict is then based on the principle that the practice is permissible if under similar economic circumstances the home country would regard the practice as permissible. Yet this today would lead to some interesting debate in the wake of the 2009 Copenhagen Climate Conference.

Type 2 conflicts are when the reasons why the host country's view is different are independent of its economic level of development. Whether or not nepotism is a useful example may be questioned in view of the discussions in Chapters 7 and 8 in the current text. Similarly, bribery may provide another example in this context. In Donaldson's algorithm, the question must then be asked: Is it possible to conduct business successfully in the host country without undertaking this particular practice? If the answer is no, the next question is: Is the practice a clear violation of fundamental international human rights? If the answer is no, then: if the practice is necessary to conduct business in the host country and it does not violate fundamental human rights, but if it does go against basic moral principles of the home country, then managers in MNC should speak against it (Donaldson, 1989, and adapted by Jackson, 1993b). Yet in a cross-cultural context, this approach may now be regarded as simplistic, but for managers working across countries, may well be too complex where companies have tended to rely (perhaps under the influence of American MNC: Chapter 5) almost exclusively on codes of ethical conduct, to which managers are expected to adhere, supplemented perhaps by training workshops, and educational materials, with special attention given to 'cultural' training prior to managers going abroad.

This now brings us to the issue of management education and training. One of the main themes throughout the current text has been 'what can we learn from other nations, societies, and by focusing on others' cultural spaces?' When Western liberal views are dismissive of Muslim attitudes towards gender relations, how can we view this differently by standing in the others' shoes? (Chapter 7). Ethical relativism has come under much criticism over the years. Yet I do not believe this is ethical relativism. Ethical relativism provides a foregone conclusion in what one should do if posed with a Donaldson-type conflict: do as the host culture does. Taking a view from nowhere is impossible despite assumptions within the positivist paradigm (Chapter 5), so taking a view from somewhere leaves us with our only option.

Starting from our own cultural space (which we attempt to make visible: Chapter 5), we can begin to understand others' cultural spaces. Yet in view of the previous discussion in this text on postcolonial theory, this is, at least in theory, difficult (Chapter 5). If the West, through historic power dynamics, has constructed the non-West in a pejorative yet exotic way (Chapter 9), how is it possible to now step in the shoes of 'the other'? Should we not then speak to 'the other'? Again we are presented with a problem through postcolonial theory: if the non-West has internalized the way the West has represented it, on behalf of the other, and if Spivak (1996) is right that the non-West cannot then speak for itself, the self-representation by the other is going to reflect the representation constructed by the West.

The other way of looking at this is: what you see is what you get – hence the concept of the Third Space (Bhabha, 1994). Through historical and ongoing geopolitical interactions involving power dynamics, cultural spaces are constructed and reconstructed. The representations of self, or 'culture', within these spaces is simply what we have ended up with at any point in time. Power dynamics allows for an element of protest and opposition to the dominant view, but these cultural Third Spaces, which have occurred through cultural crossvergence and the emergence of hybrid cultural forms, are discoverable, and can form the subject of social scientific enquiry.

In Chapter 6, the focus was on stakeholders within discourse ethics, and how discourse ethics could be used as a process of negotiation across cultures (for example, Cortina, 1998). Discovering one's own cultural space, in negotiation with discovering others' cultural spaces, could be a way forward, not withstanding my warning in Chapter 6 that Jurgen Habermas's assertion that 'in discourse the unforced force of the better argument prevails' is readily countered by postcolonial theory which suggests that despite one's attempt to neutralize power relations within such dialogue as discourse ethics, 'mimicry' in Bhabha's (1994) terms still reflects the dominant ideology in geopolitical relations. So it may be possible immediately to gain an understanding of the others' cultural space in relation to our own in immediate dialogue and effectively to neutralize power relations in what Bird (1996) has called 'good conversation'. Yet the overarching geopolitical and historical relations at the macro level may neutralize this neutralization.

So, where does that leave us, and what do we do? What is desirable in Flyvbjerg's (2001) value-rational sense? Hence back to management training and education, and to trace more methodically the implications of the content of the current text.

From Chapter 2 which focused on why ethical values might differ from one society to another, managers should first try to understand: what *choices* are available to individuals and organizations in the decisions they make; what *values* influence or govern these choices; what *rules* are followed (or not followed) in order to make such choices; how do these rules *control* the levels and nature of choice in a society or an organization; what the *power* relations are among the different stakeholders within the organization or society that control the rules and the values that influence choice; and, what different *objectives* do the different *stakeholders* have that influence choice in decision making. This provides the basis for understanding any society in terms of the dynamics that constitute its ethical context (rules, principles, structures), content (values, attitudes, ideals) and conduct (actions and interactions). In some ways this is proposing that managers, or management educators, do their own research; or at least try to understand at some level the dynamics involved.

Much research has been undertaken of course, and this might help. Yet this has largely remained at the descriptive, *what*, stage, as we explored in Chapter 4, relating this to the more general values research described in Chapter 3. The value of the type of research undertaken in the tradition of Hofstede's work is that we begin to understand why things may be different in different cultural spaces: why bribery might be regarded differently, why nepotism may not be an issue. Of course, this has its limitations. It remains at the descriptive level, has some predictive value, but does not help us in understanding what to do. Chapter 3 for example highlights the difficulty of participation, with the irony that its propagation can provide a form of tyranny. Thoroughly understanding the existing comparative literature on cultural values is perhaps a prerequisite, but does not go far enough. Similarly in Chapter 4, the growing comparative literature on management ethics is useful for understanding the structure and nature of ethical decision making and upon what type of principles it is based; what might constitute ethicality in a given society, and the implications of ethical values for the relationships between people. The shortfall in the studies presented in Chapter 4 is the lack of depth and understanding of what has been termed the *emics* of culture, or the perception of cultural values from the perspective of those societies we are interested in. This contrasts with the *etics* of culture which attempts to establish universals that can constitute the subject of study across many cultures (Peterson and Pike, 2002). Kenneth Pike, whose work on these two complementary approaches to studying culture has been taken up in the cross-cultural management literature, suggested for understanding an emic view, an *emic circle*:

See, and know.
Know, and be.
Be, and do.
Do, and see.
See, and know. (Cited in Peterson and Pike, 2002)

Much of the work of cross-cultural scholars has been trying to render culture visible. Chapter 5 tried to show how culture has been obscured from view, in a global context where even cross-cultural scholars ignore the importance and implications of geopolitical power dynamics. By trying to understand these dynamics, it may be possible to render culture visible: perhaps a prerequisite to not just understanding ethicality in different cultures, but actually what to do: the desirability of different actions. Obscuring culture and claiming universality for precepts, such as human rights, entail a particular geopolitical dynamic that should be understood. As we saw above this is not always easy, as a claim for universalism also obscures the power dynamic: a major issue in cross-cultural management studies, that itself is invisible and rarely taken cognizance of. Critical management studies rarely also integrate with cross-cultural studies, and less still are brought to the attention of managers. Hence the interest shown in postcolonial studies by critical management theorists is rarely taken up by cross-cultural scholars. Where cross-cultural management is on the agenda of, for example, MBA programmes, the critical issues raised may concern the problems of knowledge transfer from one culture to another, but often not the power dynamics of first understanding those cultural issues, and then deciding what to do. Simply understanding that it may be difficult to introduce participation to a higher Power Distance society is not the same as considering the ethicality of doing so. Even more so, the problem of understanding what is local, or indigenous, culture and what is a projection of Western culture on local cultures are thorny issues perhaps rarely discussed.

In particular Chapter 5 pointed out the following issues that may be called into question by managers:

- Home country principles are introduced that may be contrary to values in the host country: what is the ethicality of using economic power in a corporate situation to introduce one's own value system?
- Host country principles are adopted which might be contrary to home country values, and values of home country managers: what is the ethicality of adopting host country values (perhaps to gain competitive advantage, in the case of paying bribes – if indeed this is a reflection of host 'values'), which are in contradiction to value systems from one's home country?
- Supposed concepts of universal human rights are infringed because they contradict the interests of the perpetrating corporate: what is the ethicality of not living up to the high moral standards prescribed and accepted by one's home country, and ostensibly the 'international community', which have been propagated by a country's access to international power structures (such as the United Nations), but which can apparently flout those standards when it suits?

These are all issues that cannot be directly addressed by reference to studies on cultural values or ethicality in different countries. They call on value-rational thought, negotiation and often compromise. This then is the main subject of Chapter 6: discourse ethics may provide a way forward. This is examined in the European context where culture has been rendered more visible, but the subject of management ethics has often been kept to the background: it is often assumed rather than rendered explicit. Reaching understanding, or even compromising through a process of discourse ethics, renders the issues more visible. In some ways Bird's (1996) outline process of 'good conversation' is idealized. Yet the general principle of explicating one's values and issues through discursive engagement with one's business and community partners appears to be good practice. However, one should also be reminded that not all peoples from different societies are equally open to direct and open conversation, and that power dynamics may still override any such process.

One thing that Chapter 6 stressed is the importance of social partnering within a social Europe, and the role of discourse ethics within this. Chapter 7 focused on this from Islamic precepts, and the role of stakeholder relationships within this. The role that paternalism plays in this is prominent, and different to social partnering described in the context of Europe. Paternalism in the Islamic context provides protection and nurturing, and is seen as a positive feature. It also has implication for gender relations and roles, as well as *wasta*, that must be understood rather than denigrated by Western scholars and managers; and further than this, it should be learned from. Said (1978) provided a critique of Orientalism and its negative connotations of the Middle East. Ghorbani and Tung (2007) have provided a way of obviating myths of Islamic countries and how these might be explored, and possibly refuted. The major barrier to fully understanding the emics of other cultures in this way is the implicit belief in the trajectory from developing to developed economies, that 'developing' countries are backward. This is met head on in Chapter 8 in the context of Africa. Corruption is difficult for managers to deal with if they simply see it as a product of a backward economy and society. That high-level corruption is still dependent on 'developed' country managers paying bribes is an issue that needs to be taken up in this context, as should the tracing of the origins of such corruption in colonial and post-colonial administration. Much can be learned by Western managers looking at the efforts of many African managers and companies to refocus on community and humanist values that permeate sub-Saharan African communities.

Yet the denigration of the cultures of others is not so simple to understand when it is compounded with 'a taste of the exotic', as Chapter 9 explored, particularly in relation to China. Hence *guanxi* is held up almost reverentially, against a backdrop of distrust and often condemnation: a curious mixture of denigration and approbation, which reflects Said's (1978) concept of Orientalism.

This last substantive Chapter 9, heralded a new geopolitical dynamic of China, and India, in the world. Formerly management scholars reflected a view of China as a vast emerging market: somewhere where Western companies should be. Now, this is slowly changing to recognize that these 'Southern' (or non-Western) players create new dynamics in the world, and create a need for concepts that theorize the relationships of South with South. Dependency theory and postcolonial theory may now be completely inadequate to understand the relationships between China and sub-Saharan African countries, for example. Just at a time when management studies is waking up to theories that have existed in the social sciences for many years, so there is a need for new theories. A need for managers to understand these new dynamics has not been met by theories that come out of the universities. It may now be time for cross-cultural scholars to take a lead in developing new theory and concepts for understanding management ethics within this emerging dynamic.

References

Abratt, R., Nel, D. and Higgs, N. S. (1992) An examination of the ethical beliefs of managers using selected scenarios in a cross-cultural environment, *Journal of Business Ethics* 11: 29–35.

Abudu, F. (1986) Work attitudes of Africans, with special reference to Nigeria, *International Studies of Management and Organization* 16(2): 17–36.

Abuznaid, S. (2006) Islam and management: what can be learned? *Thunderbird International Business Review* 48(1): 125–39.

Acar, M. (2009) Towards a synthesis of Islam and the market economy? The Justice and Democracy Party's economic reforms in Turkey, *Economic Affairs* 29(2): 16–21.

Agbese, P. O. (1994) The state versus human rights advocates in Africa: the case of Nigeria, in E. McCarthy-Arnolds, D. Penna and J. Cruz Sobrepena (eds.) *Africa, Human Rights and the Global System*, Westport, CT: Greenwood Press.

Ahluwalia, P. (2001) *Politics and Post-Colonial Theory: African Inflections*, London: Routledge.

Alderson, S. and Kakabadse, A. (1994) Business ethics and Irish management: a cross-cultural study, *European Management Journal* 12(4): 432–40.

Ali, A. J. (1995) Cultural discontinuity and Arab management thought, *International Studies of Management and Organization* 25(3): 7–30.

(2005) *Islamic Perspectives on Management and Organization*, Cheltenham, UK: Edward Elgar.

Ali, A. J., Taqi, A. and Krishnan, K. (1997) Individualism, collectivism, and decision styles of managers in Kuwait, *Journal of Social Psychology* 137(5): 629–37.

Ali, T. (2002) *The Clash of Fundamentalism: Crusades, Jihads and Modernity*, London: Verso.

Al-Kazemi, A. and Ali, A. J. (2002) Managerial problems in Kuwait, *Journal of Management Development* 21(5): 366–75.

Amnesty International (1991) *Protecting Human Rights*, London: Amnesty International.

Annan, K. (1999) Business and the UN: a global compact of shared values and principles, *World Economic Forum*, Davos, Switzerland, and reprinted in *Vital Speeches of the Day* 65(9): 260–1.

An-Na'im, A. A. and Deng, F. (1990) (eds.) *Human Rights in Africa: A Cross-cultural Perspective*, Washington DC: Brooking Institute.

Ansari, M. A., Ahmad, Z. A. and Aafaqi, R. (2004) Organizational leadership in the Malaysian context. In D. Tjosvold and K. Leung (eds.), *Leading in High Growth Asia: Managing Relationships for Teamwork and Change*, Singapore: World Scientific, pp. 109–38.

Apressyan, R. G. (1997) Business ethics in Russia, *Journal of Business Ethics* 16: 1561–70.

Argyle, M. (1967) *The Psychology of Interpersonal Behaviour*, Harmondsworth: Penguin.

Argyris, C. (1992) *On Organizational Learning*, Oxford/Cambridge, MA: Blackwell.

Aristotle (1953) *Ethics: The Nicomachean Ethics* (trans. J. A. K. Thomson), Harmondsworth: Penguin.

Avtonomov, V. (2006) Balancing state, market and social justice: Russian experience and lessons to learn, *Journal of Business Ethics* 66: 3–9.

Aycan, Z. (2006) Paternalism: towards conceptual refinement and operationalization. In K. S. Yang, K. K. Hwang and U. Kim (eds.) *Scientific Advances in Indigenous Psychologies: Empirical, Philosophical and Cultural Contributions*, Cambridge University Press, pp. 445–66.

Aycan, Z., Kanungo, R. N. and Sinha, J. B. P. (1999) Organizational culture and human resource management practice: the model of cultural fit, *Journal of Cross-Cultural Psychology* 30(4): 501–26.

Aycan, Z., Kanungo, R. N., Mendonca, M. *et al.* (2000). Impact of culture on human resource management practices: a ten country comparison, *Applied Psychology: An International Review* 49(1): 192–220.

Ayittey, G. B. N. (1991) *Indigenous African Institutions*, New York: Transnational Publishers.

Bae, K. and Chung, C. (1997) Cultural values and work attitudes of Korean industrial workers in comparison with those of the United States and Japan, *Work and Occupations* 24(1): 80–96.

Barratt Brown, M. (1995) *Africa's Choices: After Thirty Years of the World Bank*, London: Penguin.

BBC News (2004) Q&A: Turkey and the EU, accessed from http://news.bbc.co.uk/go/pr/fr/-/1/hi/world/Europe/3682828.stm, on 13/06/09.

Beals, R. (1953) Acculturation. In A. L. Kroebner (ed.) *Anthropology Today*, University of Chicago Press.

Beaty, D. T. (1998) Colgate Palmolive in post-apartheid South Africa, reprinted in G. Oddou and M. Mendenhall, *Cases in International Organizational Behavior*, Malden, MA: Blackwell, pp. 136–42.

Becker, H. and Fritzsche, D. J. (1987) Business ethics: a cross-cultural comparison of managers' attitudes, *Journal of Business Ethics* 6: 289–95.

Beekun, I. R. and Badawi, J. A. (2005) Balancing ethical responsibility among multiple organizational stakeholders: the Islamic perspective, *Journal of Business Ethics* 60: 131–45.

Begley, T. (1998) Chang Koh Metal Ptd Ltd in China. In G. Oddou and M. Mendenhall, *Cases in International Organizational Behavior*, Malden, MA: Blackwell, pp. 151–4.

Beinart, W. (1994) *Twentieth Century South Africa*, Oxford University Press.

Berger, P. L. and Luckmann, T. (1966) *The Social Construction of Reality*, New York: Doubleday.

Berry, J. W., Poortinga, Y. H., Degall, M. H. and Dasen, P. R. (1992) *Cross-cultural Psychology: Research and Applications*, New York: Cambridge University Press.

Beschorner, T. (2006) Ethical theory and business practices: the case of discourse ethics, *Journal of Business Ethics* 66: 127–39.

Bhabha, H. K. (1994) *The Location of Culture*, New York: Routledge.

Biko, S. (1984) Some African cultural concepts, in *Frank Talk* 1(4): 29–31, and reprinted in P. H. Coetzee and A. P. J. Roux (eds.) (1998) *Philosophy for Africa: A Text with Readings*, Johannesburg: International Thomson Publishing, ch. 2, pp. 26–30.

Bilimoria, P. (1993) Indian ethics. In P. Singer (ed.) *A Companion to Ethics*, Oxford: Blackwell, ch. 4, pp. 43–57.

Binet, J. (1970) *Psychologie Economique Africaine*, Paris: Payot.

Bird, F. B. (1996) *The Muted Conscience: Moral Silence and the Practice of Ethics in Business*, Stamford, CT: Quorum.

Blanchard, K. and Peale, N. V. (1988) *The Power of Ethical Management*, New York: Cedar/ Heinemann.

Blunt, P. and Jones, M. L. (1992) *Managing Organizations in Africa*, Berlin: Walter de Gruyter.

(1997) Exploring the limits of Western leadership theory in East Asia and Africa, *Personnel Review* 26(1/2): 6–23.

Bond, M. H., Fu, P. P. and Pasa, S. F. (2001) A declaration of independence for editing an International Journal of Cross Cultural Management, *International Journal of Cross Cultural Management* 1(1): 24–30.

Boyacigiller, N. A. and Adler, N. J. (1991) The parochial dinosaur: organizational science in a global context, *Academy of Management Review* 16(2): 262–90.

Boyatzis, R. E. (1982) *The Competent Manager*, New York: John Wiley.

Brady, F. N. (1990) *Ethical Management: Rules and Results*, London: Macmillan.

Briggs, J. and Sharpe, J. (2004) Indigenous knowledge and development: a postcolonial caution, *Third World Quarterly* 25(4): 661–76.

Budhwar, P. S. (2001) HRM in India. In P. S. Budhwar and Y. A. Debrah, *Human Resource Management in Developing Countries*, London: Routledge, ch. 5, pp. 75–90.

Business Week (2005) Commentary: The Real Scandal at Volkswagen, 18 July 2005, www.businessweek.com/magazine/content/05_29/b3943064_mz054.htm, accessed 23/06/09.

Cam, S. (2002) Neo-liberalism and labour within the context of an 'emerging market' economy: Turkey, *Capital and Class* 77: 89–114.

Campbell, H. (2008) China in Africa: challenging US global hegemony, *Third World Quarterly* 29(1): 89–105.

Carlin, W. B. and Strong, K. C. (1995) A critique of Western philosophical ethics: multidisciplinary alternatives for framing ethical dilemmas, *Journal of Business Ethics* 14: 387–96.

Carlsson, J. (1998) Organization and leadership in Africa. In L. Wohlgemuth, J. Carlsson and H. Kifle (eds.) *Institution Building and Leadership in Africa*, Uppsala, Sweden: Nordiska Afrikainstitutet, pp. 13–32.

Carroll, S. J. and Gannon, M. J. (1997) *Ethical Dimensions of International Management*, Thousand Oaks, CA: Sage.

Castellino, J. (2009) *The End of the Liberal State and the First Terrorist*, London: Middlesex University Press.

CCC (Chinese Cultural Connection) (1987) Chinese values and the search for culture-free dimensions of culture, *Journal of Cross-Cultural Psychology* 18: 143–64.

Centre for Chinese Studies (2008) *The China Monitor Issue 28: China's Development Assistance to Africa*, April, University of Stellenbosch, South Africa, www.ccs.org.za/downloads/monitors/China%20Monitor%20April_2008.pdf, accessed 15/06/09.

Chakraborty, S. K. (1995) *Ethics in Management: Vedantic Perspectives*, Delhi: Oxford University Press.

Chan, G. (2008) The relevance and value of Confucianism in contemporary business ethics. *Journal of Business Ethics* 77(3): 347–60.

Chan, R. Y. K., Cheng, L. T. W. and Szeto R. W. F. (2002) The dynamics of guanxi and ethics for Chinese executives, *Journal of Business Ethics* 41(4): 327–36.

Chatterjee, P. (1986) *Nationalist Thought and the Colonial World: A Derivative Discourse*, London: Zed Books.

(1993) *The Nation and its Fragments: Colonial and Postcolonial Histories*, Princeton University Press.

Cheung, C.-K. and Chan, A. C.-F. (2005) Philosophical foundations of eminent Hong Kong Chinese CEOs' leadership. *Journal of Business Ethics* 60(1): 47–62.

Child, J. (1994) *Management in China During the Age of Reform*, Cambridge University Press.

Chomsky, N. (2003) *Hegemony or Survival: America's Quest for Global Dominance*, London: Penguin.

Christie, P. M. J., Kwon, I. G., Stoeberl, P. A. and Baumhart, R. (2003) A cross-cultural comparison of ethical attitudes of business managers: India, Korea and the United States, *Journal of Business Ethics* 46(3): 263–87.

Cicourel, A. V. (1964) *Methods and Measurement in Sociology*, New York: The Free Press.

Clarke, S. and Pringle, T. (2008) Trade unions in Russia, China and Vietnam: from governmental to non-governmental public actors, *NGPA Working Paper Series*, No. 22, London: LSE/ESRC, www.lse.ac.uk/collections/NGPA/publications/WP22_GovtoNonGov_Clark_Web.pdf, accessed 08/07/09.

Clegg, S. and Kono, T (2002) Trends in Japanese management: an overview of embedded continuities and disembedded discontinuities, *Asia Pacific Journal of Management* 19: 269–85.

Colella, A., Garcia, F., Reidel, L. and Triana, M. (2005) Paternalism: 'hidden' discrimination. Paper presented at the meeting of the Academy of Management, Honolulu, Hawaii.

Coleman, I. (2006) Women, Islam, and the new Iraq, *Foreign Affairs* 85(1): 24–38.

Cooke, B. and Kothari, U. (2001) *Participation: The New Tyranny?* London: Zed Books.

Cortina, A. (1998) Business ethics in the Catholic value system: the Spanish case. In Kumar and Steinmann (eds.).

(2008) European economic ethics research: a diagnosis, *Zeitschrift fuer Wirtschafts- und Unternehmensethik* 9(1): 10–25.

Crane, A. and Matten, D. (2004) *Business Ethics*, Oxford University Press.

Cray, D. and Mallory, G. R. (1998) *Making Sense of Managing Culture*, London: Thomson.

Cyr, D. J. and Schneider, S. C. (1998) Creating a learning organization through HRM: a German-Czech joint venture, INSEAD case collection, and reproduced as ch. 17 in G. Oddou and M. Mendenhall (eds.) (1998) *Cases in International Organizational Behaviour*, Malden, MA: Blackwell, pp. 197–210.

Dahl, R. A. (1957) The concept of power, *Behavioural Science* 2: 201–18.

Darwish, Y. (2000) Organizational commitment as a mediator of the relationship between Islamic work ethic and attitudes toward organizational change, *Human Relations* 35(4): 513–37.

de Sardan, J. P. O. (1999) A moral economy of corruption in Africa? *The Journal of Modern African Studies* 37(1): 25–52.

Decalo, S. (1992) The process, prospects and constraints of democratization in Africa, *African Affairs* 91(362): 7–35.

Deegan, H. (2009) *Africa Today: Culture, Economics, Religion, Security*, London: Routledge.

Demenchono, E. (2009) The universal concept of human rights as a regulative principle: freedom versus paternalism, *American Journal of Economics and Sociology* 68(1): 273–301.

Dia, M. (1996) *Africa's Management in the 1990s and Beyond*, Washington DC: World Bank.

Dobbs-Higginson, M. S. (1993) *Asia Pacific: Its Role in the New World Disorder*, London: Mandarin.

Dolecheck, M. and Dolecheck, C. (1987) Business ethics: a comparison of attitudes of managers in Hong Kong and the United States, *Hong Kong Managers* 1: 28–43.

Donaldson, T. (1989) *The Ethics of International Business*, New York: Oxford University Press.

Donaldson, T. and Dunfee, T. (1994) Towards a unified conception of business ethics: integrative social contracts theory, *Academy of Management Review* 19(2): 252–84.

Douglas, S., Massey, D. S. and Magaly Sanchez, R. M. (2007) Latino and American identities as perceived by immigrants, *Qualitative Sociology* 30: 81–107.

Durkheim, E. (1915/1971) *The Elementary Forms of the Religious Life* (trans. J. W. Swain), London: Allen and Unwin.

Elenkov, D. S. (1997) Differences and similarities in managerial values between US and Russia managers, *International Studies of Management and Organization* 27(1): 85–106.

Encel, S. (1970) *Equality and Authority*, London: Tavistock.

Enderle, G. (1996) A comparison of business ethics in North America and continental Europe, *Business Ethics: A European Review* 5(1): 31–46.

Erben, G. S. and Güneşer, A. B. (2007) The relationship between paternalistic leadership and organizational commitment: investigating the role of climate regarding ethics, *Journal of Business Ethics* 82: 955–68.

Escobar, A. (1995) *Encountering Development: The Making and Unmaking of the Third World*, Princeton University Press.

Etzioni, A. (1975) *A Comparative Analysis of Complex Organizations*, New York: The Free Press.

Fan, Y. (2002) Ganxi's consequences: personal gains at social cost. *Journal of Business Ethics* 38(4): 371–80.

Fang, T. (2003) A critique of Hofstede's fifth national cultural dimension, *International Journal of Cross Cultural Management* 3(3): 347–68.

Fannon, L. I. (2003) *Working Within Two Kinds of Capitalism: Corporate Governance and Employee Stakeholder: US and EU Perspectives*. Portland, OR: Hart Publishing.

Farh, J. L. and Cheng, B. S. (2000) A cultural analysis of paternalistic leadership in Chinese organizations. In J. T. Li., A. S. Tsui and E. Weldon (eds.), *Management and Organizations in the Chinese Context*, London: Macmillan, pp. 84–127.

Farh, J. L., Cheng, B. S., Chou, L. F. and Chu, X. P. (2006) Authority and benevolence: Employees' responses to paternalistic leadership in China. In A. S. Tsui, Y. Bian and L. Cheng (eds.), *China's Domestic Private Firms: Multidisciplinary Perspectives on Management and Performance*, New York: Sharpe, pp. 230–60.

Ferguson, N. (2003) *Empire: How Britain Made the Modern World*, London: Penguin.

Ferrell, O. C. and Weaver, K. M. (1978) Ethical beliefs of marketing managers, *Journal of Marketing* 42(3): 69–73.

Firth, R. (1951) *Elements of Social Organization*, London: Watts.

Flyvbjerg, B. (2001) *Making Social Science Matter*, Cambridge University Press.

Foucault, M. (1979) *Discipline and Punish*, New York: Vintage Books, p. 194.

Frank, A. G. (1969) *Capitalism and Underdevelopment in Latin America*, New York: Monthly Review Press.

Frankenberg, R. (2001) Mirage of an unmarked whiteness. In B. B. Rasmussen, E. Klinenberg, I. J. Nexica, M. Wray (eds.), *The Making and Unmaking of Whiteness*. Durham, NC: Duke University Press, pp. 72–96.

Frenkel, M. (2008) The multinational corporation as a third space: rethinking international management discourse on knowledge transfer through Homi Bhabha, *Academy of Management Review* 33(4): 924–42.

Friedman, M. (1962) *Capitalism and Freedom*. University of Chicago Press.

Fukuyama, E. (1995) *Trust: The Social Virtue and the Creation of Prosperity*. New York: Free Press.

Gannon, M. J. and associates (1994) *Understanding Global Cultures: Metaphorical Journeys Through 17 Countries*, Thousand Oaks, CA: Sage.

Gatley, S., Lessem, R. and Altman, Y. (1996) *Comparative Management: A Transcultural Odyssey*, London: McGraw-Hill.

Geertz, C. (1973) *The Interpretation of Cultures*, New York: Basic Books.

Ghorbani, M. and Tung, R. L. (2007) Behind the veil: an exploratory study of the myths and realities of women in the Iranian workforce, *Human Resource Management Journal* 17(4): 376–92.

Giddens, A. (1986) *The Constitution of Society*, Berkeley and Los Angeles: University of California Press.

Glenn, E. S., Witmeyer, D. and Stevenson, K. A. (1977) Cultural styles of persuasion, *International Journal of Intercultural Relations* 1(3): 52–66.

Glenny, M. (1993) *The Rebirth of History: Eastern Europe in the Age of Democracy*, London: Penguin.

Gluckman, M. (1956/1970) *Custom and Conflict in Africa*, Oxford: Basil Blackwell.

Goody, J. (1994) Culture and its boundaries: a European perspective. In R. Borofsky (ed.) *Assessing Cultural Anthropology*, New York: McGraw-Hill, pp. 250–61.

Gu, F. F., Hung, K. and Tse, D. K. (2008) When does guanxi matter? Issues of capitalization and its dark sides, *Journal of Marketing* 72: 12–28.

Gupta, R. K. (1991) Employees and organizations in India: need to move beyond American and Japanese models, *Economic and Political Weekly*, 25 May, 16–21.

Gutmann, B. (1995) Tandem training: the Volkswagen–Skoda approach to know-how transfer, *Journal of European Industrial Training* 19(4): 21–4.

Guy, V. and Mattock, J. (1991) *The New International Manager: An Action Guide for Cross-Cultural Business*, London: Kogan Page.

Hailey, J. (2002) Beyond the formulaic: process and practice in South Asia NGOs. In B. Cooke and U. Kothari, *Participation: The New Tyranny*, London: Zed Books, ch. 6, pp. 88–101.

Hall, E. T. (1959) *The Silent Language*, New York: Anchor Press/Doubleday.

Hansen, C. (1993) Classical Chinese ethics. In Singer (ed.), ch. 6, pp. 69–81.

Hansen, R. S. (1992) A multidimensional scale for measuring business ethics: a purification and refinement, *Journal of Business Ethics* 11: 523–34.

Harré, R., Clarke, D. and de Carlo, N. (1985) *Motives and Mechanism: An Introduction to the Psychology and Action*, London: Methuen.

Hegarty, W. H. and Sims, H. P. (1978) Some determinants of unethical decision behaviour: an experiment, *Journal of Applied Psychology* 63(4): 451–7.

(1979) Organizational philosophy, policies and objectives related to unethical decision behaviour: a laboratory experiment, *Journal of Applied Psychology* 64(3): 331–8.

Herskovits, M. J. (1948) *Man and His Works: The Science of Cultural Anthropology*, New York: Knopf.

Hickson, D. J. and McMillan, C. J. (1981) (eds.) *Organization and Nation: The Aston Programme, IV*, Aldershot: Gower.

Hickson, D. J. and Pugh, D. S. (1995) *Management Worldwide*, London: Penguin.

Hirschmann, N. J. (1998) Western feminism, Eastern veiling, and the question of free agency, *Constellations* 5(3): 345–68.

Ho, D. Y.-F. and Chiu, C.-Y. (1994) Component ideas of individualism, collectivism and social organization: an application in the study of Chinese culture, in U. Kim, H. C. Triandis, Ç. Kâğitçibaşi, S.-C. Choi and G. Yoon, *Individualism and Collectivism: Theory, Method and Application*, Thousand Oaks, CA: Sage, pp. 137–56.

Hochschild, A. (1998) *King Leopold's Ghost*, London: Macmillan.

Hofstede, G. (1980a/2003) *Culture's Consequences* (1st/2nd edns.), Thousand Oaks, CA: Sage.

(1980b) Motivation, leadership and organization: do American theories apply abroad? *Organizational Dynamics*, Summer: 42–63.

(1991) *Cultures and Organizations: Software of the Mind*, London: McGraw-Hill.

hooks, B. (1990) Marginality as a site of resistance. In Ferguson, R. *et al.* (eds.) *Out There: Marginalization and Contemporary Cultures*, Cambridge, MA: MIT Press.

Hosmer, L. T (1987) Ethical analysis and human resource management, *Human Resource Management* 26(3): 313–30.

House, R., Hanges, P. J., Javidan, M., Dorfman, P. W. and Gupta, V. (2004) *Leadership, Culture and Organizations: The GLOBE Study of 62 Societies*, Thousand Oaks, CA: Sage.

Hui, C. H. (1990) Work attitudes, leadership styles, and managerial behaviour in different cultures. In R. W. Brislin, *Applied Cross-Cultural Psychology*, Newbury Park, CA: Sage.

Hulpke, J. and Lau, C. (2008) Business ethics in China, *The Chinese Economy* 41(3): 58–67.

Human, L. (1996) *Contemporary Conversations*, Dakar, Senegal: The Goree Institute.

Hunt, S. D. and Vitell, S. J. (1986) A general theory of marketing ethics, *Journal of Macromarketing* 6: 5–16.

Husted, B. W. (1999) Wealth, culture and corruption, *Journal of International Business Studies* 30(2): 339–59.

Iankova, E. and Turner, L. (2004) Building the New Europe: western and eastern roads to social partnership, *Industrial Relations Journal* 35(1): 76–92.

ICPSR (2005) Inter-University Consortium for Political and Social Research, http://webapp.icpsr.umich.edu/cocoon/ICPSR-STUDY/03975.xml, accessed 18/12/05.

Inglehart, R. (1997) *Modernization and Postmodernization: Cultural, Economic, and Political Change in 43 Societies*, Princeton University Press.

Inglehart, R. and Baker, W. E. (2000) Modernization, cultural change, and persistence of traditional values, *American Sociological Review* 65, February, 19–51.

(2001) Modernization's challenges to traditional values: who's afraid of Ronald McDonald? *The Futurist*, March–April: 16–21.

Inglehart, R., Basanez, M. and Moreno, A. (1998) *Human Values and Beliefs: A Cross-cultural Sourcebook*, Ann Arbor, MI: University of Michigan Press.

Ip, P. K. (2009) Is Confucianism good for business ethics in China? *Journal of Business Ethics* 88: 463–76.

Izraeli, D. (1988) Ethical beliefs and behaviours among managers: a cross-cultural comparison, *Journal of Business Ethics* 7: 263–71.

Jackman, M. R. (1994) *The Velvet Glove: Paternalism and Conflict in Gender, Class, and Race Relations*, Berkeley, CA: University of California Press.

Jackson, T. (1993a) *Organizational Behaviour in International Management*, Oxford: Butterworth-Heinemann.

(1993b) Ethics and the art of intuitive management, *European Management Journal*, EAP 20th Anniversary Edition, 57–65.

(1999) Managing change in South Africa: developing people and organizations, *International Journal of Human Resource Management* 10(2): 306–26.

(2000) Management ethics and corporate policy: a cross-cultural comparison, *Journal of Management Studies* 37(3): 349–70.

(2001) Cultural values and management ethics, *Human Relations* 54(10): 1267–1302.

(2002a) The management of people across cultures: valuing people differently, *Human Resource Management* 41(4): 455–75.

(2002b) *International HRM: A Cross-cultural Approach*, London: Sage.

(2004) *Management and Change in Africa: A Cross-cultural Perspective*, London: Routledge.

Jackson, T., Amaeshi, K. and Yavuz, Y. (2008) Untangling African indigenous management: multiple influences on the success of SMEs in Kenya, *Journal of World Business* 43(3).

Jackson, T. and Aycan, Z. (2006) Editorial: from cultural values to cross cultural interfaces, *International Journal of Cross Cultural Management* 6(1): 5–13.

Jackson, T. and Bak, M. (1998) Foreign companies and Chinese workers: employee motivation in the People's Republic of China, *Journal of Organizational Change Management* 11(4): 282–300.

Jackson, T. and Calafell Artola, M. (1997) Ethical beliefs and management behaviour: a cross-cultural comparison, *Journal of Business Ethics* 16: 1163–73.

Jackson, T. and Nana Nzepa, O. (2004) Cameroon: managing cultural complexity and power. In Jackson, *Management and Change in Africa*, London: Routledge, ch. 10, pp. 208–33.

Jaeger, A. M. and Kanungo, R. N. (1990) *Management in Developing Countries*, London: Routledge.

James, E. H. (2000) Race-related differences in promotions and support: underlying effects of human and social capital, *Organizational Science* 11(5): 493–508.

Javidan, M., House, R. J. and Dorfman, P. W. (2004) A nontechnical summary of GOBE findings. In House, Hanges, Javidan, Dorfman and Gupta, pp. 29–48.

Joergensen, J. J. (1990) Organizational life-cycle and effectiveness criteria in state-owned enterprizes: the case of East Africa. In Jaeger and Kanungo (eds.), pp. 62–82.

Jones, M. T. (1999) The institutional determinants of social responsibility, *Journal of Business Ethics* 20: 163–79.

Kamoche, K. (2001) Human resource management in Kenya. In P. S. Budhwar and Y. A Debrah, *Human Resource Management in Developing Countries*, London: Routledge pp. 209–21.

Kanungo, R. N. and Jaeger, A. M. (1990) Introduction: the need for indigenous management in developing countries. In Jaeger and Kanungo (eds.), pp. 1–23.

Kaplinsky, R. (2008) What does the rise of China do for industrialization in sub-Saharan Africa? *Review of African Political Economy* 115: 7–22.

Kapoor, I. (2002) Capitalism, culture, agency: dependency versus postcolonial theory, *Third World Quarterly* 23(4): 647–64.

Katz, D. and Kahn, R. L. (1978) *The Social Psychology of Organizations* (2nd edn.), New York: John Wiley.

Kerr, C., Dunlop, J. T., Harbison, F. H. and Myers, C. A. (1960) *Industrialism and Industrial Man*, Cambridge, MA: Harvard University Press.

Kiggundu, M. N. (1989) *Managing Organizations in Developing Countries*, West Hartford, CT: Kumarian Press.

Kluckhohn, F. and Strodtbeck, F. (1961) *Variations in Value Orientation*, Westport, CT: Greenwood Press.

Koçer, R. G. (2007) 'Trade unions at whose service?' Coercive partnerships and partnership in coercion in Turkey's metal sector, *Industrielle Beziehungen* 14(3): 245–69.

Koopman, A. (1991) *Transcultural Management*, Oxford: Basil Blackwell.

Kumar, B. N. and Steinmann, H. (eds.) (1998) *Ethics in International Management*, Berlin: Walter de Gruyter.

Langlois, C. C. and Schlegelmilch, B. B. (1990) Do corporate codes of ethics reflect national character? Evidence from Europe and the United States, *Journal of International Business Studies*, Fourth Quarter, 519–39.

Larrain, J. (1979) *The Concept of Ideology*, London: Hutchinson.

Lee, K.-H. (1982) Ethical beliefs in marketing management, *European Journal of Marketing* 3: 58–67.

Lessem, R. (1994) Four worlds: the Southern African businessphere. In P. Christie, R. Lessem and L. Mbigi (eds.) *African Management: Philosophy, Concepts and Applications*, Cape Town: Knowledge Resources.

Lobel, S. A. (1997) In praise of the 'soft' stuff: a vision for human resource leadership, *Human Resource Management* 36(1): 135–9.

Lyonski, S. and Gaidis, W. (1991) A cross-cultural comparison of the ethics of business students, *Journal of Business Ethics* 10: 141–50.

Maier, K. (2000) *This House Has Fallen: Nigeria in Crisis*, London: Penguin.

Makgoba, M. W. (ed.) (1999) *African Renaissance*, Johannesburg/Cape Town: Mafube/Tafelberg.

Marsden, D. (1991) Indigenous management, *The International Journal of Human Resource Management* 2(1): 21–38.

Martin, G. S., Resick, C. J., Keating, M. A. and Dickson, M. W. (2009) Ethical leadership across cultures: a comparative analysis of German and US perspectives, *Business Ethics: A European Review* 18(2): 127–44.

Martinez, P. G. (2003) Paternalism as a positive form of leader-subordinate exchange: evidence from Mexico. *Journal of Iberoamerican Academy of Management* 1: 227–42.

Massey, D. S. and Sanchez, M. R. (2007) Latino and American identities as perceived by immigrants, *Qualitative Sociology* 30(1): 81–107.

Mbigi, L. (1997) *Ubuntu: The African Dream in Management*, Randburg, S. Africa: Knowledge Resources.

McDermott, M. and Samson, F. L. (2005) White racial and ethnic identity in the United States, *Annual Review of Sociology* 31: 245–61.

McDonald, G. M. and Pak, C. K. (1997) Ethical perceptions of expatriates and local managers in Hong Kong, *Journal of Business Ethics* 16: 1605–23.

McLaughlin, A. (2003) Americans are bringing home baby – increasingly from Africa, *Christian Science Monitor*, 4 December 2003, and reproduced at www.globalpolicy.org/component/content/article/162/27631.html, accessed 21/08/09.

McSweeney, B. (2002) Hofstede's model of national cultural differences and their consequences: a triumph of faith – a failure of analysis, *Human Relations* 55(1): 89–118.

Mellahi, K. (2006) Human resource management in Saudi Arabia. In P. S. Budhwar and K. Mellahi, *Managing Human Resources in the Middle East*, London: Routledge, ch. 6, pp. 97–120.

Mellahi, K., Frynas, J. G. and Finlay, P. (2005) *Global Strategic Management*, Oxford University Press.

Merton, R. K. (1949) *Social Theory and Social Structure*, Glencoe, IL: The Free Press.

Metcalfe, B. D. (2007) Gender and human resource management in the Middle East, *International Journal of Human Resource Management* 18(1): 54–74.

Mohan, G. (2002) Beyond participation: strategies for deeper empowerment. In B. Cooke and U. Kothari, *Participation: The New Tyranny?* London: Zed Books, pp. 153–67.

Mohanty, C. T. (1991) Under Western eyes: feminist scholarship and colonial discourses. In C. T. Mohanty, A. Russo and L. Torres (eds.) *Third World Women and the Politics of Feminism*, Bloomingdale, IN: Indiana University Press, pp. 51–80.

Montgomery, J. D. (1987) Probing managerial behaviour: image and reality in Southern Africa, *World Development* 15(7): 911–29.

Moreno, A. (2003) Corruption and democracy: a cultural assessment. In R. Inglehart (ed.) *Human Values and Social Change: Findings from the Values Surveys*, Leiden, The Netherlands: Brill, pp. 265–78.

Mulat, T. (1998) Multilateralism and Africa's regional economic communities, *Journal of World Trade* 32(4): 115–38.

Munene, J. C., Schwartz, S. H. and Smith, P. B. (2000) Development in sub-Saharan Africa: cultural influences and managers' decision behaviour, *Public Administration and Development*, 20(4): 339–51.

Mutabazi, E. (2002) Preparing African leaders. In C. B. Derr, S. Roussillon and F. Bournois (eds.) *Cross-cultural Approaches to Leadership Development*, Westport, CT: Quorum, ch. 15, pp. 202–23.

Mutwa, C. (1964/1998) *Indaba, My Children*, Edinburgh: Payback Press.

Nakano, C. (1997) A survey study on Japanese managers' views of business ethics, *Journal of Business Ethics* 16: 1737–51.

Nanji, A. (1993) Islamic ethics. In Singer (ed.), ch. 9, pp. 106–18.

Neal, M., Finlay, J. L., Catana, G. A. and Catana, D. A. (2007) Comparison of leadership prototypes of Arab and European females, *International Journal of Cross Cultural Management* 7(3): 291–316.

Neimanis, G. J. (1997) Business ethics in the former Soviet Union: a report, *Journal of Business Ethics* 16: 357–62.

Newstrom, J. W. and Ruch, W. A. (1975) The ethics of management and the management of ethics, *MSU Business Topics*, Winter, pp. 29–37.

Nonaka, I. and Toyama, R. (2007) Strategic management as distributed practical wisdom (phronesis), *Industrial and Corporate Change* 16(3): 371–94.

Noorderhaven, N. G. and Tidjani, B. (2001) Culture, governance, and economic performance: an exploratory study with a special focus on Africa, *International Journal of Cross Cultural Management* 1(1): 31–52.

Northouse, P. G. (1997) *Leadership: Theory and Practice.* Thousand Oaks, CA: Sage.

Ntuli, P. P. (1999) The missing link between culture and education: are we still chasing gods that are not our own? In Makgoba (ed.), ch. 12, pp. 184–99.

Nyambegera, S. M. (2002) Ethnicity and human resource management practices in sub-Saharan Africa: the relevance of managing diversity discourse, *International Journal of Human Resource Management* 13(7): 1077–90.

Okleshen, M. and Hoyt, R. (1996) A cross-cultural comparison of ethical perspectives and decision approaches of business students: United States of America versus New Zealand, *Journal of Business Ethics* 15: 537–49.

Ornatowski, G. K. (1999) Confucian values, Japanese economic development, and the creation of a modern Japanese business ethics. In G. Enderle (ed.) *International Business Ethics: Challenges and Approaches*, Notre Dame, IN: University of Notre Dame Press, pp. 386–405.

Paine, L. S. (1994) Managing for organizational integrity, *Harvard Business Review*, March–April, pp. 106–17.

Pakenham, T. (1991) *The Scramble for Africa*, London: Phoenix Press.

Palazzo, B. (2002) US–American and German business ethics: an intercultural comparison, *Journal of Business Ethics* 41: 195–216.

Parker, L. (2005) Uniform jilbab: inside Indonesia, in 'Sharia inspired bylaws the scourge of democracy?' *The Jakarta Post*, July–September 2005: 21–2, retrieved February 2009, www.thejakartapost.com/yesterdaydetail.asp.

Parsons, T. (1949) *The Structure of Social Action*, Glencoe, IL: The Free Press.

(1951) *The Social System*, Glencoe, IL: The Free Press.

Parsons, T. and Shils, E. (eds.) (1951) *Towards a General Theory of Action*, Cambridge, MA: Harvard University Press.

Pascale, R. T. and Athos, A. G. (1981) *The Art of Japanese Management*, New York: Simon & Schuster.

Paul, J. (1990) Participatory approaches to human rights in sub-Saharan Africa. In An-Na'im and F. Deng (eds.).

Pellegrini, E. K. and Scandura, T. A. (2006) Leader-member exchange (LMX), paternalism and delegation in the Turkish business culture: an empirical investigation, *Journal of International Business Studies* 37(2): 264–79.

(2008) Paternalistic leadership: a review and agenda for future research, *Journal of Management* 34(3): 566–93.

Peltro, P. J. (1968) The difference between 'tight' and 'loose' societies, *Transaction*, April, 37–40.

Peterson, M. F. and Pike, K. L. (2002) Emics and etics for organizational studies: a lesson in contrasts from linguistics, *International Journal of Cross Cultural Management* 2(1): 5–19.

Pickens, S. D. B. (1987) Values and value related strategies in Japanese corporate culture, *Journal of Business Ethics* 6: 137–43.

Pityana, N. B. (1999) The renewal of African moral values. In M. W. Makgoba (ed.) *African Renaissance*, Sandton: Mafube/Cape Town: Tafelberg, ch. 9, pp. 137–48.

Posner, B. Z. and Schmidt, W. H. (1987) Ethics in American companies: a managerial perspective, *Journal of Business Ethics* 6: 383–91.

Prasad, A. (ed.) (2003) *Postcolonial Theory and Organizational Analysis: A Critical Reader*, London: Palgrave Macmillan.

Priem, R. L., Love, L. G. and Shaffer, M. (2000) Industrialization and values evolution: the case of Hong Kong and Guangzhou, China, *Asia Pacific Journal of Management* 17(3): 473–92.

Puffer, S. M. and McCarthy, D. J. (1998) Business ethics in a transforming economy: applying the integrative social contrasts theory to Russia. In Kumar and Steinmann (eds.), pp. 419–37.

Radcliffe-Brown, A. R. (1952) *Structure and Function in Primitive Society*, London: Cohen and West.

Radhakrishnan, S. (1923) *Indian Philosophy*, Vol. 1, London: George Allen & Unwin.

Ralston, D. A., Gaicalone, R. A. and Terpstra, R. H. (1994) Ethical perceptions of organizational politics: a comparative evaluation of American and Hong Kong managers, *Journal of Business Ethics* 13: 989–99.

Ralston, D. A., Gustafson, D. J., Terpstra, R. H. and Holt, D. H. (1993) The impact of managerial values on decision-making behavior: a comparison of the United States and Hong Kong, *Asia Pacific Journal of Management* 10(1): 21–37.

Rawls, J. (1971) *A Theory of Justice*, Cambridge, MA: Harvard University Press.

Reader, J. (1998) *Africa: A Biography of the Continent*, London: Penguin.

Redding, S. G. (1990) *The Spirit of Chinese Capitalism*, Berlin: Walter de Gruyter.

Rees, C. J. and Althakhri, R. (2008) Organizational change strategies in the Arab region: a review of critical factors, *Journal of Business Economics and Management* 9(2): 123–32.

Reidenbach, R. E. and Robin, D. P. (1988) Some initial steps towards improving the measurement of ethical evaluation of marketing activities, *Journal of Business Ethics* 7: 871–9.

—— (1990) Towards the development of a multidimensional scale for improving evaluations of business ethics, *Journal of Business Ethics* 9: 639–53.

Robertson, D. C. (2002) Business ethics across cultures. In M. J. Gannon and K. L. Newman (eds.) *Handbook of Cross-Cultural Management*, Oxford: Blackwell, pp. 361–92.

Rohmetra, N. (1998) *Human Resource Development in Commercial Banks in India*, London: Ashgate.

Rotter, J. B. (1966) General expectancies for internal versus external control of reinforcement, *Psychological Monographs* 80(1), Whole No. 609, 1–28.

Saeed, M. and Ahmed, Z. U. (1998) An Islamic framework for international marketing ethics. In Kumar and Steinmann (eds.), pp. 341–66.

Said, E. (1978/1995) *Orientalism*, London: Penguin.

Sanyal, R. (2005) Determinants of bribery in international business: the cultural and economic factors, *Journal of Business Ethics* 59: 139–45.

Saunders, E. (1998) Leadership the South African way, *People Dynamics*, February, 31–4.

Schech, S. and Haggis, J. (2000) *Culture and Development: A Critical Introduction*, Oxford: Blackwell.

Schein, E. (2004) *Organization Culture and Leadership*, San Francisco: Jossey-Bass.

Schildkraut, D. J. (2007) Defining American identity in the twenty-first century: how much 'there' is there? *The Journal of Politics* 69(3): 597–615.

Schlegelmilch, B. B. and Robertson, D. C. (1995) The influence of country and industry on ethical perceptions of senior executives in the US and Europe, *Journal of International Business Studies*, Fourth Quarter, pp. 859–81.

Schutz, A. (1972) *Phenomenology of the Social World*, London: Heinemann.

Schwartz, S. H. (1994) Beyond individualism/collectivism: new cultural dimensions of values. In U. Kim, H. C. Triandis, Ç. Kâğitçibaşi, S.-C. Choi and G. Yoon, *Individualism and Collectivism: Theory, Method and Application*, Thousand Oaks, CA: Sage, pp. 85–119.

(1999) A theory of cultural values and some implications for work, *Applied Psychology: An International Review* 48(1): 23–47.

Schwartz, S. J., Zamboanga, B. L., Rodriguez, L. and Wang, S. C. (2007) The structure of cultural identity in an ethnically diverse sample of emerging adults, *Basic and Applied Social Psychology* 29(2): 159–73.

Selznick, P. (1949) *TVA and the Grass Roots*, Berkeley: University of California Press.

Shaw, T. M., Cooper, A. F. and Antkiewicz, A. (2007) Global and/or regional development at the start of the 21st century? China, India, and (South) Africa, *Third World Quarterly* 28(7): 1255–70.

Shenkar, O. and Ronen, S. (1987) The cultural context of negotiation: the implications of Chinese interpersonal norms, *Journal of Applied Behavioral Science* 23: 263–75.

Silverman, D. (1970) *The Theory of Organizations*, Aldershot: Gower.

Singer, P. (ed.) (1993) *A Companion to Ethics*, Oxford: Blackwell.

Singhapakdi, A., Vitell, S. J. and Leelakulthanit, O. (1994) A cross-cultural study of moral philosophies, ethical perceptions and judgements: a comparison of American and Thai marketers, *International Marketing Review* 11(6): 65–78.

Skinner, B. F. (1953) *Science and Human Behavior*, New York: Macmillan.

Smith, G. and Gilbert, N. (1985) The China guanxi. *Forbes* 136(3): 104.

Smith, P. B., Dugan, S. and Trompenaars, F. (1996) National culture and the values of organizational employees: a dimensional analysis across 43 nations, *Journal of Cross-Cultural Psychology* 27(2): 231–64.

Sorge, A. (2004) Cross-national differences in human resources and organization. In A. W. Harzing and J. Van Ruysseveldt, *International Human Resource Management*, London: Sage, ch. 5, pp. 117–40.

Sparks, A. (1990) *The Mind of South Africa*, London: Mandarin.

Spiegel (2007a) Skoda workers want VW wages: Eastern Europe pricing itself out of cheap labor market? *Spiegel Online*, 18 April 2007, www.spiegel.de/international/business/0,1518,478052,00.html, accessed 10/06/09.

(2007b) Eastern Europe's exodus: going west for the good life, *Spiegel Online*, 28 March 2007 (author: Jan Puhl) www.spiegel.de/international/europe/0,1518,474167,00.html, accessed 10/06/09.

Spivak, G. C. (1988) Can the subaltern speak? In C. Nelson and L. Grossberg (eds) *Marxism and the Interpretation of Culture*, Basingstoke, UK: Macmillan, pp. 271–313.

(1996) *The Spivak Reader*, D. Landry and G. MacLean (eds.), New York: Routledge.

Stewart, E. C. and Bennett, M. J. (1991) *American Cultural Patterns: A Cross-Cultural Perspective* (2nd edn.), Boston: Intercultural Press.

Taka, I. and Dunfee, T. W. (1997) Japanese moralogy as business ethics, *Journal of Business Ethics* 16: 507–19.

Tannenbaum, A. S. (1968) *Control in Organizations*, New York: McGraw-Hill.

Tayeb, M. H. (2000) The internationalisation of HRM policies and practices: the case of Japanese and French companies in Scotland, 11éme Congrés de l'AGRH, 16–17 November 2000, ESCP-EAP, Paris.

Taylor, H. (2002) Insights into participation from critical management and labour process perspectives. In B. Cooke and U. Kothari, *Participation: The New Tyranny*, London: Zed Books, ch. 8, pp. 122–38.

The Guardian (2009) Madonna, Mercy and Malawi : her fight to adopt a second African child, www.guardian.co.uk/music/2009/jun/12/madonna-mercy-malawi, accessed 19/08/09.

The Telegraph (2005) The great Kabbalah con exposed, www.telegraph.co.uk/culture/3634742/The-great-Kabbalah-con-exposed.html, accessed 19/08/09.

Theobold, R. (2002) Should the payment of bribes overseas be made illegal? *Business Ethics: A European Review* 11(4): 375–84.

Thomson, A. (2000) *An Introduction to African Politics*, London: Routledge.

Tönnies, F. (1887/1963) *Community and Society*, New York: Harper and Row.

Triandis, H. C. (1990) Theoretical concepts that are applicable to the analysis of ethnocentrism. In R. W. Brislin (ed.) *Applied Cross-cultural Psychology*, Newbury Park, CA: Sage, pp. 34–55.

(1994) *Culture and Social Behavior*, New York: McGraw-Hill.

(1995) *Individualism and Collectivism*, Boulder, CO: Westview.

Trimiew, D. M. and Greene, M. (1997) How we got over: the moral teaching of the African-American church on business ethics, *Business Ethics Quarterly* 7(2): 133–47.

Trompenaars, F. (1993) *Riding the Waves of Culture: Understanding Cultural Diversity in Business*, London: Nicholas Brealey.

Tsalikis, J. and LaTour, M. S. (1995) Bribery and extortion in international business: ethical perceptions of Greeks compared to Americans, *Journal of Business Ethics* 14: 249–64.

Tsalikis, J. and Nwachukwu, O. (1988) Cross-cultural business ethics: ethical beliefs differences between Blacks and Whites, *Journal of Business Ethics* 7: 745–54.

(1991) A comparison of Nigerian to American views of bribery and extortion in international commerce, *Journal of Business Ethics* 10: 85–98.

Tsutsui, W. M. (1998) *Manufacturing Ideology: Scientific Management in Twentieth-Century Japan*, Princeton University Press.

Tylor, E. B. (1871) Primitive culture, cited in C. Levi-Strauss (1963) (trans. C. Jacobson and B. G. Schoel), *Structural Anthropology*, Harmondsworth: Penguin.

Ugwuegbu, D. C. E. (2001) *The Psychology of Management in African Organizations*, Westport, CT: Quorum.

Uhl-Bien, M., Tierney, P., Graen, G. and Wakabayashi, M. (1990) Company paternalism and the hidden investment process: identification of the 'right type' for line managers in leading Japanese organizations, *Group and Organization Studies* 15: 414–30.

UN Global Compact (2000) www.unglobalcompact.org/, accessed 27/05/09.

US Census Bureau (2000) US Census 2000, www.census.gov/population/www/pop-profile/profile2000.html/www.census.gov/population/www/pop-profile/files/2000/chap16.pdf, accessed 09/05/09.

US State Department (2006) *China (includes Tibet, Hong Kong, and Macau) International Religious Freedom Report 2006*, Bureau of Democracy, Human Rights, and Labor at www.state.gov/g/drl/rls/irf/2006/71338.htm, accessed 10/09/09.

Utomi, P. (1998) *Managing Uncertainty: Competition and Strategy in Emerging Economies*, Ibadan, Nigeria: Spectrum Books.

van Luijk, H. J. L. (1997) Business ethics in Western and Northern Europe: a search for effective alliances, *Journal of Business Ethics* 16: 1579–87.

Vogel, D. (1993a) Is US business obsessed with ethics? *Across the Board: The Conference Board Magazine*, November/December.

  (1993b) Differing national approaches to business ethics, *Journal of Business Ethics* 2(3): 164–71.

Waiguchu, J. M., Tiagha, E. and Mwaura, M. (eds.) (1999) *Management of Organizations in Africa*, Westport, CT: Quorum.

Wall, J. (1990) Managers in the People's Republic of China. *Academy of Management Executive* 4(2): 19–32.

Weaver, G. R. and Agle, B. R. (2002) Religiosity and ethical behaviour in organizations: a symbolic interactionist perspective, *Academy of Management Review* 27(1): 77–97.

Werner, A. (2008) The influence of Christian identity on SME owner-managers' conceptualization of business practice, *Journal of Business Ethics* 82: 449–62.

Westwood, R. J. and Posner, B. Z. (1997) Managerial values across cultures: Australia, Hong Kong and the United States, *Asia Pacific Journal of Management* 14: 31–66.

Whipple, T. W. and Swords, D. F. (1992) Business ethics judgements: a cross-cultural comparison, *Journal of Business Ethics* 11: 671–78.

White, L. P. and Rhodeback, M. J. (1992) Ethical dilemmas in organizational development: a cross-cultural analysis, *Journal of Business Ethics* 11: 663–70.

Whiteoak, J. W., Crawford, N. G. and Mapstone, R. H. (2006) Impact of gender and generational differences in work values and attitudes in an Arab culture, *Thunderbird International Business Review* 48(1): 77–91.

Whitley, R. (1999) *Divergent Capitalisms: The Social Structuring and Change of Business Systems*, Oxford University Press.

Williams, O. F. (2004) The UN Global Compact: the challenge and the promise, *Business Ethics Quarterly* 14(4): 755–74.

Wilson, R. (2006) Islam and business, *Thunderbird International Business Review* 48(1) 109–23.

Worden, S. (2003) The role of religious and nationalist ethics in strategic leadership: the case of J. N. Tata, *Journal of Business Ethics* 47(2).

Zhuang, J. Y., Thomas, S. and Miller, D. L. (2005) Examining culture's effect on whistle-blowing and peer reporting, *Business and Society* 44(4): 462–86.

Index